Study Guide Plus
Language and Multicultural Enrichment
for

Bryjak and Soroka

SOCIOLOGY

Study Guide Plus
Language and Multicultural Enrichment
for
Bryjak and Soroka

SOCIOLOGY

Cultural Diversity in a Changing World

Diana Kendall
Austin Community College

with Contributions by

Louis Clunk
Golden West College

Allyn and Bacon

Boston • London • Toronto • Sydney • Tokyo • Singapore

Copyright © 1992 by Allyn and Bacon
A Division of Simon & Schuster, Inc.
160 Gould Street
Needham Heights, Massachusetts 02194

ISBN 0-205-13106-9

Printed in the United States of America

10 9 8 7 6 5 4   97 96 95 94 93

Table of Contents

INTRODUCTION

This study guide has been designed to aid you in studying and understanding the material presented in <u>SOCIOLOGY: CULTURAL DIVERSITY IN A CHANGING WORLD</u> by Bryjak and Soroka. Each chapter in this guide contains:

Chapter Overview
Learning Objectives
Detailed Chapter Outline
Glossary of Difficult-to-Understand Words
Key Terms to Define
Key People to Describe
Self-Tests: Multiple-Choice, True-False, Fill-in Questions,
    and Essay Questions
Answer Key to Tests With Explanations of the Correct Responses

Here are some suggestions for getting the most out of this study guide:

1.   Look over the Chapter Overview, Learning Objectives, and Detailed Chapter Outline in the study guide <u>before</u> reading each chapter in your text. This will give you a basic overview of the chapter and will help you to know what to look for as you read the chapter.

2.   While reading the chapter in your text, keep you study guide open to the Glossary of Difficult-to-Understand Words. You will not have to look up the meaning of difficult-to-understand words in the dictionary.

3.   After reading the chapter in your text, define as many of the key terms and describe as many of the key people as you can without looking back at the text. After you have finished, check your answers against the text.

4.   You may wish to use the self-tests as you complete each chapter, or you may wish to save the self-tests to use when you are studying for examinations.

5.   Whenever you choose to use the self-tests, try to take them under "testing conditions" as much as possible. Allocate about the same amount of time as you think you would have on such an exam in class. Write down your answers on paper.

6.   Next, check your answers against the key at the end of each chapter. After "grading" your own exam, look back in the text for additional information on the questions you missed.

If you read chapters as assigned and use this study guide to help you master the material, you should have a successful experience in this course. Best Wishes as you explore <u>SOCIOLOGY: CULTURAL DIVERSITY IN A CHANGING WORLD</u>!

Diana Kendall

CHAPTER ONE

THE WORLD ACCORDING TO SOCIOLOGY

Chapter 1 defines sociology and differentiates it from the other social sciences. The field of sociology is characterized by its growing international perspective. The two stages of modernization of the world are described: (1) the first stage began with the Industrial Revolution and resulted in the modernization of numerous European countries, the United States, Canada, Australia, and New Zealand; and (2) the second phase started in the aftermath of World War II and continues to unfold at different speeds and under widely different circumstances in the Third World. Sociology is described as a "debunking" science because sociologists look for levels of reality other than those presented in official interpretations of society and people's "common sense" explanations of the social world. The historical development of sociology and the early contributions of Comte and Durkheim are explored. The three major theoretical perspectives in sociology -- functional theory, the conflict model, and symbolic interactionism -- are discussed in depth. Finally, the chapter explains the methods, strengths and weaknesses of nonexperimental research designs -- such as survey research and observational studies -- and of experimental designs which utilize experimental and control groups.

LEARNING OBJECTIVES:

As you read Chapter 1, use these learning objectives to organize your notes. After completing your reading, briefly state an answer to each of the objectives, and review the text pages in parentheses.

1.   Define sociology and differentiate between sociology and the other social sciences. (2-4)

2.   State when the two phases of modernization began. (5)

3.   Discuss the increasing interdependence of the United States with Mexico and Japan. (8)

4.   Indicate why sociology is called a "debunking" science. (9)

5.   Compare "positivism" and "intuition" as means for attaining knowledge. (11)

6.   Identify Auguste Comte's contribution to the discipline of sociology, and state the major weakness of his theoretical perspective. (11-12)

7.   Explain what Emile Durkheim meant by "social facts" and how they differ from individual/psychological phenomena. (12)

8.   Describe the following regarding Durkheim's study of suicide: the basic assumption that guided his research, the four basic types of suicide, and his major contribution to our understanding of suicide. (13-16)

9.   Define "theory" and compare "grand theories" with "middle-range theories." (16)

1

10. List and briefly explain the four basic "functional requirements" that all societies must meet if they are to survive. (18-19)

11. Explain the difference in the views of functional sociologists and conflict theorists regarding the stability of society. (20)

12. State the major way in which symbolic interactionism differs from functionalist and conflict theories. (22-23)

13. Describe the role of symbols in human communication and explain why human social patterns must be understood in terms of the symbolic contexts in which they occur. (23-24)

14. Differentiate between the independent and dependent variables in scientific research. (25-26)

15. Outline the procedures, advantages and disadvantages of survey research, observational studies, and experimental research designs. (29-34)

CHAPTER OUTLINE

I. SOCIOLOGY - A GROWING INTERNATIONAL PERSPECTIVE

    A. Sociology is the study of the social organization and patterns of behavior of people in large, complex, modern, industrial societies.
        1. Cultural anthropology focuses on the social organization and behavior patterns of premodern people throughout the world.
        2. Psychology focuses on individual behavior and on how people are affected by changes in society.
        3. Economics focuses on the production, distribution, exchange, and consumption of goods and services in society.

    B. Today, sociologists are conducting more cross cultural research -- the gathering of comparable data from different societies -- to enable them to study the interrelation of political and economic institutions of societies that comprise the "global village."

II. THE MODERNIZATION OF THE WORLD

    A. The ongoing modernization of the world occurred in two broad stages:
        1. First stage: the Industrial Revolution resulting in modernization of numerous European countries, the United States, Canada, Australia, and New Zealand.
        2. Second stage: started post-World War II and continues at different speeds and under different circumstances in the Third World.

    B. Social scientists use a classification scheme placing nations on a continuum as to their degree of modernity.
        1. First World countries (e.g. United States and Japan) developed with capitalist economic systems.
        2. Second World nations (e.g. the Soviet Union, until recently) industrialized under a socialist system

3. <u>Third</u> <u>World</u> <u>nations</u> (e.g. desperately poor countries like the Sudan and Bagladesh, but also modestly rich nations like Argentina and South Korea) are characterized by rapidly increasing populations, food shortages, and large foreign debts.

C. Today, modernization is a much broader concept that focuses on the positive social changes accompanying industrialization and economic growth. For example, Mexico and Japan are at different points on the modernization continuum:
   1. Japan's first stage of development began in the latter third of the 19th century and ended with the nation's military defeat in World War II. The second stage began in the years following the war and continues today, as Japan has become one of the most powerful economic nations.
   2. Mexico began industrializing following the Revolution in 1910 but modernization did not accelerate until the post-World War II period. Today Mexico is somewhere in the middle of the modernization continuum but has important oil reserves which will make it an ever more important economic force in the future.

D. Sociology is a "<u>Debunking</u>" <u>Science</u> in that it looks for levels of reality other than those given in the everyday and official interpretations of society.

III. THE SOCIOLOGICAL STYLE: UNRAVELING HUMAN SOCIAL PATTERNS

A. Before the development of the scientific perspective, many people -- including political rulers, theologians and philosophers -- tried to make sense out of the natural and social realities that surrounded them.

B. <u>Auguste</u> <u>Comte</u> (1798-1857), the founder of sociology, sought to create a new field of inquiry that would be devoted to the scientific analysis of the human social world. He believed human societies had evolved through three historical stages, each of which had a distinctive way of explaining the world:
   1. In the <u>theological</u> <u>stage</u>, imagination dominated as the principle of understanding, and people interpreted events in terms of supernatural beings.
   2. In the <u>metaphysical</u> <u>stage</u>, observation of specific events led to rational speculation as to the nature of general events, and people derived sophisticated theoretical explanations of real-world phenomena through the power of the mind and the application of principles of logic.
   3. In the (final) <u>positivistic</u> <u>stage</u> of development, understanding of the human social world was to be generated through the adoption of the scientific method of analysis.

C. The sociological view of the world: Comte and Durkheim and the development of scientific sociology
   1. <u>Comte</u> believed the task of sociology was to discover the forces in society responsible for social statics (stability) and social dynamics (change and progress).
      a. He argued that social laws were responsible for the patterns of social integration and change found in all human societies.

        b.   Positivism -- the belief that knowledge can only be derived from people's sensory experience -- was the philosophical foundation of sociology.

        c.   He introduced the use of scientific method to the study of society and emphasized the use of observation and experimentation to test theories about social facts.

        d.   While his emphasis on turning sociology into a science was a strength of Comte's perspective, his emphasis on evolutionary theory -- that social laws determined the inevitable progress of human societies through a number of stages -- was erroneous and, as a result, held back sociology's understanding of societal change and modernization for over a hundred years.

   2.   Emile Durkheim (1858-1917) made Comte's dream of a legitimate science of society a reality by waging a sustained intellectual battle against the "reductionism" of psychologists and biologists.

        a.   Reductionists claimed that any form of social behavior ultimately can be explained as individual behavior, in terms of each person's personality, motivation, and overall state of consciousness.

        b.   Durkheim argued that social phenomena cannot be reduced to the individual level of analysis, but rather have to be understood as "social facts" which are distinguished from individual/psychological phenomena because:

           (1).   Social facts exist external to individuals.

           (2).   They constrain or influence a person independent of his/her will.

           (3).   They are shared by a significant number of people.

IV.   THINKING SOCIOLOGICALLY: THEORETICAL PARADIGMS

A.   A theory is a set of logically-coherent, interrelated concepts that attempts to explain some observable phenomena or group of facts.

   1.   A grand theory deals with the universal aspects of social life and is usually grouped in basic assumptions (as opposed to data) concerning the nature of man and society.

   2.   Middle-range theories focus on relatively specific problems in the social world (e.g. a theory of white-collar crime).

B.   Functionalist theory has its roots in natural sciences, and society was often described as a "social organism" made up of various parts, each of which had a specific function for the whole.

   1.   Early functionalist sociologists were concerned with the "problem of order" because of the major changes sweeping across Europe as a result of the Industrial Revolution.

   2.   Durkheim asserted that the stability of society was based on a shared moral order -- the consensus people reach on law, religious beliefs, and basic rules governing everyday life. The two forms of communal moral order were:

        a.   Mechanical solidarity - social cohesion in preindustrial societies resulting from a minimum division of labor, common experiences, and a strong collective conscience.

        b.   Organic solidarity - the social bond found in large industrial societies where people are dependent on one another because of a specialized, complex, highly developed, division of labor.

   3.   Twentieth century functionalist theorists have expanded the perspective beyond the problem of order and social solidarity.

a.   Talcott Parsons (1902-1979) outlined four functional requirements for social systems to survive:
   (1). Adaptation of social systems to their social and physical environment.
   (2). Goal attainment must be possible for members of society. They must have goals (or ends) and the means necessary to achieve them.
   (3). Integration of all of the components of society.
   (4). Pattern maintenance which provides occasional periods of rest for members of a social system.
b.   Robert Merton introduced concepts that permitted the study of the multiple consequences of patterns of behavior and institutions.
   (1). Manifest functions are those consequences that are intended and recognized by participants in the system.
   (2). Latent functions are consequences that are neither intended nor recognized.
c.   Contemporary functionalism has been criticized on several counts:
   (1). That it is ahistorical, concentrating on how present day events help to maintain the social system.
   (2). That it is inherently conservative and supportive of the status quo because it focuses on integration, stability and consensus while largely ignoring competition, conflict and social change.

C.   Conflict theorists argue that society is held together by the exercise of power, not by value consensus as asserted by functionalists.
   1.   Institutions, organizations, and individuals force people with less power than themselves to conform to their values and standards of conduct.
   2.   Karl Marx (1818-1883), the most influential conflict theorist, believed the fundamental conflict in capitalist societies was based on the inequality between the owners of the means of production (bourgeoisie) and the workers (proletariat) who exist by selling their labor power in the market.
      a.   The bourgeoisie become wealthier and more politically powerful by exploiting the proletariat.
      b.   The lives of the working class become so unbearable that they stage a successful revolution against the bourgeoisie.
      c.   Ultimately, class conflict ends with the end of capitalism and the rise of socialism where all of the people own the means of production and wealth is equitably distributed.
   3.   Ralf Dahrendorf asserted that in advanced capitalist societies, conflict centers around who should control the means of production, rather than ownership, as argued by Marx.
      a.   Conflict is between managers and executives (who are not owners) and the workers over authority - who will make and implement policy.
      b.   Social conflict is a struggle between those who exercise authority and those who are subject to that authority.
      c.   Such struggles over authority (and power) relationships constitute a zero-sum game, in which an increase in the power of one individual comes at the expense of loss of this commodity on the part of other individuals.
   4.   Lewis Coser argued that both internal and external conflict can have positive benefits to a group.

5

> a. Conflict which is external to the group serves to maintain the structure of the group and to strengthen its cohesion.
> b. Conflict within a group can act as a safety valve when the differences and hostilities between members are openly expressed and then negotiated.
5. Conflict theorists are criticized by functionalists for overemphasizing strife and disorder and for failing to recognize the harmonious and stabilizing aspects of group life.

D. <u>Symbolic Interactionism</u> takes a different approach from either functionalist or conflict theory in looking at social life.
1. Both functional and conflict theories are <u>macrolevel</u> paradigms which are concerned primarily with large-scale social phenomena while symbolic interaction theorists are concerned with small-scale, <u>microlevel</u> social phenomena.
2. Functional and conflict theories are <u>objectivistic</u> in orientation because they assume that objective social phenomena are of primary importance in shaping events and lives within a society; however, symbolic interaction theorists conduct their analyses from a <u>subjectivistic</u> perspective.
3. <u>Charles H. Cooley</u>, <u>George H. Mead</u>, and <u>W. I. Thomas</u> were instrumental in the development of symbolic interactionism.
> a. Cooley and Mead examined the process by which individuals acquire human personal and social characteristics, and they concluded that individuals acquire a self-identity through their interaction with significant other human beings in group situations.
> b. Thomas coined the phrase "<u>definition of the situation</u>" to describe the personal, subjective interpretation individuals give to a specific event, whether or not it is accurate and valid.
4. The symbolic interactionist perspective focuses on the many small-scale social encounters or interactions which make up larger-scale social units and examines the role of human communication in the construction of the subjective meanings that shape people's responses to their world.
> a. Human communication is unique because of its use of <u>significant symbols</u> that have attached meanings and values which are created through social interaction.
> b. Human social patterns must be understood in terms of the symbolic contexts in which they occur-- and these contexts are always subject to negotiation.
5. <u>Herbert Blumer</u>, a contemporary symbolic interaction theorist, summarized three basic ideas of the perspective:
> a. Humans respond to things on the basis of the meanings those things have for them.
> b. Meanings do not exist in the things themselves but rather are created through the process of human social interaction.
> c. Individuals interpret these meanings as they apply in specific situations, and meanings given to a thing by a particular individual vary with the situation.
6. Symbolic interactionism in its more extreme versions may be criticized for denying the existence of any sort of recognizable objective social reality. In more moderate form it permits sociologists to understand the linkage between external social realities and human social patterns that vary from one group to another.

6

V.   DOING SOCIOLOGY: IS THERE A METHOD TO THIS MADNESS?

    A.   Problems in Social Science Research
        1.   Scientific research requires the ability to empirically prove or disprove a <u>hypothesis</u> which states a relationship between independent and dependent variables.
            a.   Scientific testing of hypothesis ideally involves some sort of experiment in which the variables being studied are subjected to a series of controlled conditions according to a systematic plan developed by the researcher.
            b.   The need for controlled experiments to prove or disprove the hypothesis is problematic for research conducted regarding the human social world.
        2.   Nonempirical variables make application of the scientific method to the study of human social patterns difficult.
            a.   <u>Social constructs</u> -- such as religious beliefs, political values, or emotional states of being -- are not directly measurable.
            b.   To counteract this problem, social scientists attempt to develop <u>operational definitions</u> that specify how a phenomenon that has no direct empirical basis (for example, intelligence) is to be measured empirically.
        3.   <u>Ethical constraints</u> make it impossible to use human beings as "guinea pigs" in a sociological experiment.
            a.   People have basic moral and legal rights that include the recognition and protection of their physical and psychological well-being.
            b.   Social scientists are aware that they must not jeopardize their research subjects, and universities and research organizations have guidelines in place to protect human subjects.
        4.   The <u>Hawthorne effect</u> may occur with human subjects -- unlike the nonhuman subjects of natural science experiments -- because they know they are participating in a scientific investigation.
            a.   Subjects may change their behaviors or attitudes because they know they are being "studied" and, as a result, invalidate the research.
            b.   This problem is called the "Hawthorne effect" based on a 1930's study of an industrial plant where research subjects attempted to please researchers by doing what they thought was expected of them.

    B.   Nonexperimental Research Designs in Sociology
        1.   <u>Nonexperimental/descriptive research</u> is noncausal research aimed most often at providing accurate information about some aspect of social reality.
        2.   Nonexperimental research methods include:
            a.   <u>Survey research</u> -- a study in which the researcher asks some defined group a series of questions -- typically in an <u>interview</u> or in a <u>questionnaire</u> -- related to their behaviors or attitudes.
               (1).   A <u>representative sample</u> -- a smaller segment or subgroup of a particular <u>population</u> which reflects the attributes of that larger group -- may be used.
               (2).   Survey research is the most popular form of nonexperimental methodology because it is straightforward, not very expensive, relatively easy to conduct, and large amounts of data can be coded and computer-analyzed quickly.

   (3). Problems inherent in survey research include the difficulties of drawing truly representative samples and developing questions that ask what they are supposed to.
  b. <u>Observational studies</u> -- a research technique in which the sociologist observes subjects' behaviors directly in order to form conclusions or to make inferences about attitudes and values.
   (1). In the <u>neutral observation</u> study the subjects go about their normal activities while the researcher remains removed from the group being studied -- in terms of participation if not in actual physical distance.
   (2). In <u>participant observation</u> research the researcher does not remain an "outsider" but, rather, joins the group being studied and participates in their activities.
   (3). Problems inherent in observation research include the fact that the researcher must deceive or lie to research subjects and subjects do not give their informed consent to participate in the study -- or to refuse to participate if they so choose -- because they do not know that they are being studied. New restrictions regarding research do somewhat protect subjects today.

C. Experimental Research Designs in Sociology
 1. The objective of <u>experimental research</u> is the explanation of observed patterns and/or the prediction of future patterns.
 2. Design of experimental research includes:
  a. Systematic comparison of at least two groups of research subjects
   (1). <u>Control group</u> -- consists of those subjects who will not be exposed to the effects of the experimental condition (changes in the independent variable)
   (2). <u>Experimental group</u> -- consists of those subjects who will be exposed to the effects of the experimental condition (changes in the independent variable)
  b. Following exposure of the experimental group to the independent variable, the two groups are measured again on the dependent variable to determine what, if any, changes have occurred which may be attributed to the effects of the experimental condition.
 3. The <u>Milgram Experiment</u> raised important ethical questions about experimentation on human subjects.
  a. The purpose of Milgram's study was to discover the extent to which subjects would be willing to comply with an order to administer what they thought was a dangerous electric shock to a stranger.
  b. Because of this "obedience" experiment and the criticism it generated, there is greater concern about the rights of human research subjects today.
 4. Other critiques of experimental research
  a. It is suitable only for microlevel analysis -- small group research
  b. Social phenomena that occur in a real-world setting may be the result of hundreds of individual variables, making systematic control and manipulation of the situation virtually impossible.
  c. Much of what we know about group dynamics and the formation and development of small social groups has come from experimental studies.

GLOSSARY OF DIFFICULT-TO-UNDERSTAND WORDS

Page	Line	Col.	Term from Text	Explanation
1	6		hordes	crowd, mob, large number
1	8		infuse	instill, introduce, impart gradually
1	11		flare	burn, glow
1	13		sleighs	a vehicle on runners used to move people on snow or ice
2	7		sugarplum	small ball-shaped candy
2	9		ramshackle	ready to collapse, fall down
2	14		cast-offs	thrown away
2	17		frenetic	agitated behavior, over-excited
4	9		inception	beginning
4	14		unprecedented	remarkable, unusual
4	37		emulate	follow
4	41		proliferation	growth, multiply
4	47		vantage	different perspective
5	6		alleviate	relieve
5	14		over-simplification	to make overly simple, sometimes misunderstanding results
5	24		continuum	a line with numerous segments
7	12		aftermath	outcome, result
7	18		equitable	fair
8	4		erratic	irregular
8	14		intermeshed	locked together, woven together
8	31		endeavors	attempts, efforts
8	39		volatile	changeable, (fleeting, passing)
9	4		denigrate	belittle, scorn
9	15		construed	defined, explained, understood
9	15		indictment	accusation, charge of wrongdoing
9	25		impoverished	poor
9	36		unraveling	opening, discovering
10	16		epochs	eras, times
10	23		atone	to make up for, appease, pay the penalty
10	28		derive	infer, deduce, to obtain
11	5		underpins	supports
11	23		sensory	feeling, perceptive
11	35		overarching	all embracing, dominating
11	43		unwarranted	not justifiable, not correct
12	4		conjecture	guess, speculate
12	34		disgruntled	not content
12	34		rowdy	violent
13	30	A	impels	motivates, drives
13	28	B	disgracing	shaming
14	8	A	binds	ties, attaches
14	40	A	inextinguishable	cannot stop, cannot satisfy
14	9	B	upheavals	disorders, extreme change
14	40	B	despotism	oppression
15	43	A	"graying"	growing older, refers to median age of population, also what percentage of population is defined as elderly
15	49	A	compulsive	pressure, forceful
15	16	B	impelling	driving

Page	Line	Col.	Term from Text	Explanation
15	18	B	ethos	moral code
15	19	B	aesthetic	beauty
16	11		paradigm	example
16	13		hunch	strong feeling about an event
16	21		off-the-cuff	casual, impromptu
17	15		constituent	component, element
18	4		consensus	agreement
18	14		cohesion	sticking together, different parts coming together
18	17		precedence	takes priority
18	21		interdependency	mutual influence
18	42		fast-paced	rapidly changing, hurried
19	9		latent	dormant, not apparent
19	14		lucrative	profitable
19	25		inner-city	older more densely populated part of a city, usually the central section
19	46		ahistorical	not historical
20	8		dissension	conflict, friction, disagreement, quarreling
21	27		ceased	stopped, come to an end
22	7		rooted	part of
22	9		ubiquitous	widespread, constantly encountered
22	14		inasmuch	since
22	27		dissension	conflict
23	7		assessing	estimating, considering
23	15		small-scale	small in scope (treatment), small in the range of operation
23	42		carefree	irresponsible
25	4		methodology	procedures used in scientific inquiry
26	29		notwithstanding	however
26	31		realm	domain, influence
26	36		nonempirical	not using the senses, cannot be measured
27	11		guinea pig	a subject of scientific research
27	11		guinea pig	rodent used in scientific research
27	29		scrutinize	look at closely, inspect closely
27	29		harmless	free from injury
27	43		unobtrusive	inconspicuous, not readily noticeable
28	36		abundance	profusion, plenty
29	6		sensitizes	sharpens, responsive
29	11		immersion	plunge into, entering suddenly
29	34		feasible	possible
30	43		tenured	status granted to a teacher which protects him/her from dismissal, usually granted after a stated time in a teaching position
30	46		trustworthy	dependable
31	36		cross-check	to check from various sources, to verify accuracy
32	40		charted	outlined, plotted
32	47		farfetched	doubtful
33	22		obedience	conforming, following orders
33	41		microlevel	small
33	48		subfield	a subset, part of the whole

KEY TERMS TO DEFINE:

After studying the chapter, define each of the following terms. Then check your work by referring to the answers at the end of Chapter 1 in the Study Guide.

cross cultural research	symbolic interactionism
cultural anthropology	significant symbols
sociology	causal relationship
debunking	constructs
positivism	operational definitions
theory	Hawthorne Effect
grand theory	nonexperimental research
middle-range theory	survey research
mechanical solidarity	interview
organic solidarity	questionnaire
bourgeoisie	population
proletariat	representative sample
macrolevel	observation study
microlevel	neutral observation
objectivistic	participant observation
subjectivistic	control group
definition of the situation	experimental group

KEY PEOPLE

State the major theoretical contributions of these social scientists:

Auguste Comte

Emile Durkheim

Karl Marx

SELF-TEST

After completing this self-test, check your answers against the "Answer Key" at the end of Chapter 1 in this Study Guide and in the text on the page(s) indicated in parentheses.

MULTIPLE CHOICE QUESTIONS

Select the response which best answers the question or completes the statement:

1. The field of sociology focuses on: (3)
    a. individual behavior.
    b. the social organization and patterns of behavior in large, complex, modern, industrial societies.
    c. the social organization and patterns of behavior of premodern people throughout the world.
    d. the production, distribution, exchange, and consumption of goods and services in society.

2. Sociology developed as an attempt to understand and explain the rapid social change which occurred as a result of: (4)
    a. the Reformation.
    b. the Enlightenment.
    c. the Industrial Revolution.
    d. World War II.

3. All of the following are First World countries EXCEPT: (6-Table 1.1)
    a. the United States.
    b. Japan.
    c. Australia.
    d. the Soviet Union.

4. Sociology is a _____ science because sociologists look for levels of reality other than those given in the official interpretations of society. (8-9)
    a. "common sense"
    b. "debunking"
    c. "intuitive"
    d. "judgmental"

5. The founder of sociology who stressed the need for "scientific" analysis of society was: (10)
    a. Emile Durkheim.
    b. Auguste Comte.
    c. Karl Marx.
    d. Herbert Spencer.

6. An example of a middle-range theory would be: (16)
    a. an explanation of the universal aspects of social life.
    b. an explanation of the working of all types of societies as they progress through evolutionary stages.
    c. a "world view" of why things are the way they are.
    d. an explanation of a specific social problem such as the rate of divorce in different social groups and societies.

7. According to Emile Durkheim, the social cohesion found in preindustrial societies resulting from a minimum division of labor, common experiences, and a strong collective conscience, would be classified as: (18)
   a. mechanical solidarity.
   b. organic solidarity.
   c. a social fact.
   d. dysfunctional.

8. Manifest functions are: (19)
   a. recognized and intended consequences of a group or organization.
   b. unrecognized and unintended consequences of a group or organization.
   c. social dysfunctions of an organization.
   d. hidden and thus difficult to identify in organizations.

9. Which of the following is a latent function of professional sports? (19)
   a. making money for owners of the teams
   b. providing sports entertainment for the public
   c. providing rich role models for adolescent males
   d. providing players with high salaries and lucrative endorsements

10. _____ theory views society as a relatively harmonious, well-integrated "social system" held together by shared values and common goals. (20)
   a. Functional
   b. Conflict
   c. Symbolic interaction
   d. Zero sum game

11. _____ theorists argue that institutions, organizations, and individuals force people with less power than themselves to conform to their values and standards of conduct. (20)
   a. Functional
   b. Conflict
   c. Symbolic interaction
   d. Zero sum game

12. The most influential early conflict theorist was: (21)
   a. Auguste Comte.
   b. Emile Durkheim.
   c. Karl Marx.
   d. Herbert Spencer.

13. Symbolic interaction theorists tend to focus on: (23)
   a. small-scale, microlevel social phenomena.
   b. large-scale, social phenomena -- societies and social institutions.
   c. a group consensus orientation.
   d. a group conflict orientation.

14. The sociological perspective which asserts that human beings communicate via significant symbols to which they have attached meaning is: (24)
   a. functionalism.
   b. conflict theory.
   c. symbolic interactionism.
   d. zero sum game theory.

13

15. A hypothesis contains at least two variables. The variable which is responsible for causing a change in the other variable(s) is called the: (25-Table 1.2)
    a. independent variable.
    b. dependent variable.
    c. intervening variable.
    d. qualifying variable.

16. Which of these is an operational definition of "intelligence?" (26)
    a. Intelligence is that which is measured by an intelligence test.
    b. Intelligence is the ability to know when to come in out of the rain.
    c. Intelligence is the ability to make sense of your environment.
    d. Intelligence means different things to different people.

17. Why have universities and research organizations set up committees to evaluate proposed studies involving human subjects? (27)
    a. To insure that funding is available for the project.
    b. To insure that there will be no psychological, social, or economic harm to respondents.
    c. To insure that the study has not already been conducted.
    d. To insure that the study receives adequate media coverage.

18. The "Hawthorne Effect" refers to: (27-28)
    a. the effect that knowledge of being part of a research study has upon the subjects of that study.
    b. the distortion of a research study due to the lack of a representative sample.
    c. the lack of ethical conduct on the part of researchers in the Hawthorne study.
    d. the problem of objectivity in a participant-observation study.

19. In Durkheim's study of suicide, he used death records collected by governmental agencies. This data-collection technique is called: (28)
    a. survey research.
    b. neutral observation.
    c. participation observation.
    d. use of existing data.

20. A representative sample is defined as: (29)
    a. any partial representation of a given population.
    b. a smaller segment of a given population which reflects the attributes of that larger group.
    c. elected representatives who reflect a larger population.
    d. a systematic selection of representative cases to study.

21. Two major types of survey research are: (29)
    a. interview and questionnaire.
    b. questionnaire and observation.
    c. observation and experiment.
    d. experiment and use of existing data.

22. A researcher who observes through a special one-way mirror while an employer conducts interviews with applicants for a job is engaged in: (30)
    a. survey research.
    b. an experiment.
    c. neutral observation research.
    d. participant observation research.

14

23. Which of the following is <u>not</u> a significant problem associated with <u>observation</u> research? (31)
    a.   The researcher must deceive or lie to research subjects.
    b.   Subjects do not have the option of choosing not to participate in the study.
    c.   The control group may not be adequately matched to the experimental group.
    d.   Confidentiality of information gathered from subjects who do not know they are being studied.

24. Experimental research is used to: (31)
    a.   describe social patterns.
    b.   explain and/or predict social patterns.
    c.   generate hypotheses.
    d.   provide employment for lab technicians.

25. In all true experimental research designs, there are at least two groups. The group that is exposed to the experimental condition (change in the independent variable) is called the: (32)
    a.   experimental group.
    b.   control group.
    c.   comparison group.
    d.   guinea pig group.

TRUE-FALSE QUESTIONS

T   F   1.   Sociological research focuses on the ways in which groups affect members of human societies. (2)

T   F   2.   The first stage of modernization of the world occurred in the aftermath of the Second World War. (7)

T   F   3.   The process of modernization refers to the transformation from a traditional, usually agrarian, society to a contemporary, industrially-based state. (6-Table 1.1)

T   F   4.   Auguste Comte argued that intuition served an important function in helping scientists understand the social and physical environment. (10)

T   F   5.   Social facts are external to individuals and are shared by a significant number of people. (12)

T   F   6.   Durkheim's study concluded that the causes of suicide are external to the individual. (13)

T   F   7.   Anomic suicide is a function of overinvolvement and commitment to the group. (13)

T   F   8.   Suicide rates in the United States, Mexico and Japan are very similar. (15)

T   F   9.   The suicide rate in the United States is the highest of all now-rich countries. (15)

T   F   10. The grand theories of Comte and Marx attempted to explain the working of the human mind. (16)

15

T   F   11. Durkheim introduced the concepts of "manifest" and "latent" functions to sociology. (19)

T   F   12. According to Karl Marx, socialism signaled the final stage of economic evolution. (21)

T   F   13. Some conflict theorists believe that conflict can be beneficial to a group. (22)

T   F   14. Symbolic interactionists are preoccupied with the struggle for wealth, status and power. (23)

T   F   15. Conflict theory is a macrolevel paradigm. (23)

T   F   16. Human communication is unique among the animal world because of its use of significant symbols. (24)

T   F   17. Hypotheses are stated in terms of causal relationships. (25-26)

T   F   18. The ability of a measurement instrument to give the same results when repeated is called validity. (25-Table 1.2)

T   F   19. The ethical constraints placed on social scientists have increased in recent years. (27)

T   F   20. Most sociological studies involve experimental research. (28)

T   F   21. Sociologists prefer, whenever possible, to use data gathered by other people because it is less expensive and faster for them. (29)

T   F   22. Interviews and questionnaires are the major tools of survey research. (29)

T   F   23. In participant observation research, the researcher joins the group being studied and participates in its activities. (30)

T   F   24. Stanley Milgram discovered that many of his subjects were unwilling to comply with an order to administer what they thought was a dangerous electric shock to a stranger. (33)

T   F   25. Experimental methods are suitable for macrolevel social research. (33)

FILL-IN QUESTIONS

Fill in the blank with the word or phrase that best completes the statement.

1. _____ is the academic discipline that attempts to describe, explain, and predict human social patterns from a scientific orientation. (2)

2. When social scientists do _____ _____ research, they gather comparable data from different human populations. (3)

3. The first stage of modernization began with _____ and the second phase started after _____. (5)

4. Sociology is called a "_____" science because it looks for levels or reality other than those given in the official interpretations of society. (8-9)

5. _____ suicide results from a lack of involvement and commitment to others while _____ suicide is a function of overinvolvement and commitment to the group. (13)

6. _____suicide results from unregulated desires and ambition while _____suicide is a function of over regulation and lack of control over one's life. (13-14)

7. A _____ is a set of logically-coherent, interrelated concepts that attempts to explain some observable phenomena or group of facts. (16)

8. _____ theory deals with universal aspects of social life while _____ theories focus on relatively specific problems such as the rate of divorce. (16)

9. Marx believed that the fundamental conflict in a capitalist society was between the _____, who own and control the means of production, and the _____, who exist by selling their labor power in the market. (21)

10. The _____ orientation argues that the tangible, objective facts of social reality are of primary importance in shaping people's lives. (23)

11. According to W. I. Thomas, before people respond to an objective situation, they engage in a _____, a personal interpretation of the event. (23-24)

12. Scientists refer to components or elements of the human world which do not have a direct empirical or physical existence -- such as religious beliefs or political values -- as _____. (26)

13. A _____ _____ is a smaller segment or subgroup of a particular population which reflects the attributes of that larger group. (29)

14. _____ observation is the research technique in which the researcher remains removed or detached from the group being studied. (30)

15. Experimental research involves at least two groups of research subjects. The _____ group is exposed to the experimental condition which is the focus of the research, and the _____ group is not exposed to the experimental condition but is like the first group in all other characteristics relevant to the study. (32)

MATCH THESE SOCIAL SCIENTISTS WITH THEIR CONTRIBUTIONS:

___	1.	Emile Durkheim	A. believed conflict can be beneficial to the group
___	2.	Karl Marx	B. introduced "social facts" to explain human behavior
___	3.	Auguste Comte	
___	4.	Robert Merton	C. defined manifest and latent functions
___	5.	Ralf Dahrendorf	D. saw conflict as a class war between the bourgeoisie and the proletariat
___	6.	Lewis Coser	
___	7.	W. I. Thomas	E. argued that conflict in advanced capitalist societies centers around control, not ownership, of the means of production
			F. coined the term "sociology"
			G. coined the phrase "definition of the situation"

17

1. Discuss the two stages of modernization. Explain why the development of sociology occurred at the same time as the first stage of modernization.

2. Outline Auguste Comte's and Emile Durkheim's contributions to sociology.

3. Compare functional, conflict, and symbolic interaction perspectives on social processes and society.

4. Define these key terms in sociological research and explain their relationship: hypothesis, independent variable, dependent variable, experimental group, control group.

5. List and briefly explain each of the four types of suicide found in Durkheim's classical study. Note which of the types have been identified in contemporary studies of suicide rates in the United States, Mexico, and Japan.

ANSWERS FOR CHAPTER 1

DEFINITIONS OF KEY TERMS:

cross cultural research: the gathering of comparable data from different societies.

cultural anthropology: the study of the social organization and patterns of behavior of premodern people throughout the world.

sociology: the study of the social organization and patterns of behavior of people in large, complex, modern, industrial societies.

debunking: looking for levels of reality other than those given in the everyday and official interpretations of society.

positivism: the belief that knowledge can only be gained through people's sensory experience.

theory: a set of logically-coherent interrelated concepts that attempts to explain some observable phenonena or group of facts.

grand theory: a theory that deals with the universal aspects of social life and is usually grounded in basic assumptions (as opposed to data) concerning the nature of man and society.

middle-range theory: a theory that focuses on relatively specific phenomena or problems in the social world. A theory of white-collar crime would be a middle-range theory.

mechanical solidarity: social cohesion in preindustrial societies resulting from a minimum division of labor, common experiences, and a strong collective conscience.

organic solidarity: the social bond found in large industrial societies. In these societies people are dependent on one another because of a specialized, complex, highly developed, division of labor.

bourgeoisie: Marx's term for those people who own and control the means of production in a capitalist society.

proletariat: Marx's term for the working class in a capitalist society. According to Marx, members of the working class survive by selling their labor power to the bourgeoisie.

macrolevel: theory or research that deals with large-scale social phenomena such as societies.

microlevel: theory or research that deals with small-scale social phenomena such as families or committees.

objectivistic: orientation or viewpoint which argues that the tangible, objective facts of social reality are of primary importance in shaping people's lives and social events.

subjectivistic: orientation or viewpoint which argues that people's subjective perceptions and interpretations of reality are of primary importance in shaping their lives and social events.

definition of the situation: concept developed by symbolic interaction theorist W. I. Thomas which argued that "situations defined as real are real in their consequences."

symbolic interaction theory: sociological approach which examines the process by which members of a group or society come to define and assign meaning to their surrounding world, and the consequences or effects of the created world-view.

significant symbols: physical stimuli that have been assigned meaning and value by a social group. People respond to these symbols in terms of their meanings and values, rather than their actual physical properties.

causal relationship: an empirical association between two or more variables in which change in one factor (the independent variable) is assumed to be responsible for changes occurring in the other factor[s] (the dependent variable[s]).

constructs: components or elements of the human world which do not have a direct empirical or physical existence.

operational definitions: procedures that specify how phenomena having no direct empirical existence (constructs) are to be measured empirically.

Hawthorne effect: the effect that knowledge of being part of a research study has upon the subjects of that study. People who know they are being studied often will attempt to be "good" subjects, behaving according to their perceptions of the researcher's expectations.

nonexperimental/descriptive research: noncausal research aimed most often at providing valid, reliable information about some aspect of social reality.

survey research: type of nonexperimental study in which the researcher asks some defined group a series of questions relating to their behaviors or attitudes.

interview: survey research procedure in which the researcher asks questions through verbal interaction with the respondents.

questionnaire: survey research instrument in which questions are posed to respondents in writing for them to respond in writing.

population: name given, collectively, to all the members of a specific group being studied in a survey research design.

representative sample: a smaller segment or subgroup of a particular population which reflects the attributes of that larger group. For the sample to be representative, each member of the population must have an equal chance of being included in the sample.

observation study: research technique in which the sociologist observes subjects' behaviors directly in order to form conclusions or to make inferences about attitudes and values.

neutral observation: research technique in which researcher is identified to subject group and remains removed or detached from the group while observations are being made.

participant observation: research technique in which researcher participates in actions of subject group while observations are being made. Reseacher may be identified to the group (overt study) or researcher's identity may be kept hidden from group (covert study).

control group: in experimental research, the name given to the subject group whose members will not be exposed to the effects of the experimental condition (changes in the independent variable).

experimental group: in experimental research, the name given to the subject group whose members will be exposed to the effects of the experimental condition (changes in the independent variable).

KEY PEOPLE:

Auguste Comte, the founding father of sociology, believed that some nations were moving into the positivistic stage, the third and final phase of societal development. Positivism is the belief that reliable knowledge of the world can be gained only through people's five senses. Scientific analysis with its emphasis on observation and experimentation is grounded in positivism.

Emile Durkheim argued against the "reductionist" position that social phenomena could be reduced or explained in biological and/or psycholgocial terms. According to Durkehim, social facts exist sui generis (in and of themselves) and cannot be interpreted at the individual/psychological level of analysis. Social facts, such as laws, exist externally to the individual, constrain or influence a person's behavior, and are shared by a significant number of people.

Karl Marx, the most influential conflict theorist, argued that capitalist societies are comprised of two classes locked in an ongoing struggle. The ruling class, or bourgeoisie, own and control the "means of production." With few, if any, resources, the proletariat (working class) must sell its labor (for whatever the ruling class will pay it) in order to survive. This struggle between the "haves" and "have nots" will eventually give way to revolution and a socialist society.

ANSWERS FOR MULTIPLE CHOICE QUESTIONS

1.   b   Sociology focuses on the social organization and patterns of behavior in large, complex, modern, industrial societies. (3)

20

2.   c   Sociology originated in the mid-19th century when the Industrial Revolution was rapidly transforming European societies. Early sociologists attempted to understand the cause of these changes, and the consequences they had on societies' major institutions as well as people's behavior. (4)

3.   d   The Soviet Union has been a "Second World" -- totalitarian, socialist, industrial -- country for a number of years. It is in the process of moving toward capitalism or possibly a mixed (socialist and capitalist) economic system with increased political freedom and less government control over the day-to-day lives of its citizens. If this transformation occurs, the Soviet Union may become a "First World" country. (6 - Table 1.1)

4.   b   "Debunking" -- looking for levels of reality other than those given in the everyday and official interpretations of society -- is one of the goals of sociology. Sociologists attempt to understand and explain what "is," and are not interested in passing judgment on people, their behavior, or entire societies. (8-9)

5.   b   Auguste Comte, the founder of sociology, stressed the need for scientific analysis of society. (10)

6.   d   Middle-range theories focus on relatively specific problems in the social world -- such as the rate of divorce -- as compared with grand theories which explain the workings of entire societies. (16)

7.   a   Mechanical solidarity was the type of social cohesion found in preindustrial societies. Organic solidarity was a characteristic of industrial societies with a complex division of labor. (18)

8.   a   Manifest functions are intended and recognized by participants in the system. Latent functions are neither intended nor recognized. (19)

9.   c   The owners of professional sports teams did not intend to provide unrealistic career goals in the form of rich role models for tens of thousands of adolescent males. As a result, this outcome is a latent function or unintended consequence of their action. (19)

10.   a   Functional theory views society as a relatively harmonious, well-integrated "social system" held together by shared values and common goals. (20)

11.   b   Conflict theorists argue that institutions, organizations, and individuals force people with less power than themselves to conform to their values and standards of conduct. (20)

12.   c   Karl Marx is considered by many to be the founder of the conflict theory. He is definitely the most influential writer in this perspective. (21)

13.   a   Small-scale, microlevel social phenomena are the primary concern of symbolic interaction theorists; functional and conflict theorists focus on large-scale, macrolevel analyses. (23)

14.   c   Symbolic interactionism is the sociological perspective which analyzes human communication via significant symbols to which there are attached meanings and values. (24)

15.   a   The independent variable is the factor assumed to somehow be responsible for bringing about the observed value of the other variable (the dependent variable). (25-Table 1.2)

16.   a   "Intelligence is that which is measured by an intelligence test" is an operational definition because it specifies how a phenomenon -- intelligence -- that has no direct empirical basis is to be measured empirically. (26)

17.   b   Insuring that there will be no psychological, social, or economic harm to respondents has become a priority of universities and research organizations. Human research subjects committees evaluate proposed studies involving human subjects to ensure that no harm comes to them. (27)

21

18. a   The "Hawthorne Effect" refers to the effect that knowledge of being part of a research study has upon the subjects of that study. Knowing that they are participating in a scientific investigation, subjects may change their behaviors or attitudes in ways not fully known to the researcher, thus invalidating the results of the study. (27-28)

19. d   Use of existing data (information collected by some group or agency other than oneself) would include death records which would be collected by the equivalent of the Bureau of Vital Statistics in the various countries in which Durkheim conducted his research on suicide. (28)

20. b   A smaller segment or subgroup of a particular population which reflects the attributes of the larger group is considered to be a "representative sample;" however, it is essential that each member of the population have an equal chance of being included in the sample. (29)

21. a   Interviews and questionnaires are two major types of survey research in which the social scientist attempts to learn about people's behavior or attitudes by asking them to respond to a series of questions. Interviews are verbal; questionnaires are written. (29)

22. c   Observing through a special one-way mirror is an example of neutral observation research because the researcher remains removed from the group being studied. In this example, the researcher does not participate in group activities and is not actually physically present. (30)

23. c   Observation research does not utilize a control group and an experimental group as is the case in experimental research. The other choices are all problems associated with observation research. (31)

24. b   Explanation and/or prediction of social patterns is the objective of experimental research. (31)

25. a   The experimental group is the one exposed to the experimental condition (change in the independent variable). The control group is not exposed to the experimental condition but is used for comparison with the experimental group. (32)

ANSWERS FOR TRUE-FALSE QUESTIONS:

1.   True (2)
2.   False -- The first stage of modernization began with the Industrial Revolution. (7)
3.   True (6-Table 1.1)
4.   False -- Comte rejected intuition and embraced positivism as the means for attaining knowledge. (10)
5.   True (12)
6.   True (13)
7.   False -- Anomic suicide is a function of unregulated desires and ambition. Altruistic suicide is a function of overinvolvement and commitment to the group. (13)
8.   False -- Japan has a fairly high rate of suicide while the rate of suicide in the United States is at the low end of the continuum of now-rich countries. Mexico has a very low rate of suicide compared to either the United States or Japan. (15 and Table 1.3)
9.   False -- The United States is at the low end of the continuum of now-rich countries. (15)
10. False -- The grand theories of Comte and Marx attempted to explain the workings of all types of societies as they progressed through evolutionary stages. (16)

11. False -- Robert Merton introduced the concepts of "manifest" and "latent" functions to sociology. (19)
12. True (21)
13. True (22)
14. False -- Conflict theorists are preoccupied with the struggle for wealth, status and power. Symbolic interactionists examine the process by which members of a group or society come to define and assign meaning to their surrounding world, and the consequences or effects of the created world-view. (23)
15. True (23)
16. True (24)
17. True (25-26)
18. False -- Reliability is the ability of a measurement instrument to give the same results when repeated. Validity is the ability of an instrument to measure what it is supposed to. (25-Table 1.2)
19. True (27)
20. False -- Nonexperimental or descriptive research such as survey research and observation studies are the most frequently used methods. (28)
21. False -- Sociologists prefer to gather information themselves or, if necessary, to utilize data collected by other social scientists. (29)
22. True (29)
23. True (30)
24. False -- As the experiment progressed, Milgram was surprised and disturbed to discover that a large number of subjects were so willing to administer what they thought was an electrical shock, although many did so under protest. (33)
25. False -- Experimental methods are suitable only for microlevel social phenomena -- small group research. (33)

ANSWERS TO FILL-IN QUESTIONS:
1. Sociology (2)
2. Cross-cultural (3)
3. the Industrial Revolution; World War II (5)
4. Debunking (8-9)
5. Egoistic; altruistic (13)
6. Anomic; fatalistic (13-14)
7. Theory (16)
8. Grand; middle-range (16)
9. Bourgeoisie; proletariat (21)
10. Objectivistic (23)
11. Definition of the situation (23-24)
12. Constructs (26)
13. Representative sample (29)
14. Neutral (30)
15. Experimental; control (32)

ANSWERS TO MATCH THESE SOCIAL SCIENTISTS WITH THEIR CONTRIBUTIONS:
1. B
2. D
3. F
4. C
5. E
6. A
7. G

CHAPTER TWO

CULTURE

Chapter 2 explores the roots of culture and compares biological explanations with social and cultural perspectives on human behavior. It analyzes the importance of language in human communication, in the development of culture, and as a mechanism of social control. The chapter contrasts material and non-material culture and explains how sociologists use popular culture as a means for understanding values, norms, and patterns of behavior. Core American values are presented, and the ways in which these values are affected by one's social position, racial/ethnic identity, and experience are identified. Next, the chapter defines "norms" and discusses the hierarchy of norms. Ethnocentrism and cultural relativism are contrasted. Cultural diversity and change are analyzed in terms of subcultures and countercultures. Finally, the chapter examines the "cultural lag" between material and non-material aspects of culture in modern, industrial nations.

LEARNING OBJECTIVES:

As you read Chapter 2, use these learning objectives to organize your notes. After completing your reading, briefly state an answer to each of the objectives, and review the text pages in parentheses.

1. State the sociological definition of "culture" and discuss how it provides members of a society with a "world-taken-for granted." (38)

2. Briefly describe the main arguments of the proponents and opponents of sociobiology. (40-42)

3. Discuss the role language plays in the development of human communication and culture. (42-44)

4. Compare material and non-material culture, and give examples of each. (45-46)

5. Explain what is meant by "popular culture" and why sociologists study this aspect of culture. (47-49)

6. Discuss the core values of the United States, and identify several factors which may influence the extent to which people adhere to these values. (49-53)

7. Define folkways, mores, and laws and explain where each fits in the hierarchy of norms.(54-56)

8. Differentiate between ethnocentrism and cultural relativism. (56-58)

9. Define "culture shock" and explain when it is likely to be the most intense. (58)

10. Distinguish between subcultures and countercultures, and indicate whether countercultures are ever incorporated into the larger society. (58-60)

11. Explain how modern technology can produce cultural lag. (62-63)

CHAPTER OUTLINE

I.   INTRODUCTION

   A.   Culture is a people's way of life or social heritage that includes values, norms, institutions, and artifacts that are passed from generation to generation by learning alone.
      1. Culture provides a "world-taken-for-granted" that most people accept most of the time.
      2. Cultures set boundaries for behavior and provide standards in society -- such as the norms for beauty and physical appearance.

   B.   However, culture is not an all powerful, irresistible force that slavishly compels people to conform to an ideal standard of behavior because culture also can be altered by human beings adapting to a changing social and physical environment.

II.   THE ROOTS OF HUMAN CULTURE

   A.   The Biological Basis: One of the oldest and most controversial arguments in the biological and social sciences is whether human behavior can best be explained by biological or social explanations. The former include:
      1. Instincts -- biologically-inherited predispositions that impel most members of a species to react to a given stimulus in a specific way. Instincts once were thought to explain every aspect of behavior until scientists could not discover a core group of instincts responsible for human behavior.
      2   Biological drives -- drives experienced as a bodily imbalance or tension leading to activity that restores balance and reduces tension (such as hunger, thirst, and sex). Drives can be satisfied through learned behavior which permits the species to survive and accounts for human cultural diversity.
      3. Sociobiology -- the discipline that argues that human beings do not have instincts but do have some forms of behavior that are biologically based and transmitted genetically from one generation to another.
         a. Because some forms of behavior like altruism, aggression and homosexuality are found in virtually every human society, they must have a biological base, according to sociobiologists.
         b. Sociobiology has been criticized for its biological determinism. Many scientists argue that human beings are not predisposed to any type of behavior but, instead, have the capacity to make and to continually change their cultures virtually without limit.

   B.   Language, Thought, and Culture
      1. Importance of the development of language
         a. Human beings acquire the ability to transmit culture from generation to another.
         b. Language makes possible an ever-expanding repository of knowledge and tradition.
         c. Language provides semantic universality -- the ability to transcend time and space in communication. This is the major difference between human and non-human communication.
            (1) Human communication relies on sounds that have arbitrary meanings and can be arranged into many combinations to convey information.

25

(2) Other animals communicate by sound, odor, movement, and touch, with these signals having meaning for the animal in the <u>present</u> only.

2. Theories of how children learn to speak:
   a. The <u>imitation</u> perspective states that children simply repeat what they hear spoken by those around them.
   b. <u>Reinforcement theory</u> suggests that children are positively reinforced when they say something correctly, and negatively reinforced when they say something wrong.
   c. The <u>innateness hypothesis</u> holds that human beings learn to speak because our brains are biologically constructed or prewired to acquire language.

3. <u>The Sapir-Whorf hypothesis</u> states that language is more than just a means of communication.
   a. Language furnishes the categories by which we think, divide up, and make sense of the social world around us.
   b. Language functions as a kind of mental straight-jacket that actually forces people to perceive the social and physical environment in terms that are built into the language they speak.

4. Language as Social Control
   a. Language can be used to influence how people perceive the world and the way they think. It is a central component of a people's identity and is often linked with intense feelings of patriotism and nationalism.
   b. The importance of language as a component of a people's cultural heritage can be seen in ongoing conflicts in Canada and in the United States over what language is to be the official language of these countries.

C. Material Culture, Non-Material Culture and Popular Culture
   1. <u>Material culture</u> is the things people make and use in society.
   2. <u>Non-material culture</u> lacks a physical substance, although it was created by human beings. Examples include ideas, religious beliefs, laws, customs, and economic systems.
   3. <u>Popular culture</u> is the culture of everyday life as expressed through sport, music, hobbies, television, movies, books and other media.
      a. Popular culture is a vehicle for connecting with one's past.
      b. In addition to reflecting many of the values and patterns of behavior in contemporary society, popular culture can also be an influential factor in shaping values and behavior.

III. THE NORMATIVE ORDER

A. Core Values and National Character
   1. <u>Core values</u> are those values especially promoted by a particular culture and are often important identifying characteristics of that culture.
   2. Some social scientists use core values to generalize about the personality characteristics and patterns of behavior of an entire tribe or society; however, critics of this approach believe it is impossible to accurately determine the "national character" of a group based on core values.

B. American Values
   1. Sociologists have identified the following clusters of values in American society:

a. <u>Success</u> and related values of work, achievement, and material comfort
b. <u>Progress,</u> efficiency, rationality, and applied science (which makes it possible for people to control nature to a significant degree)
c. <u>Freedom</u>, individualism, equality, and patriotism

2. The extent to which core values are held by the American people is related to a number of factors including race, ethnicity, social class, and the experiences people have had as a result of these factors.

3. The <u>Culture</u> <u>of</u> <u>Poverty</u> thesis states that the core values of poor people are different from those of more economically successful individuals.
   a. From this perspective, values are passed down from generation to generation and contribute to a cycle of poverty from which individuals cannot escape.
   b. Other theorists reject this interpretation, arguing that lower class people do not abandon the core value of success but rather "stretch" these values so that lesser degrees of success become desirable -- and attainable.

C. Norms: Folkways, Mores and Laws
   1. <u>Norms</u> are rules stating what human beings should or should not think, say or do under given circumstances. The hierarchy of norms from least to most important is:
      a. <u>Folkways</u> -- the customary, habitual way a group does things -- <u>should</u> be followed because they represent proper etiquette, manners and the generally acceptable and approved way that people behave in social situations.
      b. <u>Mores</u> -- norms that <u>must</u> be obeyed because they are considered essential to the well being of the group (e.g. incest taboos).
      c. <u>Laws</u> -- norms that have been "codified" or formally written into a legal code. There are two types:
         (1) <u>Proscriptive</u> <u>laws</u> which state what behavior is prohibited or forbidden (e.g. criminal conduct).
         (2) <u>Prescriptive</u> <u>laws</u> which spell out what must be done, (e.g. income tax laws or traffic laws).
   3. Sanctions are attached to norms
      a. Punishments may be mild or severe
      b. Sanctions may be <u>formal</u> (handed out by organizations and institutions when rules are violated) -- or <u>informal</u> (administered by a relative or friend).
   4. Functional and conflict theorists disagree sharply concerning the manner in which norms are created and implemented (social control).
      a. Functionalists see norms originating as a result of group consensus.
      b. Conflict theorists argue that laws are a product of power relations.

D. Ethnocentrism and Cultural Relativism
   1. <u>Ethnocentrism</u> is the tendency to believe that the norms and values of one's own culture are superior to those of others, and to use these norms as a standard when evaluating all other cultures. Ethnocentric views concerning the superiority of one's group leads to stereotyping the values, attitudes and behavior of others.

        a.   A <u>stereotype</u> is a preconceived (not based on experience), standardized, group-shared idea about the alleged essential nature of a whole category of persons without regard to the individual differences of those in the category.

        b.   Stereotypes often focus on the supposed negative or humorous attributes of a group.

        c.   Historically, advertising has contributed to this type of stereotyping. In the past 15 years or so, many stereotypes have disappeared from ads.

   2.   <u>Cultural</u> <u>relativism</u> is the belief that there are no universal standards of good and bad, right or wrong; and that an aspect of any given culture can be judged only within the context of that culture.

        a.   Every culture is a unique entity and must be dealt with as such.

        b.   The main problem with cultural relativism is that any behavior can be accepted, rationalized, and justified.

E.   Culture Shock

   1.   <u>Culture</u> <u>shock</u> is the experience of encountering people who do not share one's world view that leads to feelings of disorientation, frustration, and on some occasions revulsion.

   2.   The greater the difference between a person's way of life and that of the people with whom he or she is interacting, the more intense the shock is likely to be.

IV.   CULTURAL DIVERSITY AND CHANGE

A.   Subcultures and Countercultures

   1.   <u>Subcultures</u> are groups that hold norms, values, and patterns of behavior in common with the larger society, but also have a unique design for living and world view.

        a.   Subcultures are more numerous in heterogeneous societies like the United States.

        b.   Subcultures are comprised of people from various racial and ethnic groups, different religions, geographic locations, occupations, political affiliations, and many other characteristics.

   2.   <u>Countercultures</u> are groups whose members share values, norms and a way of life that contradicts the fundamental beliefs and lifestyles of the larger, more dominant culture.

        a.   Members of a counterculture reject some or all of the core values and institutions of society, and may or may not engage in criminal behavior.

        b.   Occasionally a counterculture is incorporated into the larger society.

B.   Integration and Change

   1.   To a certain extent all cultures are <u>integrated</u>, meaning that the major material and non-material components of a society fit together and form a consistent, workable whole.

   2.   However, cultures are not completely integrated because they are constantly <u>changing</u>.

        a.   Change occurs because societies must adapt to the internal and external demands of the social, political, and physical environment.

        b.   Cultural change can be either fast or slow and accepted or resisted by various groups in society.

3. <u>Technological</u> <u>change</u> has had a dramatic impact on societies.
4. <u>Cultural</u> <u>lag</u> occurs when one aspect of culture changes faster than another aspect of culture to which it is related.
    a. In modern societies, <u>material</u> <u>culture</u> (especially technology), typically changes faster than <u>non</u>-<u>material</u> <u>culture</u> (the associated values, norms, and laws).
    b. Today human beings may be in the position of <u>reacting</u> to technological advancements rather than <u>determining</u> how they will be used.

GLOSSARY OF DIFFICULT-TO-UNDERSTAND WORDS

<u>Page</u>	<u>Line</u>	<u>Col.</u>	<u>Term from Text</u>	<u>Explanation</u>
37	4		immensely	good, great
37	6		burlesque	form of theatrical entertainment
37	6		chorus lines	dancers and singers supporting the features players in a musical comedy or review
37	10		liability	burden
37	11		prosperity	good times (economic)
37	15		disassociating	detach, separate
38	6		lanky	tall and thin
38	20		obsession	preoccupation
38	23		affliction	illness
38	24		anorexia-nervosa	a disorder where someone starves him/herself
38	26		malady	sickness
38	38		anabolicsteroids	a substance used by athletes to increase muscle mass and endurance
39	2		irresistible	impossible to withstand successfully
39	3		slavishly	submissively
39	25		alluded	referred to
39	26		adolescent	teenager
39	27		attributes	characteristics
39	33		predisposed	influenced in advance, governed
40	32		altruism	unselfish regard for others
40	33		aggression	attacking others, hostile
40	45		adaptable	flexible
40	46		distinguishes	differentiate, separate
40	49		perspective	viewpoint
40	49		paleontologist	one who studies the past from fossil remains
41	16		polymorphously	various forms
41	23		endowment	gift
42	6		linguists	one who studies languages
42	18		accumulated	collected
42	31		anticipation	hope
42	32		relies	depends on
42	42		imitation	copying
43	3		acquisition	a new ability
43	37		thrive	prosper, flourish, grow
44	16		subtle	refined, discreet
44	18		verbalized	expressed in words
44	18		reinforced	make stronger
44	22		totalitarian	central control, subordination of the individual to the state

GLOSSARY OF DIFFICULT-TO-UNDERSTAND WORDS (CONTINUED)

Page	Line	Col.	Term from Text	Explanation
44	27		abolished	to do away with, eliminate
44	29		sinister	evil
44	37		exploited	take advantage of
45	4		partitioned	separated
45	20		pluralistic	numerous members of diverse ethnic, religious, social groups, etc.
45	26		separatism	belief in being apart
45	30		assimilation	make similar
45	33		disenfranchise	deny political privileges
45	37		advocates	supports
46	8		implements	tools
46	10		proportioned	balanced
46	20		spectrum	range, continuous sequence
46	24		integrating	uniting, blending
46	27		rendered	yield, give up
46	40		ubiquitous	widespread
47	13		speculate	guess
48	4	A	fumbles	awkward, clumsily
48	11	A	doctrinaire	dogmatic, often concerns specific belief system
48	32	A	fabulous	wonderful
48	40	A	elegance	grace, refinement
48	9	B	witty	clever, humorous
48	24	B	samovar	urn for hearing water for tea-Russia
48	28	B	mendicant	beggar
48	33	B	envisioned	imagined, conceived
49	3		benevolent	kind, charitable
49	17		pursued	aimed at
49	26		virtually	almost all
49	34		cornerstones	core, importance
49	39		emphasis	special importance
50	6		motif	dominant idea
50	27		particularly	distinctly, especially
50	42		conspicuous	noticeable
50	43		rationality	reasonableness, rational understanding
51	15		minimal	least possible
51	34		corollary	something that follows
51	45		persevere	show determination
51	45		unconventionality	unusual
51	46		stubbornness	inflexibility
52	13		inability	powerlessness
52	15		ensuing	resulting
53	33		abandoning	surrendering, sacrificing
53	35		attainable	possible
53	48		awareness	knowledge of
54	1		fundamental	primary, essential
54	2		affluence	luxury, prosperity
54	8		demeanor	appearance
54	13		arbitrary	high-handed, authoritative
54	26		slurped	eating or drinking with a sucking sound
55	5		jurisdiction	domain (power)

GLOSSARY OF DIFFICULT-TO-UNDERSTAND WORDS (CONTINUED)

Page	Line	Col.	Term from Text	Explanation
55	12		mandating	requiring
55	14		transgression	offense, violation
56	1		implementation	accomplishment, fulfillment
56	3		ravaged	destroyed
56	15		proletariat	laboring class, working class
56	19		synonymous	same meaning
56	31		fanatical	overzealous, radical, extreme
56	35		commentators	critics
56	36		demeaning	degrading, meanness
57	2		pseudoscientific	false science
57	14		subservient	submissive
57	49		torture	causing intense suffering or pain
58	13		galaxies	star systems and interstellar matter
58	26		adroitly	skillfully
58	27		grotesquely	deformed, misshapen
58	32		callousness	unfeeling
59	8		inasmuch as	since
59	17		profanity	swearing
59	42		veritable	not false, real
60	20		concessions	acknowledgement, acceptance
60	38		frivolous	not serious
61	20		deprived	taken away
62	1		torpedoes	used to blow up ships under water
62	9		impunity	freedom
62	33		ingenuity	cleverness, inventiveness
62	45		proliferation	extreme growth
62	47		geopolitics	political and geographical factors characterizing a particular region
63	12	A	bedrock	base
63	25	B	emphasized	stressed
63	38	B	alienated	turned against
63	40	B	cult	worship
64	1	A	conquistadors	Spanish conquerors of North and South America in the 16th century
64	15	A	pedestal	position of honor
64	25	A	amplification	increase, enlarge, expansion
64	49	A	overwhelmingly	all-power, overpowering
65	21	A	salient	pronounced, striking
65	23	B	dishonorable	shameful
66	5	A	transgression	violation of the rules
66	34	A	diligence	industrious, busy
66	44	A	amateur	nonprofessional
66	3	B	vomit	spew, throwing up
66	28	B	endurance	tolerance
67	32	A	umpire	referee, judge
67	4	B	litigation	lawsuit
67	43	B	plaintiff	one who starts a lawsuit
67	43	B	suing	legal process, to bring action against the defendant
68	2	B	erode	eat away

KEY TERMS TO DEFINE:

After studying the chapter, define each of the following terms. Then check your work by referring the end of Chapter 2 in the Study Guide.

culture	instincts
biological drives	reinforcement theory
innateness hypothesis	material culture
non-material culture	popular culture
core values	norms
folkways	more
laws	proscriptive laws
prescriptive laws	ethnocentrism
stereotype	cultural relativism
culture shock	subcultures
countercultures	cultural lag

KEY PEOPLE

State the major contribution of each of these people:

Edward O. Wilson

Ashley Montagu

Noam Chomsky

Edward Sapir and Benjamin Whorf

Robin M. Williams

Hyman Rodman

William Graham Sumner

William Ogburn

SELF-TEST

After completing this self-test, check your answers against the "Answer Key" at the end of Chapter 2 in this Study Guide.

MULTIPLE CHOICE QUESTIONS

Select the response which best answers the question or completes the statement:

1. _____ is a people's way of life or social heritage that includes values, norms, institutions, and artifacts that are passed from generation to generation by learning alone. (38)
   a. Culture
   b. Core values
   c. Popular culture
   d. Society

2. According to sociobiologists, _____. (40)
   a. some forms of human behavior are controlled by instincts and constitute biologically-inherited predispositions that impel most members of a species to react to a given stimulus in a specific way.
   b. some forms of human behavior are biologically based and transmitted genetically from one generation to another.
   c. all human behavior can be explained by biological factors.
   d. very little of human behavior can be explained by biological factors.

3. One of the major criticisms of sociobiology is that:(40-41)
   a. sociobiology overemphasizes the role of instincts in human behavior.
   b. sociobiology relies too heavily on the importance of language in understanding human behavior.
   c. sociobiology is based on biological determinism and overstates the biological basis of human behavior.
   d. sociobiology is too heavily influenced by religious beliefs to be scientific.

4. What is the major difference between human and non-human communication? (42-43)
   a. Human communication relies to a great extent on sounds that have arbitrary meanings and can be arranged into an almost infinite number of combinations.
   b. Human communication relies on genetically predetermined signals and gestures.
   c. Human communication relies on sound, odor, movement and touch for its inherent meaning.
   d. Human communication is not as different from non-human communication as some would like to believe.

5. The Sapir-Whorf hypothesis states that language: (43)
   a. is the attaching of labels to the real world.
   b. furnishes the categories by which people interpret and make sense of the physical and social world in which they live.
   c. provides people from all cultures with similar meanings and realities.
   d. is overrated by sociologists as an indicator of social reality because it is just a means of communication.

6. According to conflict theorists, which of the following is <u>not</u> a way in which language serves as a means of social control in societies? (44-45)
   a. Language can be used to influence how people perceive the world.
   b. Language can be used to influence the way people think and behave.
   c. Language is a central component of a people's identity and is often linked with feelings of patriotism and nationalism.
   d. Language helps people to understand that they are being exploited by the ruling class.

7. Arguments that have been made for and against designating English as the "official" language in the United States show the role language plays in: (45)
   a. socializing young children in society's ways.
   b. social control and fostering a national identity.
   c. the development of popular culture.
   d. the problem of literacy.

8. Buildings, clothes and airplanes are all examples of: (45-46)
   a. material culture.
   b. non-material culture.
   c. popular culture.
   d. core culture.

9. _____ culture is the culture of everyday life as expressed through sport, movies, television, and other media. (46)
   a. Material
   b. Non-material
   c. Popular
   d. Core

10. Which of the following is <u>not</u> a core value in American society? (49-52)
    a. success
    b. aggression
    c. progress
    d. freedom

11. The extent to which core values are held by an individual is related to: (52)
    a. the length of time the person has lived in the United States.
    b. the number of years of formal education the person completed.
    c. the race, ethnicity, and social class of the individual, and the experiences the person has had as a result of these factors.
    d. the marital status of the person.

12. Rules stating what human beings should or should not think, say or do under given circumstances are called: (54)
    a. norms.
    b. core values.
    c. sanctions.
    d. reinforcement factors.

13. _____ should be followed because they represent proper etiquette, manners and the generally acceptable and approved way that people behave in social situations. (54)
    a. Taboos
    b. Folkways
    c. Mores
    d. Laws

14. Which of the following is an example of a more? (54)
    a. A sign in a restaurant reading "No Shoes, No Shirt, No Service!"
    b. Incest taboos specifying inappropriate sexual conduct.
    c. Income tax rules requiring that all wage earners file their tax returns on April 15 of each year.
    d. A requirement that a driver stopped for speeding must show his or her driver's license to the police officer who "pulls the car over."

15. _____ laws state what behavior is prohibited or forbidden while _____ laws spell out what must be done. (55)
    a. Informal; formal
    b. Formal; informal
    c. Prescriptive; proscriptive
    d. Proscriptive; prescriptive

16. The fact that residents of the United States think of, and call themselves "Americans" is seen as _____ behavior by many residents of Mexico and Latin America because they also are "Americans." (56)
    a. stereotypic
    b. ethnocentric
    c. relativistic
    d. deviant

17. The belief that there is no universal standard of good and bad, right or wrong; and that an aspect of any given culture can only be judged within the context of that culture is referred to as: (57)
    a. ethnocentrism.
    b. stereotypic behavior.
    c. cultural relativism.
    d. deviant behavior.

18. Culture shock: (58)
    a. is the experience of encountering people who do not share one's world view.
    b. may lead to feelings of disorientation, frustration, and on some occasions revulsion.
    c. is most intense when one's way of life is very different from the people with whom he or she is interacting.
    d. is all of the above.

19. Groups whose members share values, norms, and a way of life that contradicts the fundamental beliefs and lifestyle of the larger, more dominant culture are known as: (60)
    a. subcultures.
    b. countercultures.
    c. cults.
    d. subterranean groups.

20. If it is technologically possible to produce "test tube" babies without natural mothers and fathers, but there is strong societal feeling that such activity is inappropriate or immoral, sociologists would refer to this situation as: (62)
    a. cultural lag.
    b. cultural integration.
    c. cultural diffusion.
    d. cultural reproduction.

TRUE-FALSE QUESTIONS

T   F   1.   Because of cultural definitions of beauty and desirability, many women in First and Third World countries are on a calorie-reducing regime. (38)

T   F   2.   Culture is not an all powerful force because it is altered by human beings adapting to a changing social and physical environment. (38-39)

T   F   3.   Sociobiologists claim that human beings have instincts. (40)

T   F   4.   Sociologists deny that biological processes (drives) have any impact on human conduct. (42)

T   F   5.   Language is important for the transmission of culture from one generation to another. (42)

T   F   6.   The basic premise of the Sapir-Whorf Hypothesis is that the structure of language will determine how people view the world around them. (43)

T   F   7.   Popular culture reflects, but does not shape, many of the values and patterns of behavior in contemporary society. (47)

T   F   8.   Core values are those values promoted by and central to the life of a given culture. (49)

T   F   9.   The dream of making it big in the United States is the foundation for one of the core values. (49-50)

T   F   10.   Recent studies have found that Americans may be starting to reject money as the sole motivator for work. (50)

T   F   11.   Historically, fairness and equality, especially "equality of opportunity" has not been a theme in American society. (51-52)

T   F   12.   The "Culture of Poverty" thesis states that core values of poor people are different from those of economically successful individuals. (53)

T   F   13.   A man who washed his laundry in the swimming pool at his apartment complex would be violating a folkway. (54)

T   F   14.   A male sociology instructor who regularly wore an evening gown to class would be violating a more. (54)

T   F   15.   Functional and conflict theorists generally agree that norms originate as a result of group consensus and necessity. (56)

T   F   16.   In extreme forms, ethnocentrism can result in prejudice, discrimination, and war. (56)

T   F   17.   Stereotypes are often based on personal experiences which one group has had with individuals from another category of persons. (57)

T   F   18.   The major problem with the perspective of cultural relativism is that any behavior (genocide, for example) can be accepted, rationalized, and justified. (57)

T	F	19.	The greater the difference between our way of life and that of the people we are interacting with, the more intense our culture shock is likely to be. (58)
T	F	20.	Subcultures reject some or all aspects of the larger, more dominant culture. (60)
T	F	21.	Sometimes countercultures are incorporated into the larger society. (60)
T	F	22.	In modern societies, non-material culture typically changes faster than material culture. (62)
T	F	23.	The concept of macho is relatively new as a core value in Mexico. (63)
T	F	24.	Core values are similar in the United States and Japan. (65-66)
T	F	25.	Shame cultures rely on the threat of external sanctions while guilt cultures are geared to an internalized notion of sin. (66)

FILL-IN QUESTIONS

Fill in the blank with the word or phrase that best completes the statement.

1. _____ provides a "world-taken for granted" that most people accept most of the time. (38)

2. Many social scientists consider hunger, thirst, and sex to be _____ _____. (40)

3. _____ argue that some forms of behavior like altruism and aggression are transmitted genetically from one generation to another. (40)

4. Human communication relies to a great extent on sounds that have _____meanings and can be arranged into an almost infinite number of combinations to convey information about any subject imaginable. (42)

5. The _____ perspective on how children learn to speak asserts that children simply repeat what they hear spoken by those around them. (43)

6. According to the _____ hypothesis, human beings learn to speak because their brains are biologically constructed to acquire language. (43)

7. The _____ hypothesis argues that language furnishes the categories by which people interpret and make sense of the physical and social world in which they live. (43)

8. _____ culture is comprised of those things people make and use in society while _____ culture does not have physical substance, although it, too, was created by human beings. (45-46)

9. Fundamental values which provide the basis for social behavior and some of the goals pursued by members of society are called _____ values. (49)

10. The hierarchy of norms from least to most important is usually defined as _____, _____, and _____. (54)

11. Societal rules against marriage or sexual intercourse between parents and their own children are _____ _____. (54)

12. _____ laws state what behavior is prohibited or forbidden. _____ laws spell out what must be done. (55)

13. Whereas _____ is the practice of using one's culture as a basis for judging the way of life of others, _____ is the belief that there is no universal standard of good and bad, right or wrong; and that an aspect of any given culture can be judged only within the context of that culture. (57)

14. Racial and ethnic groups, individuals from different religions, geographic locations, occupations, or political affiliations are all examples of _____. (59)

15. Rapid changes in technology in the 20th century have contributed to what sociologist William Ogburn referred to as _____ _____. (62)

MATCH THESE THEORISTS WITH THEIR CONTRIBUTIONS:

____   1.   Edward Wilson   A.   identified cultural lag in contemporary societies

____   2.   Noam Chomsky   B.   hypothesized that language is more than just a means of communication

____   3.   Robin Williams   C.   developed innateness hypothesis of language acquisition

____   4.   Sapir-Whorf   D.   developed field of sociobiology

       E.   attempted to identify the

____   5.   Hyman Rodman   major values in American society

____   6.   William G. Sumner   F.   coined the term "folkways"

____   7.   William Ogburn   G.   introduced the concept of lower class value stretch

ESSAY QUESTIONS

1. Compare and contrast biological and sociological explanations of human behavior.

2. Explain the Sapir-Whorf hypothesis.

3. Specify ways in which language serves as a means of social control in societies.

4. Discuss the arguments which have been presented "for" and "against" designating English as the "official" language in the United States.

5. Compare proscriptive and prescriptive laws and give examples of each.

6. Discuss the core values in the United States, Mexico, and Japan. Explain how they are similar and how they are different.

ANSWERS FOR CHAPTER 2

DEFINITION OF KEY TERMS:

culture: a people's way of life or social heritage that includes values, norms, institutions, and artifacts that are passed from generation to generation by learning alone.

instincts: biologically inherited predispositions that impel most members of a species to react to a given stimulus in a specific way.

biological drives: drives experienced as a bodily imbalance or tension leading to activity that restores balance and reduces tension.

reinforcement theory: the language acquisition theory stating that children are positively reinforced when they say something correctly, and negatively reinforced when they say something wrong.

innateness hypothesis: according to this perspective of language acquisition, human beings learn to speak because our brains are biologically constructed or prewired to acquire language.

material culture: that aspect of culture comprised of things people make and use in society.

non-material culture: that component of culture lacking a physical substance, although created by human beings. Ideas, religious beliefs, customs, laws, and economic philosophies are examples of non-material culture.

popular culture: the culture of everyday life as expressed through sport, music, hobbies, television, movies, books, magazines, comic books, etc.

core values: those values especially promoted by a particular culture, and are often important identifying characteristics of that culture.

norms: rules stating what human beings should or should not think, say or do under given circumstances.

folkways: the customary, habitual way a group does things -- "the ways of the folk."

more: a type of norm in any given society that must be obeyed. Members of society believe that obeying mores is essential to the well being of the group.

laws: norms that have been "codified" or formally written into a legal code.

proscriptive laws: these laws state what behavior is prohibited or forbidden. For example, laws against robbing people or harming them physically are proscriptive and carry some form of punishment administered by the state.

prescriptive laws: these laws spell out what must be done. Income tax laws, traffic laws, and draft laws require people to do things at specific times, places, and under given circumstances.

ethnocentrism: the tendency to believe that the norms and values of one's own culture are superior to those of others, and to use these norms as a standard when evaluating all other cultures.

39

stereotype: a preconceived (not based on experience), standardized, group-shared idea about the alleged essential nature of a whole category of persons without regard to the individual differences of those in the category.

cultural relativism: the belief that there is no universal standard of good and bad, right or wrong; and that an aspect of any given culture can only be judged within the context of that culture.

culture shock: the experience of encountering people who do not share one's world view that leads to disorientation, frustration, and on some occasions, revulsion.

subcultures: groups that hold norms, values, and patterns of behavior in common with the larger society, but also have a unique design for living and world view.

countercultures: groups whose members share values, norms and a way of life that contradicts the fundamental beliefs and lifestyles of the larger, more dominant culture.

cultural lag: the process whereby one aspect of culture changes faster than another aspect of culture to which it is related. In modern societies, material culture (especially technology) typically changes faster than associated values, norms, and laws (non-material culture).

KEY PEOPLE:

Edward O. Wilson, a pioneer sociobiologist, argued that although human beings do not inherit an instinct that directs them to engage in specific types and quantities of agression, the "capacity" and "tendency" to engage in violent behavior is hereditary.

Ashley Montagu, an anthropologist, disagreed with the notion that human beings are predisposed to any type of behavior. He believed humans have the capacity to make and continually change their cultures virtually without limit.

Noam Chomsky, a linguist, developed an explanation of language acquisition that has been labeled the "innateness hypothesis." This hypothesis states that human beings learn to speak because their brains are biologically constructed or "prewired' to acquire language.

Edward Sapir, an anthropologist, and Benjamin Whorf, a linguist, believed that language is more than just a means of communication: that language furnishes the categories by which we think, divide up, and make sense of the social world around us. Furthermore, language functions as a kind of mental straight-jacket that actually forces people to perceive the social and physical environment in terms that are built into the language they speak.

Robin M. Williams, a sociologist, identified the major values in American society. His core values include success, progress, freedom, and patriotism.

Hyman Rodman argued against the "culture of poverty" thesis which states that the core values of poor people are differernt from those of more economically successful individuals. His "value stretch hypothesis" asserts that lower class people develop an alternative set of values without abandoning the core values of success. Lower class people "stretch" these values so that lesser degrees of success become desirable -- and attainable.

William Graham Sumner coined the term "folkways" to refer to the customary, habitual way a group does things -- "the ways of the folks."

Folkways should be followed because they represent proper etiquette, manners and the generally-acceptable and approved way that people behave in social situations.

William Ogburn identified the phenomenon of "cultural lag" -- the process whereby one aspect of culture changes faster than another aspect of culture to which it is related.

ANSWERS FOR MULTIPLE CHOICE QUESTIONS:

1. a   Culture is a people's way of life or social heritage that includes values, norms, institutions, and artificats that are passed from generation to generation by learning alone. (38)

2. b   According to sociobiologists, some forms of human behavior are biologically based and transmitted genetically from one generation to another. Response "a" is not correct because sociobiologists do not believe that human beings have instincts. Responses "c" and "d" either overstate or understate the case as seen by sociobiologists. (40)

3. c   One of the major criticisms of sociobiology is that sociobiology is based on biological determinism and overstates the biological basis of human behavior. Response "a" is not correct, once again, because sociobiologists do not believe that human beings have instincts. Responses "b" and "d" are incorrect because sociobiology does not rely on the role of language or of religious beliefs in its explanation of human behavior. (40-41)

4. a   Human communication relies to a great extent on sounds that have arbitrary meanings and can be arranged into an almost infinite number of combinations to convey information about any subject imaginable. Non-human communication relies on sound, odor, movement, and touch, with these signals having meaning for the animals' immediate environment or emotional state. (42-43)

5. b   The Sapir-Whorf hypothesis states that language furnishes the categories by which people interpret and make sense of the physical and social world in which they live. (43)

6. d   According to conflict theorists, language does not help people to understand that they are being exploited by the ruling class. This perspective argues that those in power invent a distorted language that obscures reality and keeps the masses ignorant and confused, and thus less likely to understand that they are being exploited. Responses "a," "b," and "c" are all ways in which language serves as a means of social control. (44-45)

7. b   The debate over designating English as the "official" language demonstrates the role language plays in social control and fostering a national identity. (45)

8. a   Buildings, clothes and airplanes are all examples of material culture. Material culture is comprised of those things people make and use in society. (45-46)

9. c   Popular culture is the culture of everyday life as expressed through sport, movies, television, and other media. (46)

10. b   Aggression is not one of the core values in American society. Success, progress, freedom, and patriotism are some of the most important core values. (49-52)

11. c   The extent to which core values are held by an individual is related to the race, ethnicity, and social class of the individual, and the experiences the person has had as a result of these factors. Responses "a," "b," and "d" are not indicators discussed in the text. (52)

12.   a   Norms are rules that state "what human beings should or should not think, say or do under given circumstances." (54)

13.   b   Folkways should be followed because they represent proper etiquette, manners and the generally-acceptable and approved way that people behave in social situations. (54)

14.   b   Incest taboos specifying inappropriate sexual conduct are examples of mores. Mores <u>must</u> be obeyed because they are grounded in deep-seated cultural values and are essential to the well being of the group. (54)

15.   d   <u>Proscriptive</u> laws state what behavior is prohibited or forbidden while <u>prescriptive</u> laws spell out what must be done. (55)

16.   b   The fact that residents of the United States think of, and call themselves "Americans" is seen as <u>ethnocentric</u> behavior by many residents of Mexico and Latin America because they also are "Americans." This example demonstrates that people can be ethnocentric -- believing that their own culture is superior to all others -- without even realizing they are offending another group. (56)

17.   c   Cultural relativism is the belief that there is no universal standard of good and bad, right or wrong; and that an aspect of any given culture can be judged only within the context of that culture. (57)

18.   d   Culture shock: (a) is the experience of encountering people who do not share one's world view; (b) may lead to feelings of disorientation, frustration, and on some occasions revulsion; and (c) is most intense when one's way of life is very different from the people with whom one is interacting. Thus (d), "all of the above," is the best response. (58)

19.   b   Countercultures are groups whose members share values, norms and a way of life that contradicts the fundamental beliefs and lifestyles of the larger, more dominant culture. By comparison, subcultures are groups that hold norms, values, and patterns of behavior in common with the larger society, but also have a unique design for living and world view. (60)

20.   a   "Test tube" babies are an example of cultural lag -- the process whereby one aspect of culture changes faster than another aspect of culture to which it is related. In modern societies, material culture (especially technology) typically changes faster than associated values, norms, and laws (non-material culture). (62)

ANSWERS FOR TRUE-FALSE QUESTIONS:

1.   False -- Although many middle and upper middle-class women in the United States and other First World countries are obsessed with dieting and thinness, this behavior is virtually unknown in Third World countries. (38)

2.   True (38-39)

3.   False -- Sociobiologists state that although human beings do not have instincts, some forms of behavior like altruism and aggression are transmitted genetically from one generation to another. (40)

4.   False -- Sociologists do not deny that biological processes (drives) impact human conduct, but they stress that these processes <u>interact</u> with social and cultural forces to produce behavior. (42)

5.   True (42)

6.   True (43)

7.   False -- Popular culture not only reflects many of the values and patterns of behavior in contemporary society, but it also can be an influential factor in shaping those values and behavior. (47)

8.   True (49)

9.   True (49-50)

10.   True (50)

11. False -- Fairness and equality, especially "equality of opportunity," have been persistent themes in American society for most of our history as a nation. (51-52)
12. True (53)
13. True (54)
14. True (54)
15. False -- Functional and conflict theorists disagree sharply concerning the manner in which norms are created and implemented (social control). Functionalist sociologists are more likely to see norms originating as a result of group consensus, while conflict theorists argue that laws are a product of power relations. (56)
16. True (56)
17. False -- Stereotypes are preconceived (not based on experience), standardized, group-shared ideas about the alleged essential nature of a whole category of persons without regard to the individual differences of those in the category. (57)
18. True (57)
19. True (58)
20. False -- Subcultures are groups that hold norms, values, and patterns of behavior in common with the larger society, but also have a unique design for living and world view. Countercultures reject some or all aspects of the larger, more dominant culture. (60)
21. True (60)
22. False -- Material culture (especially technology) typically changes faster than non-material culture (values, norms and laws) in modern societies. (62)
23. False -- The concept of macho can be traced back to the days of the conquistadors (i.e. the 16th century). (63)
24. False -- Core values in Japanese society are hard work, harmony, and a "shame" culture. Some of the most important core values in the United States are success, progress, freedom, and patriotism. (65-66)
25. True (66)

ANSWERS TO FILL-IN QUESTIONS:

1. Culture (38)
2. Biological drives (40)
3. Sociobiologists (40)
4. Arbitrary (42)
5. Imitation (43)
6. Innateness (43)
7. Sapir-Whorf (43)
8. Material; non-material (45-46)
9. Core (49)
10. Folkways; mores; laws (54)
11. Incest taboos (54)
12. Proscriptive; prescriptive (55)
13. Ethnocentrism; cultural relativism (57)
14. Subcultures (59)
15. Cultural lag (62)

ANSWERS TO MATCH THESE THEORISTS WITH THEIR CONTRIBUTIONS:

1. D
2. C
3. E
4. B
5. H
6. F
7. A

CHAPTER THREE

GROUPS AND SOCIAL STRUCTURE

Chapter 3 begins with the idea that the social lives of humans are structured, showing order and predictability rather than chaos and randomness. This social structuring of human activities is made possible through a shared culture that gives the members of a population a common world view. Next, the chapter contrasts "aggregates" and "categories" with "social groups." The concepts of "status" and "role" are defined, and role strain and role conflict are explained. Then, the chapter discusses the differences in membership and reference groups, in primary and secondary groups, and in formal and informal organizations. Finally, societies are defined as self-perpetuating groups of people who occupy a given territory and interact with one another on the basis of a shared culture. Societies are divided into two types: Gemeinschaft -- a traditional type of communal relationship based on personal, primary group relations -- and Gesellschaft -- a modern type of associational relationship based on formal, impersonal, and rational interaction typical of secondary groups.

LEARNING OBJECTIVES:

As you read Chapter 3, use these learning objectives to organize your notes. After completing your reading, briefly state an answer to each of the objectives, and review the text pages in parentheses.

1. Discuss the role of culture in the creation of human social structure. (73)

2. Explain how social groups differ from aggregates and categories. (73-74)

3. Differentiate between "status" and "role," and state how "role strain" and "role conflict" occur. (74-76)

4. Distinguish between membership groups and reference groups. Indicate how reference groups may play a part in an anticipatory socialization process. (76-77)

5. State the characteristics of primary groups and secondary groups, and indicate which of the two has the most lasting impact upon its members. (78-81)

6. Discuss ways in which increasing group size affects the relations among group members. (81-82)

7. List and briefly explain Amitai Etzioni's three types of formal organizations. (82-83)

8. Outline the distinguishing features of bureaucracy and identify the major strengths and weaknesses of bureaucratic organization. (83-87)

9. Define "society" and indicate how societies differ from other types of social groups. (90)

10. Differentiate between "Gemeinschaft" and "Gesellschaft" societies. (91)

CHAPTER OUTLINE

I.   THE CONCEPT OF SOCIAL STRUCTURE

A. Social structure is the organization of a societal population into various groups, and the patterned relationships that exist within and among these groups.
    1. Human social life in general is organized rather than chaotic, just as individuals' behaviors are stable rather than random.
    2. This social structuring of human activities is made possible through a shared culture that gives the members of a population a common world view.

B. Culture provides the members of a given population with a "blueprint for reality" while social structure represents the rendering of that blueprint into some sort of inhabitable residence.

II. GROUPS AND OTHER COLLECTIVITIES

A. When sociologists talk of groups, they use the term in a much more restrictive way than other people. Sociologists make the following distinctions among several different types of collectivities or situations involving more than one person:
    1. Aggregates are made up of people who occupy the same physical space at the same particular time.
    2. Categories are distinguished by common or shared characteristics of their members. The people who constitute a given category may or may not ever be physically present with one another.
    3. Social groups are made up of people who interact with one another in a regular, patterned way and who come to form a sense of common identity.
        a. Social groups display the characteristics of both aggregates and categories -- their members often share space and time, and usually share common attributes or interests as well.
        b. But, over time, these groups develop additional traits that distinguish them from either aggregates or categories: they come to form an organization or structure involving statuses and roles.

B. Status and Role
    1. In sociological usage, status means any defined or recognized position within a group or society (as compared with ordinary usage where status implies some sort of social ranking or level of prestige).
    2. Role (or formal role) is the set of expected behaviors and attitudes associated with a particular status in a group or society. Thus, the role defines what someone who occupies a particular status is supposed to do because of that position.
    3. Role performance is an individual's actual behaviors and attitudes in response to role expectations.
    4. Role strain is the inability to meet successfully all the expectations attached to a particular social role.
    5. Role conflict occurs when there are contradictory role expectations arising from two or more statuses occupied by a given individual at the same time.

45

III. TYPES OF SOCIAL GROUPS

A. Membership Groups and Reference Groups
 1. A <u>membership group</u> (or "ingroup") is a social group to which a given individual belongs and participates as a member. Sociologists believe that knowing an individual's membership groups provides a great deal of information about what that person will be like.
 2. A <u>reference group</u> is social group whose perspective is adopted by a given individual as a frame of reference for personal behaviors and attitudes.
   a. For the most part, individuals' membership groups and reference groups will be one and the same.
   b. However, sometimes an individual currently may not be a member of his or her reference group. This is especially true in the case of <u>anticipatory socialization</u> -- the early learning of appropriate behaviors and attitudes that will be required for some future social role.

B. Primary Groups and Secondary Groups
 1. <u>Primary groups</u> are social groups such as one's family or close friends that are essential in the formation of individual self-identity. According to Charles H. Cooley, relationships in primary groups have these characteristics:
   a. Total personality involvement
   b. Emotional "warmth"
   c. Spontaneity, informality
   d. Direct (face-to-face) contact
   e. Smaller size
   f. Valued as end (intrinsic rewards)
 2. <u>Secondary groups</u> are social groups such as customers and clerks that are more formal, less inclusive, and less emotional than primary groups and typically are organized for some specific purpose. Relationships in secondary groups have these characteristics:
   a. Segmented personality involvement
   b. Emotional "coolness"
   c. Patterning, formality
   d. Indirect (non face-to-face) contact
   e. Larger size
   f. Valued as means to end (extrinsic rewards)
 3. Formulations of primary and secondary groups represent what sociologists call <u>ideal types</u> -- logical constructions that present, in exaggerated and idealized form, the distinguishing features of some phenomenon.
   a. In the real social world, groups exist as combinations or mixtures of <u>both primary and secondary group characteristics</u>.
   b. Groups should be envisioned on a continuum, with different groups located along the continuum in terms of how "primary-like" or "secondary-like" the groups atmosphere and the members' interactions appear to be.
 4. <u>Group size</u> is a significant factor in the likelihood of primary-like or secondary-like relations within the group. Georg Simmel made these distinctions:
   a. A <u>dyad</u> is a social group consisting of two members. It is the most basic and intimate of all possible human groupings, and it is also the most fragile.

46

b. A _triad_ is a social group consisting of three members. The social triad marks the beginning of more complex social interaction patterns within the group and the development of an identifiable group structure.

c. The addition of further members to an exiting group dramatically increases the number of linkages within the group. As a group grows in size, formal organization becomes more necessary.

C. Formal Organizations

1. _Formal_ _organizations_ are large, deliberately-planned groups with established personnel, procedures, and rules for carrying out some particular objective or set of objectives. Sociologist Amitai Etzioni developed this classification system of formal organizations based on their members' motivations for participation:

a. _Normative_ _organizations_ -- also referred to as "voluntary associations" -- are public interest organizations such as Scouts or PTA groups that people join for non-material reasons.

b. _Coercive_ _organizations_ -- also referred to as "involuntary associations" -- are organizations such as prisons or asylums that people join involuntarily and which restrain their members from normal contact with the larger society.

c. _Utilitarian_ _organizations_ -- are organizations such as corporations or universities that individuals join for some practical, material reason.

D. Bureaucratic Organization

1. _Bureaucracy_ is an administrative device for maximizing human efficiency through the logical, orderly structuring of individual behaviors within a particular setting.

2. _Max_ _Weber_, a German sociologist, was one of the first social scientists to offer a detailed analysis of formal organizations and to define these pure or ideal-type _characteristics_ _of_ _bureaucracy_:

a. A well-defined sphere of responsibility and authority

b. Standardized, impersonal procedures for recruitment and promotion of personnel

c. An established hierarchy of communications and decision-making channels

d. Interactions based on objective and impartial secondary relationships among members _within_ the bureaucracy, as well as _between_ bureaucrats and the organization's clients or customers.

e. A distinction between organizational and personal life which divorces objective, rational, goal-directed organizational concerns from the subjective, personal, and often-emotional concerns of individuals.

E. Bureaucratic Shortcomings and Bureaucratic Ritualism

1. Bureaucracies have become known for their "red tape"

2. They often seem slow and unable to respond to novel situations demanding rapid action.

3. Things tend to "fall between the cracks" -- get lost and stay lost -- in bureaucracies if the situation needing attention does not clearly fall into any one office or area of responsibility.

4. _Bureaucratic_ _ritualism_ or _goal-displacement_ occurs when adherence to organizational rules becomes more important than fulfilling the original objectives for which the organization was created.

47

F. The Informal Organization
1. The <u>informal organization</u> is the actual set of relationships developed by the members of formal organizations as they carry out the activities defined by organizational objectives and procedures.
2. Informal organization can be either positive or negative for individuals in the organization and for the organization itself.
   a. For some individuals in large-scale organizations, primary group relationships with other employees are important for making their "organizational home" as comfortable as possible.
   b. These personal networks often can transmit information and supply (or acquire) needed resources much faster and more efficiently than established bureaucratic channels.
   c. On the other hand, informal structures may have a negative impact on the formal organization because if people see their best interests being threatened by the "official" pattern, they may use informal, primary group networks to resist or sabotage bureaucratic goals.

G. Differences in Japanese Corporate Structure and Bureaucratic Organizations in the United States:
1. In Japan, employees' relationships with the organization are more long-lasting than in the U.S.
2. Japanese hiring, promotion, and pay practices emphasize groups rather than individuals. U.S. organizations force employees to compete against one another for advancement in what amounts to a "zero-sum game" situation.
3. The Japanese corporation stresses a more generalized sphere of knowledge while U.S. organizations encourage and demand a high level of specialized expertise.
4. The Japanese corporation is much more involved in the personal lives of its workers, which many U.S. employees might consider to be an invasion of their privacy.
5. Decision-making in the Japanese organization is far less centralized and less "top-down" than in the typical U.S. bureaucracy.

IV. SOCIETIES AND SOCIETAL DEVELOPMENT

A. <u>Societies</u> are self-perpetuating groups of people who occupy a given territory and interact with one another on the basis of a shared culture. Sociologists have focused on the study of human societies and have examined important developmental changes and trends over time.
B. <u>Emile Durkheim</u> (1858-1917) argued that increasing population size, division of labor, and specialization of function led to the end of <u>mechanical solidarity</u> and the development of <u>organic solidarity</u>:
1. <u>Mechanical solidarity</u> -- structures whose members formed cohesive bonds because of their shared social attributes and cultural world view.
2. <u>Organic solidarity</u> -- a system in which cohesiveness was based on the functional interdependency created as a consequence of increasing dissimilarities among population members.
C. <u>Ferdinand Tonnies</u> (1855-1936) viewed societal change as a movement away from traditional <u>Gemeinschaft</u> organization to <u>Gesellschaft</u> organization:
1. <u>Gemeinschaft</u> is a traditional type of communal relationship based upon personal emotions and long-standing customs among the members of a societal population.

2. _Gesellschaft_ is a modern type of associational relationship based upon impersonal, rational, secondary group relations among the members of a societal population.

D. Gerhard _Lenski_ (a contemporary U.S. sociologist) formulated an evolutionary model of human development that links societal change to changes in economic technology.
   1. He views economic surpluses created through improvements in productive technology to be the catalyst for changes ranging from population size to the number and content of organized religions.
   2. This evolutionary process occurred in several stages:
      a. The first societies were hunting and gathering societies which embodied the essence of primary group relations.
         (1). These societies were small in size and very simple in organization.
         (2). They had very little social differentiation and practiced "primitive egalitarianism" in which hierarchical property, power, and prestige differences among individuals were minimal.
      b. Then, horticultural societies developed with the advent of farming. These societies created food surpluses which allowed for increased population size and a division of labor.
         (1). Some societal members were freed from actual participation in food growing and hunting and were able to pursue full-time noneconomic positions and roles (such as becoming political or religious leaders).
         (2) These leaders were able to acquire larger than average shares of social resources, and to pass these advantages along to their descendants. As a result, simple equality began to give way to simple inequality.
      c. Next, agrarian societies developed with the advent of metal tools and other "advanced" farming technologies.
         (1). These societies were characterized by much larger populations, true urban settlements, complex division of labor, and large political, economic, and military bureaucratic organizations.
         (2). Impersonal relations began to compete with more subjective, primary relations in everyday life.
         (3). Social inequalities became more complex and much larger among societal participants.
      d. Finally, industrial societies replaced agrarian societies when the development and harnessing of mechanical power sources led to a dramatic shift from agriculture to manufacturing as the major productive sources of economic wealth, power, and prestige.
         (1). Societal populations now were extremely large in size and urbanized.
         (2). Formal organizations that make up the framework of governmental, economic, educational and other major societal institutions developed to perform major functions in society.

GLOSSARY OF DIFFICULT-TO-UNDERSTAND WORDS

Page	Line	Col.	Term from Text	Explanation
71	1		plastic-wares	objects made from plastic
71	3		device	instrument
72	1		guidance	direction
72	16		affiliations	associations, combining with others
72	21		tremendously	enormously, very great
73	3		chaotic	confusion
73	20		anatomical	human body, esp. the sexual parts
73	28		blueprint	outline, sketch, plan
73	29		sort	kind, type
73	35		conjures	summons, calls up
73	36		pedestrians	strollers
74	14		disperse	scatter
74	15		ceases	to bring to an end
74	25		cluster	similar things grouped together
74	30		authentic	real, genuine
74	42		"classy"	elegant, stylish
75	2		connotations	implication, suggestion
75	22		resemble	look like
75	36		virtue	the strength
75	47		clashing	conflicting
76	12		stifled	silenced, restrained, suppressed
76	16		astonishingly	surprisingly
76	20		typologies	classifications
76	33		league	association, alliance
76	41		affiliations	connections
77	6		lesbian	female homosexual
78	2		exert	employ
78	12		aspiring	work for, aim at
78	29		deliberately	intentionally, purposefully
78	31		prolonged	drown out, lengthened
79	4		spontaneous	impulsive, free, nonpreparation
79	7		intrinsic	intimate, essential
79	18		pleasantries	agreeable, happy conversation
79	23		factually	truthfully, actually, authentically
80	7		phenomenon	object
80	9		depersonalized	impersonal, detached, objective
80	15		array	range, arrangement
80	26		homey	homelike, warm, close feeling
81	13		devoid	empty
81	18		triggered	set off
81	26		fragile	weak
81	39		proverbial	well-known, familiar
81	41		coalition	combination, union
81	43		mediator	peace-maker, umpire
82	16		peeled	searching for
82	29		analytic	logical analysis, breaking into logical parts
82	29		feasible	easier
82	32		coercive	to use force, dominate
82	35		charitable	to give (time or money), charity
83	5		tangible	concrete, solid

GLOSSARY OF DIFFICULT-TO-UNDERSTAND WORDS (CONTINUED)

Page	Line	Col.	Term from Text	Explanation
85	3		hierarchy	a series of ranks one above the other, the organization might look like a pyramid
85	9		impartial	objective, detached, fair-minded
85	26		skepticism	doubt, unbelief
85	31		realm	domain, region
85	35		slash	cut, reduce
85	37		bogged	impeded, slowed the progress
86	17	A	albeit	though, however
86	39	A	prefectural	chief officer, area governed by
87	14		limbo	transitional place, unable to take action
87	31		entrenched	established, strong defensive position, not willing to change
88	8		severe	strict, harsh, a great degree
88	24		sabotage	damage, harm, wreck
88	31		fluctuations	variations, changing
88	35		compatible	agreeable, consistent, uniform
88	38		merits	value
88	47		cradle-to-grave	birth to death--total life span
89	4		cohort	group with something in common
89	17		mandatory	required
89	18		holistic	total, whole
89	47		depicted	described, represented
90	8		adhering	sticking, binding
90	26		encompassing	enclosed, enveloped
90	29		self-perpetuating	continuing, endlessly
90	30		sustain	support, provide for
91	18		"communal"	community
91	36		cohesive	sticking tightly together
92	3		wrought	formed
92	5		buffers	cushion, protection
92	16		catalyst	spark which starts a reaction
92	28		rudiments	beginnings, basics
92	29		advent	arrival, appearance
93	11		immensely	enormous, unbounded, not confined
94	7	A	renowned	famous, noted
94	22	A	swaggering	boasting, bragging
94	36	A	turbulence	disorder, confusion
94	3	B	crucial	important
94	34	B	condescending	superior, prideful
94	52	B	revenue	income, payments
95	7	A	disdain	contempt, disregard, scorn
96	22	A	cohesion	sticking together
96	37	A	culminates	climaxes, bring to an end
96	22	B	reaffirmation	validated, confirmation
96	28	B	proliferation	multiply quickly
97	30	A	utmost	extreme, greatest amount
97	39	B	permissively	tolerant, permitting
98	2	A	benevolence	kindness
98	6	A	compliant	obedient, submissive
98	23	A	perspective	viewpoint

51

GLOSSARY OF DIFFICULT-TO-UNDERSTAND WORDS (CONTINUED)

Page	Line	Col.	Term from Text	Explanation
98	44	A	infinitesimally	too small to measure
98	48	A	manifested	obvious, evident
98	4	B	drenched	dripping wet
98	7	B	commensurate	equal in measure
98	26	B	domineering	extreme control
99	25	A	altruism	unselfish
99	40	A	antihero	lacking in admired qualities
99	9	B	introspection	self-examination
99	12	B	propelled	pushed
99	21	B	neoreligious	new religion
99	40	B	adversely	unfavorably

KEY TERMS TO DEFINE:

After studying the chapter, define each of the following terms. Then check your work by referring to the answers at the end of Chapter 3 in the Study Guide.

social structure

social collectivity

aggregate

category

group

status

role/formal role

role performance

role strain

role conflict

typologies

membership group

reference group

anticipatory socialization

primary groups

secondary groups

ideal types

dyad

triad

formal organizations

normative organizations

coercive organizations

utilitarian organizations

bureaucracy

goal-displacement/bureaucratic ritualism

informal organization

societies

Gemeinschaft

Gesellschaft

KEY PEOPLE

State the major theoretical contributions of each of these people.

Charles Horton Cooley

Georg Simmel

Amitai Etzioni

Max Weber

Emile Durkheim

Ferdinand Tonnies

Gerhard Lenski

SELF-TEST

After completing this self-test, check your answers against the "Answer Key" at the end of Chapter 3 in this Study Guide and in the text on the page(s) indicated in parentheses.

MULTIPLE CHOICE QUESTIONS

Select the response which best answers the question or completes the statement:

1. The organization of a societal population into various groups and the patterned relationships that exist within and among them is referred to as a(n): (73)
    a. social collectivity
    b. social structure
    c. aggregate
    d. category

2. A collection of pedestrians waiting to cross a busy intersection would be classified by sociologists as a(n): (74)
    a. aggregate
    b. category
    c. social group
    d. status group

3. In sociological usage, status is: (74)
    a. a level of prestige in society
    b. a high social ranking
    c. any defined or recognized position within a group or society
    d. the set of expected behaviors and attitudes associated with a particular position in a group or society

4. A Pre-Law Association at a university and a Future Business Leaders' Club at a high school are examples of: (78)
    a. primary groups
    b. reference groups
    c. coercive groups
    d. expressive groups

5. The term "primary group" was coined by: (78)
    a. Emile Durkheim
    b. Ferdinand Tonnies
    c. Gerhard Lenski
    d. Charles H. Cooley

6. Which of the following is an example of a primary group? (78)
    a. delegates to the Democratic National Convention
    b. students in an 8:00 a.m. sociology class
    c. friends who get together every Monday night to watch football on television
    d. an attorney hosting a holiday party for her clients

7. Married couples, two "best friends," and a brother and sister are all examples of: (81)
    a. dyads
    b. triads
    c. aggregates
    d. categories

8. The classical sociologist who focused on the effects of group size on the nature and the strength of the social bonds that formed between group members was: (81)
    a. Gerhard Lenski
    b. Amitai Etzioni
    c. Ferdinand Tonnies
    d. Georg Simmel

9. A formal organization has which of the following characteristics? (82)
    a. spontaneity, informality
    b. established personnel, procedures, and rules for carrying out some objective
    c. total personality involvement
    d. emotional rewards for participants

10. People join _____ organizations because they perceive their goals as being socially or morally worthwhile. (82)
    a. normative
    b. coercive
    c. utilitarian
    d. informal

11. Corporations and universities are examples of _____ organizations: (83)
    a. normative
    b. coercive
    c. utilitarian
    d. informal

12. Which of these is an example of a coercive group? (82-83)
    a. college students in a lecture hall taking a required final exam
    b. new employees of a corporation attending a mandatory orientation session
    c. Scouts on a wilderness hiking trip required for a merit badge
    d. inmates at a state prison facility

13. Max Weber was the first sociologist to offer a detailed analysis of: (83-84)
    a. primary and secondary groups
    b. bureaucracy
    c. normative, coercive and utilitarian organizations
    d. Gemeinschaft and Gesellschaft

14. Which of the following is not an element of "pure" bureaucracy? (84-85)
    a. well-defined spheres of responsibility and authority
    b. standardized, impersonal procedures
    c. recruitment and promotion on the basis of technical expertise
    d. blending of organizational and personal life

15. Bureaucratic ritualism occurs when: (87)
    a. adherence to organizational rules becomes more important than fulfilling the original objectives for which the organization was created
    b. adherence to organizational rules is forced on participants who have been removed from normal contact with the larger society
    c. organizational participants develop informal networks and "grapevines" to create a better working environment for themselves
    d. organizational participants perceive that their group's goals are morally worthwhile

16. A(n) _____ is the actual set of relationships developed by the members of formal organizations as they carry out the activities defined by organizational objectives and procedures. (87-88)
    a. Formal organization
    b. Informal organization
    c. Bureaucratic organization
    d. Normative organization

17. Studies of employees in Japanese corporations, as compared with U.S. workers, indicate that: (88-89)
    a. Japanese workers have longer-lasting relationships with their organizations than do most workers in the U.S.
    b. Japanese employees move together as they advance through the ranks of the organization, rather than having to compete against one another for advancement as U.S. workers do
    c. Japanese workers experience much more involvement of the corporation in their personal lives than do employees in the U.S.
    d. all of the above

18. Which of the following is not a characteristic of societies? (90)
    a. Societies are self-perpetuating
    b. Societies occupy a given territory
    c. Societies are less encompassing than other types of human groups
    d. Societies are made up of people who interact with one another on the basis of a shared culture

19. A society in which people interact with one another on the basis of long-standing customs and with personal emotions is called: (91)
    a. Gemeinschaft
    b. Gesellschaft
    c. Organic solidarity
    d. Inorganic solidarity

20. A society in which impersonal, rational, secondary group relations dominate people's daily lives is called: (91)
   a. Gemeinschaft
   b. Gesellschaft
   c. Organic solidarity
   d. Inorganic solidarity

21. Which of the following sociologists linked changes in productive technology with the larger economic surpluses which occurred as societies developed through various stages? (92)
   a. Charles H. Cooley
   b. Max Weber
   c. Gerhard Lenski
   d. Georg Simmel

22. Cities, complex divisions of labor, and bureaucratic organizations first developed in _____ societies. (92-93)
   a. hunting and gathering
   b. horticultural
   c. agrarian
   d. industrial

TRUE-FALSE QUESTIONS

T   F   1. Social structure represents the attempts of a given human population to translate its particular view of the world into concrete terms. (73)

T   F   2. From the sociological perspective, all social groups are examples of collectivities, and all collectivities are social groups. (74)

T   F   3. A category is a number of people who share the same physical space at the same time. (74)

T   F   4. A status is a recognized position within a group while a role is the set of expected behaviors and attitudes associated with a particular status. (74-75)

T   F   5. Role conflict is the inability to meet successfully all the expectations attached to a particular social role. (75)

T   F   6. Individuals belong to and participate in membership groups, but they may or may not actually belong to reference groups. (76-77)

T   F   7. An individual's membership group affiliations provide a great deal of information about what that person is like. (76)

T   F   8. A major difference between primary groups and secondary groups is that primary groups are essential to the formation of an individual's self-concept. (78-79)

T   F   9. Generally, members of secondary groups are interchangeable. (79)

T   F   10. According to Georg Simmel, the triad is the most fragile of social groups. (81)

56

T   F   11.   Normative organizations attract members who are seeking some sort of tangible, material benefit from their participation. (82)

T   F   12.   According to Max Weber, bureaucracy is a device for maximizing human efficiency. (84)

T   F   13.   Bureaucracies have a unique ability to deal with people, things, or situations that don't fit recognized patterns. (85)

T   F   14.   Secretaries who establish primary group relations with other secretaries in the same corporation are an example of informal organizational structure. (88)

T   F   15.   Informal structures always work to the formal organization's advantage. (88)

T   F   16.   While the Japanese model of formal organization seems to have worked well in that society, it is doubtful that the same principles could be applied to the U.S. with equal effect. (89)

T   F   17.   Societies are less encompassing and self-perpetuating than other types of human groups. (90)

T   F   18.   According to Tonnies, as societies increased in size and became more highly differentiated, the quality of social relations changed. (91)

T   F   19.   Lenski's evolutionary theory of societal development includes hunting and gathering groups, horticultural villages, agrarian societies, and industrial societies. (92-93)

T   F   20.   Durkheim, Tonnies, and Lenski disagree about the general course of societal development. (93)

FILL- IN QUESTIONS

Fill in the blank with the word or phrase that best completes the statement.

1.   A(n) _____ is a social collectivity whose members occupy the same physical space at the same time while a(n) _____ is a social collectivity whose members are clustered statistically on the basis of common or shared characteristics. (74)

2.   The concept of _____ _____ is used to indicate an individual's actual behaviors and attitudes in response to role expectations. (75)

3.   _____ _____ occurs when contradictory role expectations arise from two or more statuses occupied by a given individual at the same time. (75)

4.   Ordering systems that sort and classify individual groups on the basis of distinguishing characteristics are referred to as _____by sociologists. (76)

5.   _____ groups are those groupings in which a given individual objectively belongs and participates as a member. _____ groups are those social groups whose values, norms, beliefs, and behaviors serve as the basis for the individual's personal life. (76-77)

6. Social groups such as an accountant and her clients that are more formal, less inclusive, and less emotional than primary groups and typically are organized for some specific purpose are _____ groups. (79)

7. _____ is an administrative device for maximizing human efficiency through the logical, orderly structuring of individual behaviors within a particular setting. (84)

8. Self-perpetuating groups of people who occupy a given territory and interact with one another on the basis of a shared culture are referred to as _____. (90)

9. A(n) _____ is characterized by a traditional type of communal relationship based upon personal emotions and long-standing customs among the members of a societal population while a(n) _____ is a modern type of associational relationship based upon impersonal, rational, secondary group relations among the members of a societal population. (91)

10. Based on Lenski's theory of societal development, agrarian societies gradually were replaced by _____ societies as a result of the development and harnessing of mechanical power sources. (92-93)

MATCH THESE IMPORTANT CONCEPTS WITH THEIR DEFINITIONS:

___	1.	Aggregate	A.	An organizational structure characterized by well-defined spheres of responsibility and authority, standardized, impersonal procedures, and emphasis on technical merit
___	2.	Category	B.	Any defined or recognized position within a group or society
___	3.	Group	C.	Social groups such as one's family or close friends that are essential in the formation of individual self-identity
___	4.	Status	D.	Social collectivity whose members occupy the same physical space at the same time
___	5.	Role	E.	Social group to which a given individual belongs and in which the individual participates as a member
___	6.	Membership group	F.	Social collectivity whose members are clustered statistically on the basis of common or shared characteristic(s)
___	7.	Reference group	G.	The set of expected behaviors and attitudes associated with a particular status in a group or society
___	8.	Primary group	H.	Social collectivity whose members possess a feeling of common identity and who interact in a regular, patterned way
___	9.	Secondary group	I.	Social groups such as customers and clerks that are more formal, less inclusive, less emotional than primary groups and typically organized for some specific purpose
___	10.	Bureaucracy	J.	Social group whose perspective is adopted by a given individual as a frame of reference for personal behaviors and attitudes

ESSAY QUESTIONS

1. Explain the role of culture and social structure in creating order and predictability in the social lives of humans.

2. Compare aggregates, categories, and social groups. Give examples of each from your own experience.

3. Indicate why reference groups may have such a strong influence on individuals who may not even be members of the group.

4. Discuss Max Weber's ideal characteristics of bureaucracy. Note several specific ways in which contemporary bureaucracies differ from these ideal characteristics.

5. Explain why it would be difficult for corporations in the United States shift from bureaucracy to Japanese organizational structure.

ANSWERS FOR CHAPTER 3

DEFINITIONS OF KEY TERMS:

social structure: the organization of a societal population into various groups, and the patterned relationships that exist within and among these groups.

social collectivity: any collection or situation involving more than one person.

aggregate: social collectivity whose members occupy the same physical space at the same time.

category: social collectivity whose members are clustered statistically on the basis of common or shared characteristic(s).

group: social collectivity whose members possess a feeling of common identity and who interact in a regular, patterned way.

status: any defined or recognized position within a group or society.

role/formal role: the set of expected behaviors and attitudes associated with a particular status in a group or society.

role performance: an individual's actual behaviors and attitudes in response to role expectations.

role strain: the inability to meet all the expectations attached to a particular social role.

role conflict: contradictory role expectations arising from two or more statuses occupied by a given individual at the same time.

typologies: ordering systems that classify individual phenomena into categories or "types" on the basis of distinguishing characteristics.

membership group: social group to which a given individual belongs and in which the individual participates as a member.

reference group: social group whose perspective is adopted by a given individual as a frame of reference for personal behaviors and attitudes.

anticipatory socialization: the early learning of appropriate behaviors and attitudes that will be required for some future social role.

primary groups: as described by Charles H. Cooley, social groups such as one's family or close friends that are essential in the formation of individual self-identity.

secondary groups: (a term implied but not used by Cooley himself), social groups such as customers and clerks that are more formal, less inclusive, less emotional than primary groups and typically are organized for some specific purpose.

ideal types: logical constructions that present, in exaggerated and idealized form, the distinguishing features of some phenomenon.

dyad: a social group consisting of two members.

triad: a social group consisting of three members.

formal organizations: large, deliberately-planned groups with established personnel, procedures, and rules for carrying out some objective or set of objectives.

normative organizations: also called "voluntary associations." In Amitai Etzioni's typology, public interest organizations such as Scouts or PTA groups that people join for non-material reasons.

coercive organizations: in Amitai Etzioni's typology, organizations such as prisons or asylums that people join involuntarily and which restrain their members from normal contact with the larger society.

utilitarian organizations: in Amitai Etzioni's typology, organizations such as corporations or universities that individuals join for some practical, material reason.

bureaucracy: in Max Weber's formulation, an administrative device for maximizing human efficiency through the logical, orderly structuring of individual behaviors within a particular setting. Bureaucracies are characterized by well-defined spheres of responsibility and authority, standardized, impersonal procedures, recruitment and promotion on the basis of technical expertise, and a distinction between organizational and personal life.

goal-displacement/bureaucratic ritualism: phenomenon often found within bureaucracies, in which adherence to organizational rules becomes more important than fulfilling the original objectives for which the organization was created.

informal organization: the actual set of relationships developed by the members of formal organizations as they carry out the activities defined by organizational objectives and procedures.

societies: self-perpetuating groups of people who occupy a given territory and interact with one another on the basis of a shared culture.

Gemeinschaft: according to Ferdinand Tonnies, a traditional type of communal relationship based upon personal emotions and long-standing customs among the members of a societal population.

Gesellschaft: according   to   Ferdinand   Tonnies,   a   modern   type   of   associational relationship based upon impersonal, rational, secondary group relations among the members of a societal population.

KEY PEOPLE:

Charles   Horton   Cooley   (1864-1929)   was   one   of   the   first   sociologists   to   differentiate between primary and secondary group relations. According to Cooley, primary groups -- such   as   the   family   --   are   essential   to   the   formation   of   individual   self-concept.   In contract,   secondary   groups   --   such   as   employees   in   corporations   or   students   in universities -- are more formalized groupings created and organized for some specific purpose.

Georg   Simmel   (1858-1918),   a   German   sociologist,   analyzed   the   dyad   --   a   two-person group -- and the triad -- a three-person social group. The dyad is the most basic and intimate of all possible human groupings. The social triad marks the beginning of more complex   social   interaction   patterns   within   the   group   and   the   development   of   an identifiable group structure.

Amitai   Etzioni,   a   contemporary   sociologist,   classified   formal   organizations   into   three types   of   based   on   their   members'   motives   for   participation: (1)   normative   organizations -- such as charitable and community service groups -- are joined because people perceive their goals as being socially or morally worthwhile, and individuals derive non-material   rewards   for   their   participation;   (2)   coercive   organizations   --   such   as prisons   or   asylums   --   force   people   to   join   and   typically   remove   them   from   normal contact   with   the   larger   society   for   the   duration   of   their   membership;   and   (3) utilitarian   organizations   --   such   as   corporations   or   universities   --   attract   members who are seeking some sort of tangible, material benefit from their participation.

Max   Weber   (1864-1930),   a   German   sociologist,   was   one   of   the   first   social   scientists   to offer a detailed anlaysis of formal organizations. According to Weber, bureaucracy is a   device   for   maximizing   human   efficiency   through   the   logical,   orderly   structuring   of individual behaviors within a particular setting.

Emile   Durkheim   (1857-1917),   a   French   sociologist   previously   discussed   in   Chapter   1, saw   the   development   of   human   societies   as   tied   to   the   division   of   labor   and specialization   of   function   in   societies.   He   theorized   that   as   occupational   structures became more complex, the mechanical solidarity of a community held together by common values   and   beliefs   began   to   be   replaced   by   an   organic   solidarity   grounded   in   the interdependency and interlocking of these differentiated statuses.

Ferdinand   Tonnies   (1855-1936)   was   the   German   sociologist   who   coined   the   terms "Gemeinschaft"   and   "Gesellschaft."   Gemeinschaft   societies   are   characterized   by   a traditional type of communal relationship based on personal emotions and long-standing customs   among   the   members   of   a   societal   population.   Gesellschaft   societies   are characterized   by   a   modern   type   of   associational   relationship   based   on   impersonal, rational, secondary group relations among the members of a societal population.

Gerhard   Lenski,   a   contemporary   U.S.   sociologist,   refined   an   evolutionary   model   of human   development   that   links   societal   change   to   changes   in   economic   technology.   In Lenski's   view,   economic   surpluses   created   through   improvements   in   productive technology   have   been   the   catalyst   for   changes   ranging   from   population   size   to   the number and content of organized religions.

ANSWERS FOR MULTIPLE CHOICE QUESTIONS

1. __b__ Social structure is defined as "the organization of a societal population into various groups, and the patterned relationships that exist within and among these groups." (73)

2. __a__ Members of social aggregates share the same physical space at a particular moment in time -- such as the pedestrians waiting to cross a busy intersection -- but not necessarily anything else. (74)

3. __c__ Sociologically speaking, "status" is any defined or recognized position within a group or society. It does not indicate social ranking or level of prestige. (74)

4. __b__ People who are in the process of preparing for some future social status often adopt the perspective and behaviors of this sought-after group before they actually gain admission to it. At this point, the groups function as "reference groups" for them, such as the Pre-Law Association or the Future Business Leaders' Club. (78)

5. __d__ Charles H. Cooley coined the term "primary group." (78)

6. __c__ Friends who get together every Monday night to watch footbal on television constitute a primary group because these social groups are made up of one's family or close friends. Responses "a," "b," and "d" are examples of secondary groups which are more formal, less inclusive, less emotional than primary groups and typically are organized for some specific purpose. (78)

7. __a__ Married couples, two "best" friends, and a brother and sister all constitute dyads -- social groups consisting of two members. (81)

8. __d__ Georg Simmel focused on the effects of group size on the nature and the strength of the social bonds that formed between group members. (81)

9. __b__ Formal organizations (which also could be referred to as "secondary groups") are characterized by established personnel, procedures, and rules for carrying out some objective. Responses "a," "c," and "d" are characteristics of primary groups. (82)

10. __a__ People join normative organizations because they perceive their goals as being socially or morally worthwhile. Rewards in normative organizations are non-material in nature. (82)

11. __c__ Corporations or universities are examples of utilitarian organizations because members receive some sort of tangible, material benefits from their participation. (83)

12. __d__ Inmates at a state prison facility are examples of a coercive group because they "join" involuntarily and are restrained from normal contact with the larger society. In Responses "a," "b," and "c," participants have "joined" voluntarily and, theoretically, could leave if they chose to do so. (82-83)

13. __b__ Max Weber was the first sociologist to offer a detailed analysis of bureaucracy. (83-84)

14. __d__ In "pure" bureaucracy, a clear distinction is made between organizational life and personal life. (84-85)

15. __a__ Bureaucratic ritualism occurs when adherence to organizational rules becomes more important than fulfilling the original objectives for which the organization was created. (87)

16. __b__ Informal organization is the actual set of relationships developed by members of formal organizations as they carry out the activities defined by organizational objectives and procedures (in formal organizations). (87-88)

17. __d__ All of the responses are true. Studies of employees in Japanese corporations indicate that Japanese workers have longer-lasting relationships with their organizations, that they advance together through the ranks, and that they experience much more involvement of the corporation in their personal lives. (88-89)

18.   c   Instead of being <u>less</u> encompassing, societies are <u>more</u> encompassing than other types of human groups, in the sense that they include many more individuals than any other group within the same geographic area. (90)

19.   a   In Gemeinschaft societies people interact with one another on the basis of long-standing customs and with personal emotions. (91)

20.   b   Gesellschaft societies are characterized by impersonal, rational, secondary group relations. (91)

21.   c   Gerhard Lenski linked changes in productive technology with the larger economic surpluses which occurred as societies developed through various stages. (92)

22.   c   Agrarian societies first developed cities, complex division of labor, and large political, economic, and military bureaucratic organizations. (92-93)

ANSWERS FOR TRUE-FALSE QUESTIONS

1.   True (73)

2.   False -- While all social groups are examples of collectivities, <u>not</u> <u>all</u> collectivities are groups, as in the distinctions among "aggregates," "categories," and "social groups." (74)

3.   False -- A <u>category</u> is a number of people who share some common characteristic(s). An <u>aggregate</u> is a number of people who share the same physical space at a particular moment in time, but not necessarily anything else. (74)

4.   True (74-75)

5.   False -- <u>Role</u> <u>conflict</u> occurs when contradictory role expectations arise from <u>two</u> <u>or</u> <u>more</u> <u>statuses</u> occupied by a given individual at the same time. <u>Role</u> <u>strain</u> is the inability to meet successfully all the expectations attached to <u>a</u> <u>particular</u> (one) social role. (75)

6.   True (76-77)

7.   True (76)

8.   True (78-79)

9.   True (79)

10.   False -- The <u>dyad</u> is the most fragile of social groups because it depends so heavily upon the particular characteristics of the specific people involved that if either party leaves the relationship the character of that group will be destroyed. (81)

11.   False -- Normative organizations attract members who are seeking some sort of <u>non</u>-material <u>benefit</u> for their participation in organizations such as charitable and community service groups. <u>Utilitarian</u> organizations attract members who are seeking some sort of tangible, material benefit from their participation. (82)

12.   True (84)

13.   False -- One of the major criticisms of bureaucracies is their lack of ability to respond to novel situations or to deal with people, things, or situations that don't fit recognized patterns. (85)

14.   True (88)

15.   False -- Informal structures do not always work to the formal organization's advantage. In fact, if personnel in bureaucracies see their best intersts being threatened by the use of "official" patterns, they may use informal, primary group networks to resist or sabotage bureaucratic goals. (88)

16.   True (89)

17.   False -- Societies are <u>more</u> encompassing and self-perpetuating than other types of human groups. (90)

18.   True (91)

19.   True (92-93)

20. False -- Although Durkheim, Tonnies, and Lenski use different terminology and have different foci, they all are in agreement about the general course of societal development: from small to immensely large, from simple to enormously complex, and from passive responders to active planners of events. (93)

ANSWERS TO FILL-IN QUESTIONS
1. Aggregate; category (74)
2. Role performance (75)
3. Role conflict (75)
4. Typologies (76)
5. Membership; reference (76-77)
6. Secondary (79)
7. Bureaucracy (84)
8. Societies (90)
9. Gemeinschafts; Gesellschafts (91)
10. Industrial (92-93)

ANSWERS TO MATCHING QUESTIONS:
1. D
2. F
3. H
4. B
5. G
6. E
7. J
8. C
9. I
10. A

CHAPTER FOUR

SOCIALIZATION

Chapter 4 describes the socialization process by which most human behavior is learned. First, biological versus cultural factors influencing human behavior are analyzed. Case studies of young children who were isolated from normal social contact are used to demonstrate the importance of early socialization experiences in human development. Next, three perspectives on personal development are presented: (1) Sigmund Freud -- the interplay of conscious and unconscious personality forces, (2) Charles Cooley -- the "looking-glass" self, and (3) George H. Mead -- the "generalized other." Various agents of socialization -- families, schools, peer groups, and mass media -- are identified. Finally, the chapter looks at adult socialization and resocialization, and it discusses the "oversocialized" conception of human beings (the mistaken view that all aspects of human lives are controlled by society through the socialization process).

LEARNING OBJECTIVES:

As you read Chapter 4, use these learning objectives to organize your notes. After completing your reading, briefly state an answer to each of the objectives, and review the text pages in parentheses.

1. Describe ways in which human social behaviors differ from the behaviors of non-human beings. (105-106)

2. Explain why early contact with other humans is so important for the social development of children. (106-107)

3. Discuss the role that human interaction plays in the process of individual personality development. (108-111)

4. State the main reason why successful socialization is an important objective in all human societies. (111-112)

5. Indicate how the family functions as a critical socialization agent in most societies. (112-113)

6. Analyze the role of formal education in the socialization process of modern societies like the United States and Japan. (113-116)

7. Explain why peer groups have such a significant influence on their members, especially among adolescents. (116-117)

8. Describe ways in which mass media such as television have become critical agents of social learning in modern societies. (117-120)

9. Discuss the need for increasing amounts of adult socialization in contemporary human societies. (120-121)

10. Explain how the process of resocialization differs from other forms of socialization. (121)

CHAPTER OUTLINE

I.   INTRODUCTION

A.   Socialization is the social learning process through which individuals
     develop their human potentials and also acquire the established patterns of
     their culture.
     1.   Most human behaviors -- including those we might regard as natural --
          are acquired through the socialization process.
     2.   This process not only is essential for the survival of individuals but
          also for the adaptability and survival of societies.

B.   People in contemporary societies have the ability to reshape their daily
     activities and values dramatically to meet the demands of changing
     realities.   Responses to changing world energy and environmental conditions
     are an example:
     1.   As traditional societies modernized, many people changed their
          orientation from one of protecting the physical environment to one of
          exploiting it for their own gain.
     2.   Today, a world of depleted resources and rapidly-decaying natural
          environments create a challenge to human adaptability and require
          significant changes in peoples' perspectives.

II. ON BEING HUMAN: BIOLOGY AND "HUMAN NATURE"

A.   As previously discussed in the Culture chapter, if there is such a thing as
     "human nature," it defines only general behavioral possibilities (and
     impossibilities) rather than specific behavior.

B.   For human beings, culture provides the set of specific behavioral responses
     to the world that instincts supply for non-human beings.

C.   Since culture represents a human creation rather than an inherited
     biological program, it must be learned by the individuals who live under
     its influence.   This learning normally occurs as a by-product of the close
     and sustained contact with other human beings that all individual humans
     require by virtue of their biological make-up.

III. ON BEING HUMAN: SOCIAL LEARNING AND "HUMAN NATURE"

A.   Biological inheritance provides all humans with a pool of behavioral
     potentials.   It is the quality and quantity of individual humans' social
     and cultural experiences that largely decide which of these potentials will
     be actualized.
     1.   Since human infants are biologically helpless, they must depend
          entirely upon other humans for their physical survival.
     2.   The resulting prolonged physical contact between human infants and
          their caretakers creates an environment of close social interaction.
     3.   This interaction is essential to the development of that set of
          attributes we normally think of as "human" characteristics --
          including verbal and written language, rational thought, and the
          formation of a self-concept.
B.   Case studies of children who were isolated from normal social contact
     shortly after birth suggest that early socialization experiences are
     critical for the development of language skills and other human
     characteristics.

66

1. The cases of Anna, Isabelle, and Genie were very similar in that they had been subjected to extreme social deprivation from the first year or two of their lives.
    a. Isabelle was more fortunate than Anna and Genie because she was with her mother, a deaf-mute.
    b. Anna and Genie had been shut away in closet-like rooms and had almost no interaction with other human beings outside of the occasional physical contact needed to provide for their minimal physical needs.
2. When discovered, none of these girls could talk, feed or dress herself, or otherwise demonstrate an ability to interact "normally" with other human beings. After being removed from captivity, their ability to be socialized varied widely:
    a. Isabella, who had been with mother, was able to acquire written and verbal language skills, and seemed on her way living a normal life.
    b. Anna and Genie never were completely able to develop normal human language skills or social behaviors appropriate for persons of their ages.
3. These cases demonstrate that involvement in human social interaction must occur early in an individual's life if that person is to become fully human.

IV. THEORIES OF SOCIALIZATION AS HUMAN DEVELOPMENT

   A. Most social scientists agree that social learning experiences are critical in the creation of "human" beings. Psychologists tend to stress the interplay between internal conscious or unconscious personality forces and external social factors.
      1. The work of Sigmund Freud (1854-1939), a famous psychiatrist and psychoanalyst, is a conflict interpretation of the human socialization process. He argued there was a conflict between the individual and society, and that the socialization process consists of the progressive development of a social conscience and the increasing submission of individual impulses to societal wishes and requirements.
      2. Freud believed the human personality has three components:
         a. The id is that unconscious part of the human personality representing inherited aggressive and sexual impulses. The id is individualistic and pleasure-directed.
         b. The superego is that unconscious part of the human personality representing internalized cultural values and norms. The superego is the social conscience which counteracts the anti-social impulses of the id.
         c. The ego is that conscious part of the human personality that negotiates and mediates between the opposing forces of id and superego.

   B. Socialization as Self-Development: Cooley and Mead
      1. Charles H. Cooley (1864-1929) argued that human development is a product of interaction with other humans in social group situations (rather than the belief that human nature is determined by genetic heritage and biological maturation).
         a. He coined the phrase the "looking glass self" to refer to the process by which individuals acquire a self-concept (a sense of personal identity) through interactions with other people. According to Cooley, the process has three steps:

67

            (1).   The individual imagines how he or she must appear to other people.

            (2).   The individual imagines what sort of judgment these other people are making about him or her.

            (3).   The individual experiences some sort of self-feeling reflecting his or her perceptions of how these other people have seen and judged him or her.

     b.   Cooley's analysis of the relationship between group interaction and personal development reshaped social scientists' thinking on the issue of human development.

2.   George H. Mead (1863-1931), a social philosopher, argued that both mind and self are social products which represent the outcomes of the individual's interactions with others in social situations rather than the outcomes of biological inheritance.

     a.   Mead argued that language, involving the use of significant symbols -- physical stimuli which have been given socially-created, culturally-defined value and meaning -- is fundamental to the human developmental sequence.

     b.   He portrayed socialization as a three-step process in which increasing social contact between the individual and others creates role playing and role-taking activities:

            (1).   In the play stage, young children pretend to be some specific person -- such as mother or father -- going about some specific task. In the process of imitating the behaviors of the other person (role-playing), the child begins to view and evaluate the world from that other person's frame of reference (role-taking).

            (2).   In the game stage, the child interacts with others in group situations, developing a sense of social structures and the relationships among different statuses and roles. Continued experience in interacting with others brings a growing awareness of the concept of group structure and a group perspective to the child.

            (3)   In the final stage, the child comes to form a sense of self based on the demands and expectations of the larger social and cultural community of which the child is a member -- the generalized other -- which ultimately provides the frame of reference from which the child views the world and itself.

     c.   According to Mead, the social self -- the human personality structure that results from the individual's interaction with others through play and game activities -- is divided into two parts:

            (1).   the "me" component, which is the objective, predictable part of the social self that corresponds to one's social statuses and roles; and

            (2).   the "I" component, which is the subjective, creative, individual part of the social self.

     d.   Mead argued that the self is never a fully finished product, but rather is subject to significant modification throughout one's lifetime, as individuals' social statuses and social relationships change over time.

V. SOCIALIZATION AS SOCIAL LEARNING

A. The Family
    1. In premodern societies, the family was the single most important source of information and learning about the surrounding world.
        a. Extended family groups, which typically included several generations of blood-related individuals (and their spouses and offspring) occupying a single household under the authority of a household head, provided new members of premodern societies with their introduction to social realities.
        b. Primary socialization is the term given to this first social learning experience by individuals, typically in the setting of the family. This process includes:
            (1). Establishment of one's initial societal position;
            (2). Internalization of proper cultural values and beliefs; and
            (3). Learning of appropriate communication and social interaction patterns with others.
        c. In traditional societies, the family enjoyed a near monopoly as the agent of socialization for members of the society.
    2. In modern societies, the differentiation and elaboration of more specialized social units have eroded much of the family's traditional role as the exclusive source of social learning experiences.
        a. Nuclear family patterns, composed of two spouses and their children, largely have replaced the extended family, and young children now spend considerable time outside the family.
        b. Despite these changes, the family still fulfills these functions for most people in modern societies:
            (1). The family constitutes the initial setting of social interaction for newly-born individuals, and is likely to be the major source of the child's contact with the social world over an extended period of time.
            (2). It provides the first experiences most people have with primary group relations, thus having an enormous impact on the child's developing self-concept.
            (3). It continues to function as the initial and continuing determinant of the individual's social class position in modern societies.
        c. In modern societies, the family is still very important in the socialization process; however, a number of other agents of socialization now also play a major role in this process.

B. The School
    1. In traditional societies, formal education was virtually unknown to most individuals.
    2. In modern societies, formal education for the masses is the norm.
        a. Individuals enter the world of formal education at a much earlier age than in the past.
        b. People are exiting the system at a much later age than before because they must spend a significantly longer amount of time in school to become acquainted with the growing volume of existing information.
    3. Education serves several manifest functions (activities that are known to, and intended by the individuals involved) for society, including:
        a. Creating and transmitting academic skills and cultural knowledge
        b. Training in important job-related skills to prepare people for entry into the occupational system.

4. Education also serves to generate a number of other consequences for individuals and for society. Some of these less-recognized effects -- the "informal" or "hidden curriculum" of education -- include:
    a. Entering school represents the beginning of the individual's socialization into a large-scale, depersonalized social structure which evaluates and places its members on the basis of performance criteria rather than personal identities.
    b. The school is an important instrument of <u>anticipatory socialization</u> -- the early learning of attitudes and behaviors that will be needed for some future social roles.
    c. <u>Political socialization</u> occurs in schools in virtually every industrial nation. This "political" agenda may occur overtly or subtly.
        (1). <u>Overt</u> political socialization includes courses -- such as civics -- in the curriculum, celebration of patriotic holidays, and the pledge of allegiance to the flag.
        (2) <u>Subtle</u> political socialization includes activities such as the selection of textbooks based on their political content as much as on their academic content.
5. The school is an important agent of socialization because it is a microcosm of the larger society, with its own culture, social stratification system, political apparatus, networks of primary and secondary groups, and mechanisms of political socialization which legitimize existing social and cultural arrangements in society.

C. <u>Peer Groups</u>
1. <u>Peer group</u> (or <u>peers</u>) refers to people of approximately the same social position and same age as oneself.
    a. Peers serve as a buffer between the individual and the larger society for adolescents:
        (1). Peer groups provide some degree of freedom from adult control.
        (2). They provide an opportunity to explore aspects of life -- such as smoking or drinking -- normally discouraged and punished by parents or other authority figures.
        (3). Peer groups provide personalized, primary group relations in exchange for conformity to the values and standards of behavior of the group.
    b. Adults also can be profoundly affected by peer groups.
        (1). Peer pressure in the workplace typically causes adult workers to conform to the informal expectations of their coworkers.
        (2). Although the classical study to document the impact of peer pressure on workers was done in an industrial setting with blue-collar workers, this type of pressure now occurs in all occupational and professional categories.
2. Throughout life, most individuals never outgrow their peer group affiliations, and these peer groups never really stop educating people about the social world and their place in it.

D. <u>The Mass Media</u>
1. In contemporary societies, mass media such as television have become important sources of knowledge and social learning.
    a. Modern societies depend upon the smooth, continuous flow of information. Political and economic policy-making rely heavily on up-to-the-minute data and statistics.

b. Mass media also play a multifaceted and profound role in the human social learning process. For example, schools use many audio-visual resources.

2. Mass media -- and especially television -- has had a tremendous impact on the American public.

a. On average, American adults spend more than half of their waking lives with some form of mass media -- television, radio, magazines, newspapers, and other sources -- for entertainment and information.

b. People expect programs that are meant to inform to present a truthful portrayal of reality; however, some researchers have found that the news is a social construct determined by media personnel.

3. Children have a more difficult time than adults in sorting out media facts from media fiction.

a. A major area of criticism revolves around the effects of televised violence on children's developing personalities and social behaviors.

b. Whether or not television viewing is directly responsible for acts of aggression, it is evident that television is an important element in many children's social learning experiences.

E. Adult Socialization and Resocialization

1. Secondary socialization is the social learning experienced during adolescence and, in particular, during adulthood. In modern and in developing societies, secondary socialization is very important.

a. In many instances, values, beliefs and practices taught to individuals during childhood do not translate to the situations confronting them as adults.

b. For most people, secondary socialization occurs in the context of marital and occupational roles.

(1). Today, individuals experience a wider array of family situations because of increases in the divorce rate and in the number of women entering the full-time paid workforce.

(2). Occupational roles also have changed considerably in contemporary societies. For example, most children no longer learn how to perform occupational roles from their parents, and professionals have to continue to learn even after many years of formal education.

2. Resocialization is the rapid and dramatic secondary socialization experience in which established behaviors and attitudes are removed and new patterns are created.

a. Sociologist Erving Goffman studied the resocialization process which occurs in total institutions, which he defined as places -- such as prisons, monasteries, or asylums -- where large numbers of people who are cut off from the larger society have all aspects of their lives planned and controlled by agents of the institution.

b. As part of the resocialization process in total institutions, personal identities and differences -- such as individual clothing and hair styles -- are taken away and replaced with a new, categorical identity -- common uniforms and a number rather than a name.

c. After individual resistance is broken down, the persons being resocialized are exposed to new, mandated behaviors with the assumption that new attitudes will follow.

71

VI. SOCIALIZATION, OVERSOCIALIZATION, AND SOCIAL CONTROL

A. Every society has a fundamental interest in ensuring that its members internalize the established societal patterns.
   1. The continued survival of the society depends upon the successful transmission of these patterns to each new generation.
   2. Most people act as their own agents of social control because they have internalized the norms of society.

B. While socialization agents in all societies greatly shape the lives of their members, they never control them completely.
   1. Dennis H. Wrong, a sociologist, cautioned against accepting what he termed the "oversocialized conception of human beings" -- the mistaken view that all aspects of human lives are controlled by society through the socialization process. This view portrays people as puppets who have been socialized by their society to believe everything they have been taught and to act blindly on the basis of these beliefs.
   2. Because modern societies are heterogeneous -- with diverse racial, ethnic, class, religious, and other subcultural groups -- there will be no single integrated world view shared by all population members.

GLOSSARY OF DIFFICULT-TO-UNDERSTAND WORDS

Page	Line	Col.	Term from Text	Explanation
103	4		cartel	business organization designed to limit competition
103	5		lubricating oil	oil to reduce wear
103	14		siphoning	emptying
104	1		escalate	to increase
104	5		retrench	find a new way
104	11		hippies	usually young people who reject societies' ways
104	11		freaks	unusual people
104	19		scavenging	removing and using discarded material
104	39		fragile	easily broken
105	33		aborigines	natives
105	33		dine	eat
105	36		compel	force
107	7		premise	idea
107	35		offset	balance
107	35		deprivation	absence
107	41		full-fledged	fully developed
108	5		irreversible	cannot be changed
108	27		bundle	group
109	28		anesthetist	a medical doctor
109	32		contingent	dependent
110	7		diaper pin	fastens the cloth between a baby's legs
110	7		initiate	begin
110	41		genuine	real
110	43		campout	to sleep outside in a tent, etc.
111	10		badges	a patch, usually of cloth, to honor a deed
112	14		eroded	destroyed

GLOSSARY OF DIFFICULT-TO-UNDERSTAND WORDS (CONTINUED)

Page	Line	Col.	Term from Text	Explanation
113	22		virtually	honestly
113	24		sophisticated	worldly
113	34		curricula	course of study
113	48		credentialled	documented; for example, one is credentialed to teach
115	29		embedded	to place firmly
115	33		whims	sudden ideas
116	14		pedagogical	teaching
116	17		indigenous	original
116	26		microcosm	small community
116	29		apparatus	device
116	33		legitimizing	make lawful
116	46		age-stratified	ranking by age
114	30	A	prosaically	matter of fact
114	12	B	immunization	shots given to resist disease
114	13	B	erratic	no fixed course
114	22	B	disparities	differences
114	46	B	stipend	given sum of money
115	6	B	augmented	made greater
118	5		multifaceted	many parts
119	20		allocated	distribute
119	30		susceptible	predisposed, have a tendency to
120	7		clonelike	identical
120	36		proliferation	rapid growth
120	46		minted	created and approved
121	6		implanted	learned and incorporated within the self
121	12		barracks	housing
121	18		mandated	required
122	4		karma	destiny
122	22		severe	stern
122	38		portrayed	description
122	42		heterogenous	mixed
123	12	A	upheavals	disturbance
123	18	A	paternalistic	the government acts like a father
123	5	B	impoverishment	poverty
123	26	B	streamlining	new type, modern
124	3	A	perpetuating	continuing
124	9	A	permeates	spreads to
124	31	A1	pathological	diseased
124	34	A	dysfunctional	impaired, injured, not able to perform
124	51	A	promiscuous	immoral, loose
124	2	B	ambiguity	uncertainty
125	38	B	corollary	result
126	35	B	pervasive	diffused, spread, scatter
127	36	A	acquisition	attainment, gained
128	25	A	infrastructure	basic framework
128	9	B	egalitarian	promoting human equality
128	15	B	inegalitarian	promoting human inequality
128	26	B	ordeal	trial, experience
128	41	B	curriculum	set of courses
130	13	A	regimen	regular course of training
130	50	A	mock	ridicule, make fun of

Page	Line	Col.	Term from Text	Explanation
130	50	A	defy	are, challenge
131	2	A	hefty	very large
131	30	A	intensifies	becomes stronger

KEY TERMS TO DEFINE:

After studying the chapter, define each of the following terms. Then check your work by referring to the answers at the end of Chapter 4 in the Study Guide.

socialization	"me"
socialization agents	"I"
superego	primary socialization
id	nuclear family
ego	anticipatory socialization
self	peers/peer group
significant others	secondary socialization
looking-glass self	resocialization
significant symbols	total institutions
play	oversocialized conception of human beings
role-playing	extended family
role-taking	patriarchal family
game	external migration
the generalized other	internal migration
social self	

KEY PEOPLE

State the major theoretical contributions of each of these people.

Sigmund Freud

Charles H. Cooley

George H. Mead

Erving Goffman

Dennis H. Wrong

SELF-TEST

After completing this self-test, check your answers against the "Answer Key" at the end of Chapter 4 in this Study Guide and in the text on the page(s) indicated in parentheses.

MULTIPLE CHOICE QUESTIONS

Select the response which best answers the question or completes the statement:

1. The social learning process experienced by individuals from the day they are born until the day they die is: (104)
   a. socialization.
   b. resocialization.
   c. social interaction.
   d. imitation.

2. The cases of Anna, Isabelle, and Genie, who were isolated as children, demonstrate that: (107-108)
   a. nuclear families no longer work in modern societies.
   b. involvement in human social interaction must occur early in our lives if we ever are to become fully "human".
   c. isolation helps children to develop survival skills that other children do not possess.
   d. isolation does not make as much difference in the development of children as researchers previously had thought.

3. Which of the following is not one of the parts of the human personality, based on the studies of Sigmund Freud? (108)
   a. "me"
   b. "id"
   c. "ego"
   d. "superego"

4. Charles H. Cooley called the sense of personal identity that individuals acquire through interactions with other people: (109)
   a. the generalized other.
   b. the socialized other.
   c. the anticipatory socialization process.
   d. the looking glass self.

5. George H. Mead argued that _____ is (are) fundamental to the entire human development process. (109)
    a. emotions
    b. biological factors
    c. language
    d. unconscious motives

6. According to Mead, the type of behavior in which the child pretends to be some specific person -- such as Mommy or Daddy -- occurs during which of these stages? (110)
    a. game
    b. play
    c. generalized other
    d. significant other

7. Primary socialization entails: (112)
    a. the establishment of one's initial societal position.
    b. the internalization of proper cultural values and beliefs.
    c. the learning of appropriate communication and social interaction patterns with others.
    d. All of the above.

8. Modern societies are characterized by which of these family patterns? (112-113)
    a. extended family
    b. nuclear family
    c. atomic family
    d. monolocal family

9. All of the following are manifest objectives of education, except: (113-116)
    a. creation and transmission of academic skills and cultural knowledge.
    b. preparation for entry into the occupational system.
    c. training in important job-related skills.
    d. legitimization of existing social and cultural arrangements in society.

10. The early learning of behaviors and attitudes that will be needed for some future social role is: (115)
    a. anticipatory socialization.
    b. primary socialization.
    c. secondary socialization.
    d. resocialization.

11. Civics classes, the celebration of patriotic holidays, and the pledge of allegiance to the flag are all examples of: (116)
    a. anticipatory socialization.
    b. primary socialization.
    c. political socialization.
    d. resocialization.

12. People of approximately the same social position and same age are referred to as: (116)
    a. the generalized other.
    b. the looking glass self.
    c. significant others.
    d. peers.

13. Peer groups typically have their most profound impact on: (116-117)
    a. young children.
    b. adolescents.
    c. young adults.
    d. senior adults.

14. Which of the following is <u>not</u> discussed in your text as one of the most important agents of socialization in modern societies? (112-120)
    a. the family
    b. the mass media
    c. the church
    d. the school

15. On average, American adults spend more than _____ of their waking lives with some form of mass media. (119)
    a. one-tenth (10%)
    b. one-quarter (25%)
    c. one-half (50%)
    d. three-quarters (75%)

16. Young children primarily come in contact with mass media through: (119)
    a. watching television.
    b. reading books.
    c. attending movies.
    d. playing video games.

17. Social learning experienced during adolescence and, in particular, during adulthood is referred to as: (120)
    a. primary socialization.
    b. secondary socialization.
    c. anticipatory socialization.
    d. resocialization.

18. Adult socialization involving rapid and dramatic social learning experiences in which old, established attitudes or behaviors are removed and new patterns are implanted is referred to as: (121)
    a. primary socialization.
    b. secondary socialization.
    c. anticipatory socialization.
    d. resocialization.

19. Which of the following is <u>not</u> an example of a total institution? (121)
    a. a convent
    b. an army barracks
    c. a university
    d. a prison

20. The mistaken view that all aspects of human lives are controlled by society through the socialization process is: (122)
    a. the oversocialized conception of human beings.
    b. the undersocialized conception of human beings.
    c. the misconception about human beings.
    d. the distorted view of human beings.

T   F   1.   In modern societies the socialization process takes place only from infancy through adolescence. (104)

T   F   2.   Scientific research indicates that biological factors significantly affect -- but don't absolutely determine -- the behaviors of human beings. (105-106)

T   F   3.   Culture is a human creation rather than an inherited biological program. (106)

T   F   4.   The cases of Anna, Isabelle, and Genie demonstrate that the long-term effects of isolation were more severe on Isabelle, because she was hidden away with her mother, who was a deaf-mute. (107-108)

T   F   5.   Psychological interpretations of socialization -- such as Sigmund Freud's -- focus on the interplay of conscious and unconscious personality forces. (108)

T   F   6.   Charles Cooley proposed that human development is a product of interaction with other humans in social group situations. (109)

T   F   7.   The theories of socialization developed by Sigmund Freud, Charles Cooley, and George H. Mead are all very similar in focus. (109)

T   F   8.   According to George H. Mead, individuals can develop a human personality even without language skills. (109-110)

T   F   9.   Mead's "play stage" becomes an exercise in role-taking and role-playing. (110)

T   F   10.   The "me" component of the social self is the subjective, creative, individually unique aspect of the person. (111)

T   F   11.   Primary socialization typically occurs in schools and through the mass media. (112)

T   F   12.   The extended family generally includes a variety of relatives in addition to parents and siblings. (112)

T   F   13.   Formal education was virtually unknown to most individuals in traditional societies. (113)

T   F   14.   The school is an important instrument of resocialization in society. (115-116)

T   F   15.   Formal education contains a "political" agenda which may be advanced either overtly or in more subtle ways. (116)

T   F   16.   Schools tend to question existing social and cultural arrangements in society. (116)

T   F   17.   For adolescents, peers serve as a buffer between the individual and the larger society. (116-117)

T F 18. Adolescents are not the only age grouping subject to important peer group influence. (117)

T F 19. Research has proven conclusively that violence on television causes aggressive behavior in many children who watch television frequently. (119)

T Γ 20. A great deal of adult socialization occurs in the context of marital and occupational roles. (120)

FILL-IN QUESTIONS

Fill in the blank with the word or phrase that best completes the statement.

1. _____ is the social learning process through which individuals develop their human potentials and also acquire the established patterns of their culture. (104)

2. Sigmund Freud believed that the human personality had three parts: the _____ , the _____, and the _____. (108)

3. In Charles Cooley's theory, the sense of personal identity individuals acquire through interactions with other people is called the _____ _____ _____. (109)

4. According to George Mead, language involves the use of _____ _____ , which are physical stimuli which have been given socially-created, culturally-defined value and meaning. (109)

5. In Mead's theory, the _____ _____ is the surrounding cultural and social community of which the child is a member, and it ultimately provides the frame of reference from which the child views the world and itself. (111)

6. _____ socialization is the first social learning experienced by individuals, typically in the setting of the _____. (112)

7. _____ socialization is the social learning experienced during adolescence and, in particular, during adulthood. (120)

8. _____ is a rapid and dramatic secondary socialization experience in which established behaviors and attitudes are removed and new patterns are created. This process typically occurs in _____ _____. (121)

MATCH THESE THEORISTS WITH THEIR KEY CONCEPTS:

____	1.	Sigmund Freud	a.	the looking glass self
____	2.	Dennis H. Wrong	b.	the generalized other
____	3.	Charles H. Cooley	c.	the oversocialized conception of human beings
____	4.	George H. Mead	d.	total institutions
____	5.	Erving Goffman	e.	"id," "ego," and "superego"

ESSAY QUESTIONS

1. Identify ways in which human social behaviors differ from the behaviors of nonhuman beings.

2. Discuss the cases of Anna, Isabelle, and Genie and explain what these cases tell us about the social development of children.

3. Analyze the formal and informal or "hidden" curriculum in education.

4. Distinguish between primary and secondary socialization, and indicate the settings in which each takes place.

5. Explain how resocialization differs from other types of adult socialization.

ANSWERS FOR CHAPTER 4

DEFINITIONS OF KEY TERMS:

socialization: the social learning process through which individuals develop their human potentials and also acquire the established patterns of their culture.

socialization agents: parents, teachers, and other important groups involved in the socialization of individual societal members.

superego: in Freudian theory, that unconscious part of the human personality representing internalized cultural values and norms.

id: in Freudian theory, that unconscious part of the human personality representing inherited aggressive and sexual impulses.

ego: in Freudian theory, that conscious part of the human personality that negotiates and mediates between the opposing forces of id and superego.

self: an individual's awareness and concept of personal identity.

significant others: people who are important in the creation of an individual's self-concept.

looking-glass self: in Cooley's theory, the sense of personal identity individuals acquire through interaction with other people.

significant symbols: in human communication, physical stimuli which have been given socially-created, culturally-defined value and meaning.

play: in Mead's theory, behavior in which children pretend to be parents or other specific people.

role-playing: process in which, during play, children begin to duplicate the behaviors and attitudes of the specific people being imitated.

role-taking: during play activities, the process in which children begin to view and evaluate the world from the perspective of the people being imitated.

game: in Mead's theory, any organized group behavior that requires the child to interact with other people.

the generalized other: in Mead's theory, the surrounding social and cultural community of which the child is a member, which ultimately provides the frame of reference from which the child views the world and itself.

social self: in Mead's theory, the human personality structure that results from the individual's interaction with others through play and game activities.

"me:" in Mead's terminology, the objective, predictable part of the social self that corresponds to one's social statuses and roles.

"I:" in Mead's terminology, the subjective, creative, individual part of the social self.

primary socialization: the first social learning experienced by individuals, typically in the setting of the family.

nuclear family: in modern societies, the typical family unit consisting of two spouses and their immediate offspring.

anticipatory socialization: the early learning of behaviors and attitudes that will be needed for some future social role.

peers/peer group: people of approximately the same social position and same age as oneself.

secondary socialization: social learning experienced during adolescence and, in particular, during adulthood.

resocialization: rapid and dramatic secondary socialization experiences in which established behaviors and attitudes are removed and new patterns are created.

total institutions: places such as prisons, monasteries, or asylums where large numbers of people who are cut off from the larger society have all aspects of their lives planned and controlled by agents of the institution. These total institutions often are the settings within which resocialization takes place.

oversocialized conception of human beings: the mistaken view that all aspects of human lives are controlled by society through the socialization process.

extended family: family arrangement characterized by several generations of blood-related individuals (and their spouses and offspring) occupying a single household under the authority of a household head.

patriarchal family: family structure in which males dominate females, married couples reside with the husband's parents, and family descent is traced through the male lineage.

external migration: the movement of people from a given society to another society.

internal migration: the movement of people from one area to another area within the same society.

KEY PEOPLE:

Sigmund Freud (1854-1939), a famous psychiatrist and psychoanalyst, saw the socialization process as one of conflict between the individual and society. He focused on the interplay of conscious and unconscious personality forces in socialization. He argued that the superego -- the social conscience -- was necessary to counteract the anti-social impulses of the id -- the bundle of unconscious aggressive and sexual drives. The ego -- the conscious mechanism by which individuals are able to engage in deliberate decision-making -- acts as a mediator between the id and the superego.

Charles H. Cooley (1864-1929) was one of the earliest sociologists to propose that human development is a product of interaction with other humans in social group situations. Cooley termed his perspective the looking-glass self because he believed that humans get an impression of who and what they are as mirrored through others' images of themselves. He thought this occurred in a three-step process: (1) the reaction of other people causes a person to imagine how he or she appears to others; (2) they then imagine what sort of judgment the other people are making about them; and (3) they experience some sort of self-feeling reflecting their own perception of how the others have seen and judged them.

George H. Mead (1863-1931), a social philosopher, saw language, involving the use of significant symbols, as fundamental to the human development process. He divided the self into two parts: the "I" -- the subjective, creative, individually unique aspect of the person -- and the "me" -- the objective, status-holding, role-playing aspect of the person. He believed there was continuing interaction between the "I" and the "me."
Mead divided the socialization process into three stages: (1) play -- behavior in which children pretend to be parents or other specific people; (2) game -- any organized group behavior that requires the child to interact with other people; and (3) the generalized other -- the surrounding social and cultural community of which the child is a member, which ultimately provides the frame of reference from which the child views the world and itself.

Erving Goffman (1922-1982), a sociologist, defined total institutions as places where large number of people who are cut off from the larger society live and work for an extended period of time in a carefully-controlled atmosphere.

Dennis Wrong, a contemporary sociologist, wrote a famous article which cautioned social scientists against accepting what he termed an oversocialized conception of human beings. He thought it was incorrect to portray people as puppets who have been socialized by their society to believe everything they have been taught and to act blindly on the basis of these beliefs.

ANSWERS FOR MULTIPLE CHOICE QUESTIONS

1. a   Socialization is the lifelong social learning process through which individuals develop their human potentials and acquire the established patterns of their culture. (104)
2. b   Cases of individuals who were isolated as children indicate the importance of early and sustained human social interaction for them to become fully "human." (107-108)
3. a   Freud's theory of the human personality includes the id, ego, and superego. The "me" is not in Freud's theory: it is the objective, predictable part of the social self in Mead's theory. (108)
4. d   Cooley's theory was the looking-glass self. The generalized other is Mead's theory. Responses "b" and "c" are not a part of Cooley's perspective. (109)
5. c   Mead argued that language is fundamental to the human development process. He argued that language involves the use of significant symbols -- physical stimuli which have been given socially-created, culturally-defined value and meaning (109)
6. b   According to Mead, it is in the play stage that children pretend to be parents or other specific people. (110)

82

7.   **d**   Primary socialization entails the establishment of one's initial societal position, the internalization of proper cultural values and beliefs, and the learning of appropriate communication and social interaction patterns with others, thus making response "d" -- all of the above -- correct. (112)

8.   **b**   The nuclear family, consisting of two spouses and their immediate offspring, is the predominant family pattern in modern societies. (112-113)

9.   **d**   Responses "a," "b," and "c" are all manifest objectives or "functions" of education; response "d" -- legitimization of existing social and cultural arrangements in society -- is an informal or hidden curriculum of education. (113-116)

10.   **a**   Anticipatory socialization is the early learning of behaviors and attitudes that will be needed for some future social role. (115)

11.   **c**   Civics classes, the celebration of patriotic holidays, and the pledge of allegiance to the flag are all types of <u>political socialization</u> in schools which promote and legitimize the societal status quo. (116)

12.   **d**   <u>Peers</u> are people of approximately the same social position and same age as oneself. (116)

13.   **b**   Although peer groups influence people of all ages, these groups typically have the most profound impact on <u>adolescents</u> because peers serve as buffers between the individual and the larger society, provide some degree of freedom from adult control, allow for exploration of previously forbidden behaviors, and provide primary group ties in return for conformity to the values and standards of behavior of the peer group. (116-117)

14.   **c**   Although the church is considered to be an agent of socialization, many sociologists believe that the church is losing significance as compared with the role of the family, the mass media, and the school in modern societies. (112-120)

15.   **c**   On average, American adults spend more than half (50%) of their waking lives with some form of mass media -- including television, radio, magazines, newspapers, etc. (119)

16.   **a**   Watching television is the primary way in which young children come in contact with mass media. Many children spend as much time watching television as they do in school or interacting with parents and other traditional socialization agents. (119)

17.   **b**   Secondary socialization is the social learning experienced during adolescence and, in particular, during adulthood. (120)

18.   **d**   Resocialization is the rapid and dramatic secondary socialization experience in which established behaviors and attitudes are removed and new patterns are created. (121)

19.   **c**   A university is not a total institution because people are not completely cut off from the larger society, and they do not have all aspects of their lives planned and controlled by agents of the institution -- although to students it sometimes may seem like a total institution! Convents, army barracks, and prisons fit the definition of total institutions. (121)

20.   **a**   The oversocialized conception of human beings is the mistaken view that all aspects of human lives are controlled by society through the socialization process. (122)

ANSWERS FOR TRUE-FALSE QUESTIONS

1.   False -- Socialization is a social learning process which individuals experience from birth to death. (104)

2.   True (105-106)

3.   True (106)

4. False -- Isabelle appears to have been somewhat more fortunate than Anna and Genie because she was hidden away with her mother. When she was removed from captivity, Isabelle was able to make more progress in developing social and intellectual skills than the other two girls. (107-108)
5. True (108)
6. True (109)
7. False -- Freud's perspective had a biological focus (as do most psychological theories) in that he emphasized the interplay between internal conscious or unconscious personality forces and external social factors. Cooley and Mead emphasized the social contexts within which socialization occurred. (109)
8. False -- George Mead emphasized the importance of language in the development of human personality. (109-110)
9. True (110)
10. False -- The "I" component of the social self is the subjective, creative, individually unique aspect of the person. The "me" in Mead's terminology, is the objective, predictable part of the social self. (111)
11. False -- Primary socialization typically occurs in the family and in peer groups. Secondary socialization occurs in schools and through the mass media. (112)
12. True (112)
13. True (113)
14. False -- The school is an important instrument in secondary socialization. Resocialization typically occurs in prisons, boot camps, monasteries, asylums, etc. (115-116)
15. True (116)
16. False -- Schools tend to reinforce the existing social arrangements -- the status quo -- in society rather than questioning these arrangements. (11-12)
17. True (116-117)
18. True (117)
19. False -- The issue of whether violence on television causes aggressive behavior in children is far from settled. Some studies believe there is a strong relationship between the violence and children's aggression; however, other studies have suggested that the relationship may be weaker and more complex than first believed. (119)
20. True (120)

ANSWERS TO FILL-IN QUESTIONS

1. Socialization (104)
2. Id, ego, superego (108)
3. Looking-glass self (109)
4. Significant symbols (109)
5. Generalized other (111)
6. Primary (112)
7. Secondary (120)
8. Resocialization; total institutions (121)

ANSWERS TO MATCHING QUESTIONS

1. E
2. C
3. A
4. B
5. D

CHAPTER FIVE

SOCIAL STRATIFICATION

Chapter 5 examines social stratification -- the systematic division of a societal population into categories that are defined and treated as social unequals. Four major explanations for social inequality are presented and evaluated: (1) Natural Superiority Theory, (2) Functionalist Theory, (3) Marxian Class-Conflict Theory, and (4) the Weberian Multiple-Hierarchies Model. Objective and Subjective Class Analyses are the primary methods used in stratification research. In objective class analysis, groups are defined on the basis of quantifiable differences such as income, education, and occupation. In subjective class analyses, groups are defined either on the basis of individuals' self-perceptions of their own class position, or other people's judgments of the individuals' social class. Social mobility -- the movement of individuals and groups within and between social levels in a stratified society -- is discussed. Differences between open-class and closed-caste systems are examined, as are the factors involved in intergenerational and intragenerational mobility and in voluntary and structural mobility. Social stratification generates many significant consequences for members of human societies in regard to physical and mental health, political involvement, criminal justice, and education.

LEARNING OBJECTIVES:

As you read Chapter 5, use these learning objectives to organize your notes. After completing your reading, briefly state an answer to each of the objectives, and review the text pages in parentheses.

1.   Explain why some theorists believe that social stratification is "natural" in human societies. (136-137)

2.   State the basic assumptions of functionalists like Davis and Moore regarding social inequality, and note the major criticisms of this perspective. (138-139)

3.   Identify the basic assumptions of conflict theorists like Marx regarding social stratification. (140-142)

4.   Explain why Weber was so critical of Marx's class-conflict theory of stratification. Note the main points in Weber's multiple-hierarchies model as compared with Marx's class-conflict theory of stratification. (142-144)

5.   Discuss the major approaches employed to study social class in contemporary societies like the U.S. (144-149)

6.   Differentiate between open-class and closed-caste stratification systems and give descriptions of each system. (149-152)

7.   Distinguish between intergenerational and intragenerational mobility and between structural and voluntary mobility. (153)

8.   Explain the relationship between social class position and physical and mental health, political involvement, crime and criminal justice, and education. (154-158)

CHAPTER OUTLINE

I. INTRODUCTION

A. Social stratification is the systematic division of a societal population into categories which are defined and treated as social unequals. Populations are structured into layers or ranks based on each of these dimensions:
1. Property -- income, wealth, and other material resources
2. Prestige -- reputation or social honor
3. Power -- the ability to accomplish desired objectives even in the face of opposition

B. Social inequality systems apparently have been a persistent fact of life since the formation of settled, horticultural-based societies thousands of years ago, but the amount of stratification has varied significantly from society to society.

II. EXPLANATIONS AND INTERPRETATIONS OF STRATIFICATION

A. Natural Superiority Theory
1. The Natural Superiority Theory predated the beginning of the discipline of sociology. Early sociologists Herbert Spencer and William Graham Sumner contributed to Social Darwinism which had its roots in the Natural Superiority perspective.
2. Social Darwinism was a social and political philosophy that believed in the existence of natural laws of social evolution and argued for a "hands-off" approach to human social affairs:
a. Social life was viewed as a competitive struggle for existence among individual human beings -- "survival of the fittest."
b. The best social policy was that of a laissez-faire, "hands-off" approach since social inequalities were grounded in natural human differences.
3. Although the Natural Superiority argument originally was intended as an explanation of social differences among individuals, it was adapted as an explanation -- and justification -- as to why certain kinds of people might occupy socially superior or inferior positions in a society.
a. This approach justified the superiority of men over women, whites over nonwhites, and Anglo-Saxons over non-Anglos.
b. It also justified immigration quota laws designed to halt or limit the flow of "inferior," undesirable people into the U.S.
4. Even though this approach has been largely discredited as a valid scientific explanation of social inequality, it is still used by some people in the modern world to justify the inequality experienced by many categories of individuals.

B. Functionalist Theory
1. The classic Functionalist statement concerning social inequality -- known as the Davis-Moore Theory -- argues that social stratification is a natural and perhaps inevitable part of social life that is necessary for the continued survival of society. The Davis-Moore Theory argues:
a. Virtually all human societies have differentiated social statuses that receive unequal amounts of property, power, and prestige rewards.

    b.   People with unequal kinds and amounts of talent must be encouraged to assume and to perform various social tasks.

    c.   To meet the challenge of matching talented people to critical social roles, all societies offer individuals incentives -- property, power, and prestige -- proportional to the skill requirements and the functional importance of the positions they are being asked to fill.

2.   According to the Functionalist approach, the system of stratification is functional and necessary for the continued well-being of the <u>society</u> <u>itself</u>.

    a.   Motivating individuals to fill important positions means that these positions will be filled by the most qualified and competent and that tasks necessary for social survival will be fulfilled.

    b.   The Functionalist argument translated into a "hands-off" approach to social policy even though some of the effects of social stratification might be dysfunction for individuals or groups.

3.   Critics of the Functionalist model -- such as Melvin Tumin -- claim it is impossible to assess the degree of difficulty of various types of work and to determine the actual functional importance to society of specific social statuses. Two major criticisms are:

    a.   "Strangulation of talent" occurs: different levels of rewards for different social statuses initially may encourage occupational competition in which the most qualified people win; however, over time, the competition becomes less open -- children with successful parents have an advantage over children with less successful parents, even where ability levels of the children are identical.

    b.   The role of <u>power</u> in the creation and maintenance of social inequality systems is ignored. Power is treated solely as a type of reward attached to individual social statuses. Davis and Moore did not investigate the use of power by individuals or groups to restrict access to highly-valued, highly-rewarded statuses.

C.   Marxian Class-Conflict Theory

1.   Conflict theorists like <u>Karl</u> <u>Marx</u> (1818-1883) focused on power factors to explain inequality:

    a.   <u>Class</u> <u>conflicts</u> -- power struggles between unequal groups that occur in all stratified societies -- were seen as the driving force of human social history.

    b.   The single most important fact of life for every human population was its <u>mode</u> <u>of</u> <u>production</u> -- the mechanism by which wealth was produced in a given society.

    c.   This economic <u>substructure</u> shaped all other significant material and nonmaterial aspects of societal life.

    d.   <u>Superstructures</u> -- social or cultural forms like law, politics, and art -- are derived from and reflect the society's economic <u>substructure</u>.

2.   Marx argued that societies would polarize into two distinct <u>objective</u> <u>classes</u> -- groups defined on the basis of relationship to the economic system:

    a.   The <u>Bourgeoisie</u> -- owners of the <u>means</u> <u>of</u> <u>production</u> -- possess great economic, political, social, and other power resources, and they exist as a <u>subjective</u> <u>class</u> which is conscious and aware of its own collective position and interests in the mode of production.

    b.   The <u>Proletariat</u> -- workers who sell their labor to the owners -- generally lack effective economic, political, and social power. Initially, they are not a <u>subjective</u> <u>class</u> because they do not recognize their historical role in the economic productive process and are dominated and exploited by the owners.

    3.   Marx predicted that when the workers became unable to maintain minimal survival standards, they would become a <u>subjective</u> <u>class</u> -- conscious of their own collective position -- and a class struggle would ensue, leading to a revolution by the workers and to a violent overthrow of the property-based, capitalist system.

    4.   Thus far, history has failed to verify Marx's predictions, and, if anything, recent events in Eastern-bloc socialist societies would seem to signal that Marxist class-conflict theory may no longer be valid.

D.   Weberian Multiple-Hierarchies Model

    1.   <u>Max</u> <u>Weber</u> (1864-1920), a German sociologist, developed a rebuttal to Marx's economic based, class conflict theory.

    2.   Weber rejected Marx's materialistic determinism and exclusive focus upon economic stratification:

        a.   He argued that individuals and groups are ranked in hierarchies across a number of important dimensions in modern, complex societies.

        b.   <u>Life</u> <u>chances</u> -- access to basic opportunities and resources in the marketplace -- define the individual's class position in modern societies -- not just ownership of private property, as in Marx's view.

    3.   Weber asserted that two other dimensions of inequality are crucial -- in addition to economic conditions -- to an understanding of modern stratification:

        a.   <u>Social</u> <u>hierarchy</u> -- individuals are ranked according to the level of prestige or honor accorded them by others, thus coming to occupy a particular level, or <u>stratum</u>, in this hierarchy by virtue of a certain <u>life</u> <u>style</u> -- a distinctive orientation or relationship to the social world.

        b.   <u>Political</u> <u>hierarchy</u> -- individuals are ranked as <u>parties</u> by virtue of their different abilities to mobilize and employ power.

    4.   According to Weber, the connections among economic, social, and political hierarchies are flexible and change over time.

III. METHODS AND ISSUES IN STRATIFICATION ANALYSIS

A.   Objective Class Analysis

    1.   <u>Objective</u> <u>class</u> <u>analysis</u> is a technique for defining and measuring social class based upon objective factors such as income, education, and occupation.

    2.   How objective class analysis is conducted:

        a.   A given population is divided into hierarchies of income, occupational, educational, or other objectively-defined categories.

        b.   Researchers establish the boundaries for these groupings based on either observed or predicted significant differences in attitudes or behavior among the categorized groups.

        c.   Findings often are reported in the form of a composite portrait of the class structure which simplifies reality for the sake of clarity.

B. Subjective Class Analysis: Self-Placement
    1. <u>Subjective</u> <u>self-placement</u> is a technique for defining and measuring social class based upon respondents' perceptions of their own positions within the class hierarchy.
    2. How subjective class analysis using <u>self-placement</u> is conducted:
        a. Social class is treated as a subjective self-identification. It is assumed that an individual's subjective socioeconomic self-identification has significant consequences for personal values, beliefs, and behaviors.
        b. Researchers ask population members to locate themselves within a class hierarchy which is either established by the respondents themselves or is predetermined by the researchers.
    3. This approach operates on the assumption that the individual's self-perception is the true measure of that individual's social class position, and that individuals can and will locate themselves accurately within the inequality system.

C. Subjective Class Analysis: Reputation
    1. <u>Subjective</u> <u>reputation</u> is a technique for defining and measuring social class based upon <u>other</u> people's evaluations of an individual's position within the class hierarchy.
    2. Conducting class analysis using the <u>reputational</u> approach:
        a. The individuals making the evaluations are people who know the individual well enough to judge his or her relevant socioeconomic status characteristics.
        b. The reputational approach portrayals social class (at least in the U.S.) as primarily a matter of status or prestige considerations.
    3. Over fifty years ago, W. Lloyd Warner and his associates conducted the landmark series of community stratification studies in the U.S. using the subjective reputation approach:
        a. Social classes were seen as self-aware groups largely based on status inequalities rather than economic ones.
        b. Subjective evaluations were used to determine the "evaluated participation" of individuals in the community based on their income, wealth, occupation, and other "objective" factors.
    4. Warner set up an hierarchy of six social class groups -- upper-upper, lower-upper, upper-middle, lower-middle, upper-lower, and lower-lower -- and concluded that members of a given class shared a certain level of reputation among their community peers.
        a. It was <u>not</u> the possession of objective socioeconomic traits <u>per se</u> that defined who was and who was not a member of a particular class group.
        b. It was the evaluations made of individuals -- and the reputations generated by these evaluations -- that were the critical factors.
    5. Since people in large, contemporary industrial societies do not know each other well enough to make accurate evaluations of the social positions of others, some researchers today use a combination of methods and survey research instruments to do stratification research.

IV. OPEN AND CLOSED STRATIFICATION SYSTEMS: CLASS, CASTE, AND SOCIAL MOBILITY

A. The Open-Class System: (Nearly) All Things Are Possible
    1. Characteristics of open-class systems:
        a. <u>Social mobility</u> -- the movement of individuals and groups within and between social levels -- is possible.

	b.	Positions at all levels are filled on the basis of achievement.

       b.   Positions at all levels are filled on the basis of achievement.

       c.   Social class boundaries are vague and overlapping.

       d.   Relatively low levels of class awareness exist.

       e.   Individuals engage in primary and secondary relationships outside their own membership groups.

    2.   In class-oriented societies such as the U.S., it is presumed that educational credentials and occupational levels provide access to upward social mobility for individuals.

B.   The Closed-Caste System: Stay Where You Were

    1.   Closed-caste systems -- found in traditional societies such as 19th century India -- are characterized by maximum inequalities of condition and of opportunity:

       a.   If there was any movement in an individual's lifetime, it would be downward, but not upward.

       b.   Socialization practices discouraged the thought of upward caste movement. Individuals were taught to accept their caste positions.

    2.   Caste positions were assigned to individuals on the basis of ascription -- the principle of filling social positions on the basis of personal characteristics (such as sex, race, and age) over which an individual had no control.

       a.   In traditional India, the caste position of one's parents, acquired from them at birth, was the critical factor.

       b.   No amount of accomplishments in economic, educational, or occupational efforts was sufficient to offset the overriding effect of birth-caste level.

       c.   Caste behaviors and boundaries were clearly-defined and understood by all members of society, and caste awareness was a central part of individual and collective identities.

       d.   Individuals were limited to forming relationships only with others in their own membership groups.

C.   Social Mobility Principles and Patterns

    1.   Social mobility refers to the movement of individuals and groups through social space within stratification systems. There are several types of social mobility:

       a.   Horizontal mobility is the movement of people in the social space within a given level of the stratification hierarchy.

       b.   Vertical mobility is the movement of people from one level of the social hierarchy to a different level.

          (1).   Movement may be either upward or downward.

          (2).   In the U.S., upward mobility ("social climbing") is the American Dream; downward mobility ("skidding") is the American Nightmare.

    2.   When sociologists study social class mobility, often they actually are examining occupational mobility because occupations can be defined more clearly and measured more easily than "social class."

       a.   Sociologists may look at intergenerational mobility -- the movements of people within the social structure across several different generations -- or at intragenerational mobility -- the extent of social movement experienced by individuals within their own occupational career lifetimes.

       b.   Social mobility may also be analyzed in terms of voluntary mobility -- social movement that results from individual efforts-- and _structural_ _mobility_ -- social movement that results from changes in economic or other social structures.

V. THE CONSEQUENCES OF SOCIAL STRATIFICATION

A. Physical and Mental Health
   1. People from higher socioeconomic status groups become ill less often and less seriously than members of lower socioeconomic groups.
   2. When in need of medical care, people from higher socioeconomic status groups can avail themselves of high quality medical and health care facilities.
   3. People in higher classes are far less likely than those in the lowest classes to experience serious psychological disturbances or impairments, but when they are in need of health treatment, they have access to individual therapists and private psychiatric care facilities.

B. Political Involvement
   1. Upper-middle and upper-class individuals are more likely than the members of lower-ranked groups to be involved in political activities.
   2. Lower social class members largely have opted out of the electoral process of voting, of becoming involved in campaign activities, or of running for elected office.

C. Crime and Criminal Justice
   1. Members of the lower rungs on the social ladder have a much higher probability of becoming either victims or perpetrators of crime, including patterns of family violence and homicide.
   2. Middle and upper-class individuals who are involved in criminal activity tend to commit white-collar, corporate, and elite offenses which often go unrecognized and unpunished.
   3. Lower class individuals tend to commit conventional or street crime which receives more attention from police and courts and is likely to be more severely punished.

D. Education
   1. Formal educational level is both an indicator of current social class position and an important resource for attaining higher future social class positions.
      a. Modern societies are "credential" systems which feature occupations that increasingly demand formal certification of competency.
      b. Higher education provides the certification necessary to gain entry to high status/high salary jobs.
      c. Cross-cultural studies of social mobility indicate the critical role of formal education in the status attainment process.
   2. Historically, formal education has been an escape mechanism for many members of the lower classes who otherwise would have remained stuck at the bottom of the social hierarchy.
      a. In traditional societies, formal education was reserved solely for the use of the nobility and other privileged classes.
      b. Peasants or serfs were not considered to need formal education because they were considered to be intellectually inferior.
      c. In developing countries where only the established upper classes can appreciate and afford education, such experiences today are still reserved for societal elites.

91

3.   In the United States, upper-middle and upper-class children are more likely to attend a college or university than their counterparts in the working and lower classes.
   a.   Throughout their experiences with formal education, children from high-status families receive instruction at elite, prestigious schools from pre-kindergarten through university levels.
   b.   Lower-class children are disadvantaged by their lack of early school experiences which give upper socioeconomic children an edge in their competition for formal educational credentials.

GLOSSARY OF DIFFICULT-TO-UNDERSTAND WORDS

Page	Line	Col.	Term from Text	Explanation
135	1		gymnastics	exercise
135	16		horticulture	growing crops with human labor
136	6		theoretical	academic, hypothetical, speculative, questioning
136	7		conflicting	disagreeing, opposing
137	10		trait	characteristic, quality
137	20		purging	make pure, make clean
137	26		laissez-faire	free choice, no government interference
137	41		catastrophe	disaster
137	47		exert	employ with continued force
138	10		controversy	disagreement
138	28		precedents	something from the past which is used as an example
138	43		irrelevant	immaterial, not important
138	44		tangible	concrete, solid
139	4		jeopardized	in danger, in risk, in peril
139	10		nonintervention	not getting involved
139	19		ultimately	finally
139	26		affluent	wealthy, rich
139	27		criteria	yardstick, standard
139	29		stifling	suppressing, depriving
140	5		ensued	would be attained, would be followed
140	18		polarize	break into opposing groups
141	47	B	cadets	training to be police officers
142	11		plight	condition, bad state of affairs
142	31		bolster	reinforce, boost, support
142	31		besieged	beset, attached
142	36		obsolete	outdated, outmoded, dated
142	42		multidimensional	numerous, related segments
142	48		rebuttal	a response to an argument
143	2		simplistic	overly simple
142	23		virtue	by authority of
143	29		reputation	esteem, good name, high regard
143	46		bedfellows	allies, close associates, partners
144	7		enormous	huge, vast
144	15		precise	accurate
144	23		inhabitants	members, occupants
144	28		conceptualize	to form a though, to interpret a thought
145	4		leisure	spare time, freedom, free time
146	4		affiliations	combinations, to associate with
146	9		terminology	words

Page	Line	Col.	Term from Text	Explanation
149	3		inevitable	ultimate, certain, unable to avoid
149	17		reconcile	adjust
149	20		biases	prejudice, slant, pre-judgement
149	20		distortions	misrepresentation, a statement which is not true
149	41		elaborating	expanding, detail, all the parts
150	9		discrepancies	differences
150	20		deliberately	willfully, intentionally
151	16		credentials	documents, diplomas
151	23		contemporary	current, present time
151	30		reincarnation	rebirth in new form
151	48		bequeathed	leave, give
152	2		disparities	differences
152	25		linkages	bonds, ties, relationships
154	4		demean	be mean to, degrade, make little of
154	5		receptive	open to suggestion and ideas
154	16		avail	take advantage of, use
155	20		opted	made a choice
155	39		aggravated	angry and annoying
155	39		homicide	to kill, murder
156	15		perpetrators	involved in committing
157	9		prestigious	honored
158	13	A	reconcile	adjust
158	18	A	macrolevel	highly balanced
158	27	A	typology	classification
158	29	A	agrarian	farming with labor other than human
158	40	B	apex	tip, very top
159	6	A	halted	stopped
159	18	A	ideologies	philosophies
159	30	B	protracted	long
160	14	A	petroleum	oil
160	2	B	oversaturated	much excess
161	2	A	marginal	on the edge
161	6	B	impeded	slow the progress
162	11	A	spectacular	wonderful, marvelous
162	14	A	miracle	marvel, wonder
162	23	A	versus	against
162	10	B	rigor	strictness
162	49	B	mandatory	required
163	15	A	sacrifices	forfeits
163	30	A	echelon	level
163	1	B	terminated	ended
163	41	B	mind-boggling	confusing, puzzling

KEY TERMS TO DEFINE:

After studying the chapter, define each of the following terms. Then check your work by referring to the answers at the end of Chapter 5 in the Study Guide.

social stratification

property

prestige

power

Social Darwinism

Davis-Moore Theory

class-conflicts

mode of production

substructure

superstructure

objective classes

subjective classes

multidimensional model

life chances

class

social hierarchy

stratum

life styles

political hierarchy

parties

objective class analysis

subjective self-placement

subjective reputation

open-class society

closed-caste structure

social mobility

exogamy

ascription

endogamy

horizontal mobility

vertical mobility

intergenerational mobility

intragenerational mobility

voluntary mobility

structural mobility

KEY PEOPLE

State the major theoretical or methodological contributions to our knowledge of social stratification made by each of these people:

Herbert Spencer and William Graham Sumner

Kingsley Davis and Wilbert Moore

Melvin Tumin

Karl Marx

Max Weber

W. Lloyd Warner

After completing this self-test, check your answers against the "Answer Key" at the end of Chapter 5 in this Study Guide and in the text on the page(s) indicated in parentheses.

MULTIPLE CHOICE QUESTIONS

Select the response which best answers the question or completes the statement:

1. The systematic division of a population into categories which are defined and treated as social unequals is known as: (135)
    a. class consciousness
    b. social structure
    c. objective class
    d. social stratification

2. Which of the following attempted to explain social inequality in wealth, power, and prestige as reflections of innate inequalities in mental and physical abilities among individuals? (136-137)
    a. class-conflicts theory
    b. natural superiority theory
    c. multidimensional model
    d. life chances model

3. The classic Functionalist statement concerning the question of social inequality was made by: (138)
    a. Herbert Spencer and William Sumner
    b. Karl Marx and Max Weber
    c. Kingsley Davis and Wilbert Moore
    d. W. Lloyd Warner and his associates

4. _____ theory focuses on power factors to explain inequality structures. (140)
    a. Natural superiority
    b. Functionalist
    c. Class-conflict
    d. Social Darwinist

5. Karl Marx believed that the single most important fact of life for every human population was its: (140)
    a. mode of production
    b. reproductive capacity
    c. life changes
    d. life style

6. Karl Marx argued that capitalist societies ultimately would break down into the following classes: (140)
    a. labor and management
    b. bourgeoisie and proletariat
    c. upper, middle and lower
    d. upper-upper and lower-lower

7. In Max Weber's model, life chances referred to: (143)
    a. access to basic opportunities and resources in the marketplace
    b. ranking according to the level of prestige or honor accorded to an individual by others
    c. ranking according to one's ability to mobilize and employ power
    d. an inequality hierarchy defined on the basis of power differences

8. Max Weber referred to individuals who were ranked according to the level of prestige or honor accorded them as a(n): (143)
    a. interest group
    b. subjective class
    c. political hierarchy
    d. social hierarchy

9. The research method used by W. Lloyd Warner and associates in their community stratification studies is an example of: (147-148)
    a. subjective class analysis using the self-placement approach
    b. subjective class analysis using the reputational approach
    c. objective class analysis using the statistical approach
    d. objective class analysis using the non-statistical approach.

10. A major difference between an open-class system and a closed-caste system is that: (150-152)
    a. in an open-class system, individuals acquire positions at all levels on the basis of achievement
    b. in a closed-caste system, individuals acquire positions at all levels on the basis of achievement
    c. in an open-class system, class behaviors and boundaries are clearly-defined and understood by all members of society
    d. in a closed-caste system, caste behaviors and boundaries are vague and members of society have relatively low caste awareness

11. The movement of individuals and groups within and between social levels in a stratified society is: (152-153)
    a. social hierarchy
    b. social mobility
    c. occupational mobility
    d. intergenerational mobility

12. When Charles starts his career in the grocery business, he makes $800 a month as a stocker. By the time he retires, he owns a chain of grocery stores and has a net worth of $80 million. This is an example of: (153)
    a. social hierarchy
    b. upward social skidding
    c. intergenerational mobility
    d. intragenerational mobility

13. _____ mobility represents the effects of significant changes in economic or other social institutions in a society. (153)
    a. Social
    b. Horizontal
    c. Structural
    d. Voluntary

14. As discussed in your text, which of the following is a consequence of social stratification? (154-155)
    a. People in higher classes are far more likely than those in the lowest classes to experience serious psychological disturbances because of the stresses of their high-powered positions.
    b. People in lower social classes are less likely to become ill because they cannot afford to do so.
    c. People in higher classes tend to opt out of the electoral process because they know the elected officials will decide things in favor of the upper classes.
    d. People in lower social classes tend to display much less interest in and knowledge of political issues.

15. Which of the following types of crime receive more attention from police and court agencies? (156)
    a. white collar crime
    b. conventional or street crime
    c. corporate crime
    d. elite offenses

16. In modern societies, formal education:(156-158)
    a. is a critical resource for economic and occupational success
    b. is becoming a less critical resource because of changes in the global economy
    c. is losing its close association with the social class system
    d. is readily available to children from all social class backgrounds because of a system of free, public education

17. In regard to the consequences of social stratification, your text concludes that: (157-158)
    a. the social level of one's specific membership group in an open-class society does not have much impact on an individual's life
    b. it is difficult to conclude from research what, if any, impact one's position in the social hierarchy has on that person's life
    c. the social level of one's specific membership group in an open-class society is possibly one of the most important facts in an individual's life
    d. if individuals do not believe in the reality of structured social inequality, they probably will not even notice that it exists in an open-class society

TRUE-FALSE QUESTIONS

T   F   1.   Social stratification is found in most human societies throughout the world. (135)

T   F   2.   Sociologists only recently have begun to study social stratification in societies. (136)

T   F   3.   According to conflict theorists, differences in people's wealth and privilege are the result of individual differences in physical strength or intellectual capacity. (137)

T   F   4.   The Natural Superiority argument has been used to explain why certain kinds of people occupy socially superior or inferior positions in a given society. (137)

T   F   5.   Functionalists such as Davis and Moore have argued that social stratification may be necessary for the continued survival of society. (138-139)

T   F   6.   The underlying assumption of the functionalist perspective is that individuals can be motivated to help others if they know they will be rewarded for doing so. (138)

T   F   7.   The functional approach acknowledges that some of the effects of social stratification may be dysfunctional for particular individuals or groups. (139)

T   F   8.   One of the most serious criticisms of the functional (Davis-Moore) interpretation of stratification is that it ignores the role of power in the creation and maintenance of social inequality. (139)

T   F   9.   According to Marx, the interests of owners and workers were inherently incompatible. (140)

T   F   10. Marx argued that social stratification was natural and inevitable. (142)

T   F   11. For Marx, human social history was a series of revolutionary conflicts. (142)

T   F   12. Since both Marx and Weber were conflict theorists, their explanations of social inequality systems were quite similar. (143)

T   F   13. Weber argued modern stratification systems rank people socially and politically as well as economically. (143)

T   F   14. Sociologists believe that it is necessary to understand multiple inequality systems to comprehend the realities of social stratification in the modern world. (143-144)

T   F   15. The objective class analysis method has its conceptual underpinnings in the writings of Marx and Weber. (144)

T   F   16. According to recent research, voting, child-rearing practices, and other behaviors associated with socioeconomic status position show clear, natural breaking points with respect to income, educational, and occupational levels. (145)

T   F   17. Some approaches to subjective class analysis assume that the individual's self-perception is the true measure of that individual's social class position. (146)

T   F   18. Warner and associates concluded that the U.S. stratification system was made up of three social class groups: upper, middle, and lower. (147)

T   F   19. When sociologists construct "ideal types" of stratified societies, they are making value judgments about what types of systems would be "best." (149)

T F 20. In open-class systems people are free to engage in secondary and primary relationships outside one's own membership group. (150-151)

T F 21. Positions in open-class systems are based on ascription. (150-151 - Table 5.2)

T F 22. Intergenerational studies focus on mobility patterns within a given generation. (153)

T F 23. Historically, the relatively high rates of mobility in the class structure experienced by various ethnic immigrants to the U.S. may be attributed to structural mobility. (153)

T F 24. Excessive drug use is the single most frequent cause of death among young African American males in the lower classes of U.S. society. (155-156)

T F 25. Formal education has been an escape mechanism from the lower classes for some individuals, but, at the same time, education may serve an important role in the preservation of existing stratification hierarchies. (156)

FILL-IN QUESTIONS

Fill in the blank with the word or phrase that best completes the statement.

1. In societies characterized by social stratification, populations are structured into layers or ranks based on _____, _____, and _____. (135)

2. _____ _____ was a social and political philosophy that believed in the existence of natural laws of social evolution and argued for a "hands-off" approach to human social affairs. (137)

3. The _____ _____ Theory argues that people with unequal kinds and amounts of talent somehow must be encouraged to assume and to perform various social tasks. (138)

4. In Marxian theory, the economic _____ shaped all other significant material and nonmaterial aspects of societal life. _____ were social or cultural forms like law, politics, and art that derived from the society's economic foundation. (140)

5. Max Weber developed a _____ model of modern stratified societies which argued that modern societies are characterized by several hierarchies of inequality. (143)

6. According to Weber, _____ _____ were the levels of access to basic opportunities and resources in the marketplace that defined individuals' positions in the economic inequality hierarchy. (143)

7. In _____ _____ research, a researcher may ask respondents to place themselves in terms of their own social class position. (145-146)

8. Social movement within a given level in the stratification hierarchy is _____ mobility, while social movement between different levels in the stratification hierarchy is _____ mobility. (152)

9. _____ mobility studies chart the movements of people within the social structure across several different generations. _____mobility refers to the extent of social movement experienced by individuals within their own occupational career lifetimes. (153)

10. Social movement that results from individual efforts is referred to as _____ mobility, while social movement that results from changes in economic or other social structures is _____ mobility. (153)

MATCHING

____1. prestige

____2. property

____3. power

____4. class-conflicts

____5. life chances

____6. class

____7. stratum

____8. life styles

____9. parties

____10. social mobility

____11. horizontal mobility

____12. vertical mobility

____13. intergenerational
        mobility

____14. intragenerational
        mobility

____15. voluntary mobility

____16. structural mobility

A. social movement within a given level in the stratification hierarchy

B. individuals characterized by a given life style in the social hierarchy

C. income, wealth, or other material resources

D. social movement that results from changes in economic or other social structures

E. reputation or social honor

F. groups composed of individuals sharing a given level of power

G. social movement between different levels in the stratification hierarchy

H. the ability of an individual or group to accomplish desired objectives even in the face of opposition

I. the social movement of individuals within their own lifetimes

J. power struggles between unequal groups that, according to Marx, occurred in all stratified societies

K. social movement that results from individual efforts

L. levels of access to basic opportunities and resources in the marketplace

M. individuals characterized by a common level of life chances in the economic hierarchy

N. the movement of individuals and groups within and between social levels in a stratified society

O. a distinctive orientation or relationship to the social world that formed the basis for prestige or honor

P. social movement from one generation to another; for example, the social position of sons compared to fathers

1. Differentiate between the functional and conflict perspectives on social inequality. State the causes of social inequality, and indicate whether social inequality is good or bad for individuals and for society from each viewpoint.

2. Explain Marx's class-conflict theory of stratification and discuss the major reasons why Weber was critical of this theory.

3. Discuss objective class analysis and subjective class analysis based on self-placement and on reputation. Note the major strengths and weaknesses of each approach.

4. Compare open-class systems and closed-caste systems. Explain the role social mobility plays in each of the systems.

5. State specific reasons why sociologists assert that prestige, power, and fortune seem to foster levels of physical and psychological well-being that may make happiness more likely. Give specific examples regarding health, political involvement, crime, or education.

ANSWERS FOR CHAPTER 5

DEFINITIONS OF KEY TERMS:

social stratification: the systematic division of a societal population into categories which are defined and treated as social unequals.

property: income, wealth, and other material resources.

prestige: reputation or social honor.

power: the ability of an individual or group to accomplish desired objectives even in the face of opposition.

Social Darwinism: a social and political philosophy that believed in the existence of natural laws of social evolution and argued for a "hands-off" approach to human social affairs.

Davis-Moore Theory: a functionalist interpretation of social stratification that attempts to explain social inequality in terms of its contribution to social survival.

class-conflicts: power struggles between unequal groups that, according to Karl Marx, occurred in all stratified societies.

mode of production: the mechanism by which wealth was produced in a given society. (Marx)

substructure: the economic system that shaped all other significant material and nonmaterial aspects of societal life. (Marx)

superstructure: social or cultural forms like law, politics, and art that derived from and reflected the society's economic substructure.

objective classes: groups defined on the basis of relationship to the economic system. In modern society, the two major classes are bourgeoisie (owners) and proletariat (workers).

subjective classes: groups whose members were conscious and aware of their own collective position and interests in the mode of production.

multidimensional model: an interpretation of stratification developed by Max Weber which argued that modern societies are characterized by several hierarchies of inequality.

life chances: the levels of access to basic opportunities and resources in the marketplace that defined individuals' positions in the economic inequality hierarchy. (Weber)

class: individuals characterized by a common level of life chances in the economic hierarchy. (Weber)

social hierarchy: an inequality hierarchy based upon prestige or social honor considerations. (Weber)

stratum: individuals characterized by a given life style in the social hierarchy. (Weber)

life styles: a distinctive orientation or relationship to the social world that formed the basis for prestige or honor. (Weber)

political hierarchy: an inequality hierarchy defined on the basis of power differences. (Weber)

parties: in Weber's model, groups composed of individuals sharing a given level of power.

objective class analysis: a technique for defining and measuring social class based upon objective factors such as income and occupation.

subjective self-placement: a technique for defining and measuring social class based upon respondents' perceptions of their own positions within the class hierarchy.

subjective reputation: a technique for defining and measuring social class based upon other people's evaluations of an individual's position within the class hierarchy.

open-class society: a social system in which inequalities of condition and of opportunities are minimized.

closed-caste structure: a society characterized by maximum inequalities of condition and of opportunity.

social mobility: the movement of individuals and groups within and between social levels in a stratified society.

exogamy: social interaction system in which individuals are free to form relationships with others outside their own membership groups.

ascription: the principle of filling social positions on the basis of personal characteristics (e.g., sex, race, age) over which one had on control.

endogamy: social interaction system in which individuals are limited to forming relationships only with others in their own membership groups.

horizontal mobility: social movement within a given level in the stratification hierarchy.

vertical mobility: social movement between different levels in the stratification hierarchy.

intergenerational mobility: social movement from one generation to another

intragenerational mobility: the social movement of individuals within their own lifetimes.

voluntary mobility: social movement that results from individual efforts.

structural mobility: social movement that results from changes in economic or other social structures.

KEY PEOPLE:

Herbert Spencer and William Graham Sumner were among the earliest sociologists to contribute to the Natural Superiority Theory with their work in Social Darwinism, which believed in the existence of natural laws of social evolution and argued for a "hands-off" approach to human social affairs.

Kingsley Davis and Wilbert Moore are responsible for the classic functionalist statement concerning the question of social inequality. The Davis-Moore Theory argued that social stratification is a natural and perhaps inevitable part of the human condition -- a part of social life that in fact may be necessary for the continued survival of society.

Melvin Tumin provided a strong criticism of the Davis-Moore (Functional) Theory of social stratification. He argued that any system of stratification created to promote the search for individual ability and talent ultimately would have the opposite consequence, which he termed the "strangulation of talent" effect.

Karl Marx was a conflict theorist who focused on power factors to explain inequality structures. He believed that differences in property ownership created objective classes whose opposed interests put them into conflict with one another. As these classes (owners and workers) became subjectively aware of their respective situations, the class struggle would lead to a revolution by the workers and the violent overthrow of the property-based, capitalist system.

Max Weber criticized Marx's theory for its oversimplicity and its exclusive reliance on economic factors to explain inequality. Weber argued that modern stratification systems rank people socially and politically as well as economically. Weber's multidimensional model of stratification has guided a great deal of stratification research over the past fifty years.

W. Lloyd Warner and associates conducted the landmark reputational approach study about fifty years ago. Warner believed that social class in the United States is largely a matter of status, rather than economic, inequalities. In his study, it was not the possessed objective socioeconomic traits a respondent had that defined who was a member of a particular class group, but, rather, evaluations made by other individuals -- and the reputations generated by these evaluations -- that were the critical factor. He portrayed the social class structure as having six groups: upper-upper, lower-upper, upper-middle, lower-middle, upper-lower, and lower-lower.

ANSWERS TO MULTIPLE CHOICE QUESTIONS:

1. d The systematic division of a population into categories which are defined and treated as social unequals is known as social stratification. (135)

2. b The Natural Superiority Theory asserted that social inequality was the result of individual differences in physical strength, mental agility or intellectual capacity or some other "natural" human traits with which individuals were born. (136-137)

3. c Kingsley Davis and Wilbert Moore made the classic functionalist statement concerning the question of social inequality. The functionalist theory of stratification is often called the "Davis-Moore Theory." (138)

4. c Class-conflict theory focuses on power factors to explain inequality structures. Natural Superiority, Functionalist, and Social Darwinist theorists typically do not analyze power as a factor in social stratification. (140)

5. a For Marx, the single most important fact of life for every human population was its mode of production, the mechanism by which wealth was produced in the given society. (140)

6. b Marx argued that modern industrial societies would polarize into two objective classes: the bourgeoisie (owners) and the proletariat (workers). (140)

7. a Weber thought that life chances -- access to basic opportunities and resources in the marketplace -- defined the individual's class position within the larger society. (143)

8. d Social hierarchy, according to Weber, referred to individuals who were ranked according to the level of prestige or honor accorded them. By contrast, in the political hierarchy, individuals were ranked as parties by virtue of their different abilities to mobilize and employ power. (143)

9. b The research by Warner and associates utilized subjective class analysis using the reputational approach. Warner believed that objective class status was not as important as the evaluations made of individuals -- and the reputations generated by these evaluations -- that were the critical factors in shaping virtually all other significant aspects of the lives of individuals. (147-148)

10. a One of the major differences in an open-class system as opposed to a closed-caste system is the fact that individuals acquire positions in open-class structures based on achievement while they acquire positions in closed-caste structures based on ascription. (150-152)

11. b Social mobility is the movement of individuals and groups within and between social levels. Occupational mobility refers to measuring "social class" based on upward or downward mobility exclusively based on occupational levels. Intergenerational mobility is the movement of people across several generations. (152-153)

12. d The upward movement of Charles from an $800-a-month stocker to an $80 million grocery chain owner is an example of intragenerational mobility -- the extent of social movement experienced by individuals within their own occupational career lifetimes. (153)

13. c   Structural mobility represents the effects of significant changes in economic or other social institutions in a society. For example, the Industrial Revolution provided opportunities for many immigrants who otherwise might have remained frozen in place at the bottom of an agrarian class hierarchy. (153)

14. d   Research indicates that people in lower social classes tend to display much less interest in and knowledge of political issues. Upper-middle and upper-class groups tend to maintain control of the political structure. Responses "a" and "b" are stated in reverse: It is the people in the lower classes who are more likely to experience serious psychological disturbances and to have major physical health problems than those in the higher classes. (154-155)

15. b   Conventional or street crimes are likely to receive more attention from police and court agencies. Lower class people receive more frequent and more serious punishments for their offenses. Middle and upper-class individuals tend to be involved in white-collar, corporate, and elite offenses which often go unrecognized and unpunished. (156)

16. a   Formal education is a critical resource for economic and occupational success in modern societies. Members of developing societies also are very concerned about acquiring a "good" formal education so that they will have good career opportunities. The other responses are incorrect because education is becoming even more important in the global economy. For example, U.S. workers have to compete in the world marketplace with Japanese workers who often have received better levels of education. Children from upper social classes have much better opportunities for high quality education in the U.S. than do children from lower social class backgrounds in spite of a system of free, public education. (156-158)

17. c   According to your text -- and the writings of many other sociologists as well -- one's social class position in an open-class society is possibly one of the most important facts in an individual's life. As the authors note, "It often can be a matter of life and death itself." (157-158)

ANSWERS TO TRUE-FALSE QUESTIONS

1. True (135)
2. False -- The continuing and seemingly-universal presence of social inequalities has made the study of social stratification a basic part of sociological concern since the beginning of the field. (136)
3. False -- Natural Superiority approaches interpret social inequalities as reflections of natural inequalities in mental and physical abilities among individuals. Conflict theorists strongly deny this assertion. (137)
4. True (137)
5. True (138-139)
6. False -- The underlying assumption of the functional perspective is that individuals can be motived best -- or only -- by appealing to their individual desires for prestige, fortune, and power -- not "to help others." (138)
7. True (139)
8. True (139)
9. True (140)
10. False -- According to Marx, social stratification was neither natural nor inevitable; nor did it serve the best interests of societal survival. (142)
11. True (142)

12. False -- Although they would both be classified as "conflict" theorists, the perspectives of Marx and Weber diverged widely on a number of issues. For example, Marx's view of inequality focused exclusively upon economic stratification. Weber argued that economic-based inequalities were only one component of stratification systems. (143)
13. True (143)
14. True (143-144)
15. True (144)
16. False -- Although research has demonstrated social class differences in voting, child-rearing practices, and other behaviors, no clear natural breaking points have been determined with respect to income, educational, and occupational levels. For example, there is no single yearly income figure that marks the precise boundary line between those who vote and those who don't. (145)
17. True (146)
18. False -- Warner and associates concluded that the U.S. stratification system was made up of six social class groups: upper-upper, lower-upper, upper-middle, lower-middle, upper-lower, and lower-lower. (147)
19. False -- When sociologists use the term "ideal types," they do not mean "best." In this chapter, "ideal types" refers to logically-extreme forms of social inequality that may be thought of as the endpoints in a continuum of such inequalities. (149)
20. True (150-151)
21. False -- Positions in open-class systems are based on achievement. In caste-closed structures, societal positions are based on ascription. (150-151 - Table 5.2)
22. False -- Intergenerational studies focus on mobility patterns between generations. Intragenerational studies focus on mobility patterns within a given generation. (153)
23. True (153)
24. False -- Murder is the single most frequent cause of death among young African American males in the lower classes of U.S. society, not excessive drug use. (155-156)
25. True (156)

ANSWERS TO FILL-IN QUESTIONS

1. Property, prestige, power (135)
2. Social Darwinism (137)
3. Davis-Moore (138)
4. Substructure; superstructures (140)
5. Multidimensional (143)
6. Life chances (143)
7. Subjective self-placement (145-146)
8. Horizontal; vertical (152)
9. Intergenerational; intragenerational (153)
10. Voluntary; structural (153)

ANSWERS TO MATCHING

1.	E	7.	B	12.	G
2.	C	8.	O	13.	P
3.	H	9.	F	14.	I
4.	J	10.	N	15.	K
5.	L	11.	A	16.	D
6.	M				

CHAPTER SIX

RACIAL AND ETHNIC MINORITIES

Chapter 6 distinguishes between majority and minority groups, and between racial and ethnic minorities. Race and ethnicity are concepts subject to a great deal of confusion and misunderstanding. Racial minorities consist of people who are (or who are thought to be) genetically and physically different from the majority group. Ethnic minorities are composed of people culturally different from the dominant societal group. Both racial and ethnic minority groups face stereotyping, prejudice and discrimination by the majority. Six patterns of majority-minority racial and ethnic groups relations are described: assimilation, pluralism, legal protection of minorities, population transfer, continued subjugation, and extermination. The experiences of various racial and ethnic groups -- African Americans, Native Americans, Hispanic Americans, and Asian Americans -- are discussed. The relationship between racial and ethnic minority group linkages and the social stratification system in the United States is analyzed in terms of the nature and extent of economic gains made by various groups over the past forty years. The chapter concludes with an analysis of William J. Wilson's controversial hypothesis on race, class, and poverty, and an assessment of the future of minority group relations in the U.S. Although many favorable changes have occurred for some members of racial and ethnic groups during the past forty years, race-related problems in the United States are far from being resolved.

LEARNING OBJECTIVES:

As you read Chapter 6, use these learning objectives to organize your notes. After completing your reading, briefly state an answer to each of the objectives, and review the text pages in parentheses.

1. Differentiate between majority groups and minority groups. (167-168)

2. Explain how prejudice differs from discrimination. (168)

3. State the difference between the concepts of "race" and of "ethnicity." (169-171)

4. Outline and briefly describe the six patterns of majority-minority racial and ethnic group relations. Indicate which of the patterns are closest to the functionalist and conflict perspectives. (171-176)

5. Indicate how the experience of slavery continues to affect relations between whites and African Americans in the United States. (177-178)

6. Discuss the major reasons why Native Americans remain the most severely disadvantaged minority group in terms of income, education, occupation, and other quality of life indicators. (179-180)

7. Specify the factors which account for the high levels of poverty and low levels of education among many Hispanic American groups. (180-183)

8. Explain why Asian Americans have been portrayed as a "superminority" while at the same time they have experienced "Asian bashing." (183-184)

9. Analyze the future prospects for racial and ethnic relations in the United States. (184-189)

OUTLINE

I. INTRODUCTION

   A. A minority group is composed of people who possess traits that make them distinctively different from dominant majority societal groups and which are negatively-valued in the larger society.
      1. Minority groups are denied equal access to educational, occupational, and other opportunity structures.
      2. They often are relegated to subordinate positions at the bottom of the stratification hierarchies of their societies.

   B. Minority group stratification represents a prime example of the continued existence of Natural Superiority thinking, with its emphasis upon ascribed, personal qualities which often are presented as stereotypes.
      1. Stereotypes are categorical portrayals of all members of a specific group as being essentially identical to one another and essentially unlike all members of other groups. Stereotypes foster a climate that encourages the development of prejudice and discrimination.
      2. Prejudice is an irrational, negative feeling or belief about members of a certain group, based upon presumed characteristics of that group.
      3. Discrimination is unequal, unfair treatment toward members of some specific group.

II. RACE AND ETHNICITY

   A. Race -- a population that differs from others in the relative frequency of some gene or genes -- is a widely misunderstood concept.
      1. Although ethnologists have divided racial groups into three categories -- Caucasoid or "white," Negroid or "black," and Mongoloid or "yellow" -- this classification scheme is imprecise and inaccurate
      2. Many variations in physical and other characteristics exist, and there has been a tremendous amount of amalgamation -- biological reproduction across different racial group lines.

   B. Ethnic groups consist of people who possess a distinctive, shared culture and a sense of common identification based on that culture.
      1. Although ethnicity itself has nothing to do with biological differences among people, many ethnic groups in fact possess specific physical characteristics that differentiate them from other ethnic groups.
      2. People who appear indistinguishable on the basis of physical characteristics may be members of vastly different ethnic groups.
      3. In the United States, "ethnic groups" include groups which are recognizably different on the basis of cultural characteristics, physical characteristics, or some combination of the two.

III. PATTERNS OF RACIAL AND ETHNIC GROUP RELATIONS

   A. Assimilation is the process by which minority groups become absorbed or incorporated into the majority group's sociocultural system, thereby eventually losing their individual cultural and/or physical identities.

108

According to Milton Gordon, there are several types or stages of assimilation:

1. Cultural assimilation (acculturation) involves changes in behaviors, beliefs, values, and attitudes among minority group members to approximate more closely the patterns of the dominant societal group.

2. Structural assimilation involves the gradual acceptance and admittance of minority group members into secondary and primary group relationships by members of the majority group.

3. Marital/physical assimilation (amalgamation) involves large-scale intermarriage and biological reproduction across majority-minority group lines, resulting in the gradual decline of distinctive physical features that may be associated with particular minority groups.

    a. Melting Pot theory, which was one of the most enduring images of the United States for almost two centuries, envisioned the assimilation of individual immigrant groups into society as an amalgamation of cultural and physical traits.

    b. In actuality, the "Melting Pot" did not occur, at least in part, because of ethnocentrism -- the belief in the superiority of one's own way of life and a corresponding belief in the inferiority of others' ways of life -- and emphasis on Anglo-Conformity -- the philosophy and policy that immigrants to the U.S. must abandon their old ways and conform to prevailing Anglo-Saxon cultural patterns.

    c. The functionalist perspective has tended to regard assimilation as the most desirable form of intergroup relations because it promotes social and cultural unity, as well as stability for society as a whole.

B. Pluralism refers to the retention of minority group identities and diversities, with individual racial and ethnic groups (majority and minorities) accommodating themselves to one another's individual differences. Modern Switzerland is perhaps the best example of successful pluralism in action.

C. Legal Protection of Minorities refers to a variety of legal/political actions designed to establish or maintain the civil or other rights of recognized minority groups.

D. Population Transfer is the voluntary or involuntary movement of minority group members from situations of contact with other specific groups to a different geographic area. An example of Population Transfer is the relocation of Native American tribes to reservations during the 19th century.

E. Continued Subjugation refers to intergroup patterns in which minority groups are kept in a subordinate social and economic position. The system of apartheid, or racial segregation, in South Africa is perhaps the most obvious example.

1. Conflict theorists argue that the subjugation and exploitation of racial and ethnic minorities by powerful majority groups remains a continuing part of the history of the U.S. and other modern societies.

2. According to the conflict view, while assimilation may be the stated or formal goal of many modern societies, the actual social and political policy has been one of domination of minorities.

3. Marxian conflict theorists have argued that majority-minority group conflicts ultimately are a subset of class conflicts and that prejudice and discrimination against racial or ethnic groups are motivated by the economic exploitation of the group. Several versions of this economic-based argument exist:

   a. One version argues that direct competition between members of the majority group and a specific minority group for such rewards as jobs, education, and housing leads to the creation of hostilities which are expressed through prejudicial attitudes and acts of discrimination against the "threatening" minority group.

   b. A second version views the economic decline of the majority group as the underlying source of prejudice and discrimination against minority group members -- thus minorities are made into scapegoats -- innocent targets for the majority group's frustration and aggression.

4. From the standpoint of symbolic interaction theory, the power struggles that are so characteristic of majority-minority group interactions might be interpreted as the outgrowth of the differing world views of these groups.

   a. When people who share the same societal space do not share a common symbolic (cultural) perspective, divergent group values and meanings may cause economic and political conflict.

   b. A new world view acceptable to all parties (the Melting Pot model) or triumph of one world view over the others (the Anglo Conformity model) would be necessary to resolve the conflict.

F. Extermination/Genocide refers to attempts to physically destroy or annihilate members of particular minority groups. For members of the majority group, intergroup relations problems are solved by eliminating the offending minority group(s).

IV. RACIAL AND ETHNIC INTERGROUP RELATIONS IN THE UNITED STATES

A. African Americans

1. African Americans constitute the largest racial or ethnic minority in the United States, and are the only group in this society to have been held in slavery.

2. History of slavery and persistence of discrimination:

   a. African Americans originally were brought to the U.S. involuntarily, and for a period of nearly 250 years, they endured incredibly demeaning and dehumanizing conditions.

   b. The system of slavery was formally destroyed by the Civil War; however, soon thereafter, segregation laws -- the so-called "Jim Crow laws" -- were established to effectively bar the newly-freed slaves from any real participation in society on a par with whites.

   c. Brown v. Board of Education (U.S. Supreme Court - 1954) -- declared racially-segregated school facilities unconstitutional and opened the assault on the Jim Crow system -- eventually leading to Civil Rights legislation during the 1960's and 1970's:

      (1). Civil Right legislation dismantled the formal de jure segregation system

      (2). However, what had been formal and legally- supported mechanisms of repression now became informal, de facto, practices which were embedded within established institutional structures. These practices are referred to as <u>institutional</u> <u>racism</u> by sociologists.

    d. Recent attempts to legislate racial equality through measures designed to deal with the subtle, but persistent, consequences of such institutionalized practices seem to have had an opposite effect.

        (1). A series of Reagan-era Supreme Court rulings effectively narrowed the scope of previous minority-rights legislation.

        (2). The Civil Rights Act of 1990 was vetoed by President Bush.

3. African Americans remain significantly below whites in most quality of life indictors:

    a. Excessive mortality rates among African American men living in Harlem exist compared with other segments of the U.S. population.

    b. There are significant differences in median incomes between African American and white families and in the proportion of African American families living below the government-defined poverty line.

    c. Substantially higher rates of unemployment exist for African American than for whites.

    d. Homicide rates are higher, and life expectancy rates are lower, for African Americans than for whites.

B. Native Americans

1. Though Native Americans preceded white European settlers in the United States, they lacked the newcomers' military technology and were overwhelmed by the colonists.

2. By the mid-19th century, all Native American tribes living in the U.S. had been forcibly relocated west of the Mississippi River.

3. Subsequently, Native Americans were removed to reservations because of their lack of assimilation to Anglo culture, and their lives became controlled by the U.S. Government's Bureau of Indian Affairs.

    a. It was the goal of the Bureau to force assimilation to white cultural patterns and the breakup of tribal groupings.

    b. This resulted in the Native Americans' way of life being destroyed and their tribal resources squandered or sold away.

4. In the 1960's and 1970's, Native Americans protested and organized a <u>Pan</u>-<u>Indian</u> <u>Movement</u> -- an intertribal political coalition united to promote the common interests of Native Americans in the U.S.

5. Native Americans remain today perhaps the most disadvantaged American minority group in terms of economic, educational, physical and mental health, and other quality of life factors.

C. Hispanic Americans

1. Hispanic Americans consist of people from Spanish or Latin American origins, including Mexican Americans, Cubans, and Puerto Ricans. For many Anglos, Hispanics form a perceived threat for several reasons:

    a. Hispanic Americans represent a sizeable portion of the U.S. population and are one of the fastest-growing racial or ethnic groups, having already gained a numerical majority in portions of several states.

    b. There has been a large in-flow of documented and undocumented workers who work at wages substantially lower than those paid to Anglos.

       c.   Language differences also contribute to the potential for conflict between Hispanics and Anglos, as evidenced by the passage of laws making English the official state language in a number of states.

    2.   The life situations of many Hispanics in the U.S. are characterized by significantly lower economic, educational, occupational, housing, and other quality of life standards.

    3.   In recent years, Hispanic groups have attempted to organize a pan-Hispanic coalition in an effort to strengthen their political power position, but they have been hampered by diversities and disagreements among various segments of their own group.

D.   Asian Americans
    1.   Asian Americans have been portrayed as a "superminority" because of their educational and economic successes.
        a.   Asian Americans demonstrate the highest levels of median family income of all ethnic groups in the U.S.
        b.   They have the highest average level of formal education of any group in this society, including whites.

    2.   The picture is not this bright for all Asian Americans.
        a.   Many have low-paid, poorly-compensated service occupations.
        b.   They have begun to experience prejudice and discrimination from many top-rung universities which may fear an "over-representation" of Asian students at the expense of whites.
        c.   Many Asian refugees who have arrived in recent years have sunk to the bottom rungs of the occupational and income ladders; however, governmental assistance programs do not assume they need help because of the "superminority" image.

    3.   Historically, Asian Americans have been victims of prejudice and discrimination.
        a.   Chinese Americans were victims of violent attacks in the mid-1800s in California.
        b.   Immigration restrictions specifically targeted Chinese for exclusion in 1881.
        c.   During World War II, Japanese Americans were subjected to forced relocation and internment in special camps.
        d.   New fears of the "yellow peril" occurred with the large flood of political and economic refugees from southeast Asia.

V.   MINORITIES AND POVERTY IN THE UNITED STATES: A DECLINING SIGNIFICANCE OF RACE?

A.   Historically, white ethnics -- who physically resembled the dominant WASP (White Anglo-Saxon Protestant) societal group -- were able to overcome initial rejection by and subjugation to the majority group; however, racial minority groups remained physically distinctive from the dominant group even after cultural assimilation had occurred.
    1.   This made racial minority groups vulnerable to continuing prejudice and discrimination.
    2.   Warner states that caste rather than class factors continue to mark relations between racial majority and racial minority groups.

B.   Racial and ethnic minorities are overrepresented among those living in poverty in the U.S.; however, the specific factors responsible for this observed pattern remain the subject of much dispute.
    1.   Poverty, or economic deprivation, is a politically and socially sensitive issue that lends itself to a variety of interpretations.

a. <u>Relative</u> <u>poverty</u> is the situation of being economically deprived compared to some other particular group.

b. <u>Absolute</u> <u>poverty</u> refers to the inability to maintain physical survival on a longtime basis.

2. The "American Underclass" consists of the hardcore poor for whom poverty has become a permanent life situation, and who increasingly are becoming separated and isolated from mainstream American life.

3. William J. Wilson offered a highly-controversial hypothesis that asserts that today it is class-related factors of occupational skills and educational levels -- and not racial group status -- that keep some people trapped in poverty.

a. Wilson acknowledges that racial factors may have once been important in pushing minority people into poverty situations.

b. He argues that race <u>per</u> <u>se</u> has declined as an important determinant of socioeconomic status, and changes in the occupational structure now perpetuate socioeconomic inequality.

c. Wilson's hypothesis has been criticized: especially his assertion that race and racism no longer are significant factors in the structuring of African Americans' stratification experiences.

VI. THE FUTURE OF MINORITY GROUP RELATIONS IN THE UNITED STATES

A. The objective life situations of many racial and ethnic groups have improved significantly during the past forty years.

1. Civil rights of minorities are now protected by laws that prohibit discrimination.

2. Various affirmative action directives and court decisions have served the advancement of these groups.

3. Substantial gains have been made in minority group education, income, and occupational situations.

B. However, many of these gains are more apparent than real, and some of these may have begun to deteriorate.

1. Some problems are the result of direct competition for jobs and economic well-being.

2. Other problems relate to the erosion of minority group gains during the Reagan Administration.

3. There has been a resurgence of negative feelings and behaviors against many minorities.

GLOSSARY OF DIFFICULT-TO-UNDERSTAND WORDS

Page	Line	Col.	Term from Text	Explanation
167	2		whirlwind	confused, disordered, or mixed-up rush
167	7		slum	densely populated area of the city with run-down housing and poverty
167	8		alleged	questionable, to make a statement without proof
167	15		subordinate	interior, low-ranking
168	3		relegated	assigned
168	9		stigmatizing	branding, labeling
168	22		recurring	repeated
168	24		distort	misrepresent

GLOSSARY OF DIFFICULT-TO-UNDERSTAND WORDS (CONTINUED)

Page	Line	Col.	Term from Text	Explanation
168	26		foster	promote
168	37		ranging	swinging, spanning
169	22		drastic	extreme
169	25		blatant	unpleasant, vulgar
169	33		manifest	show
169	36		straightforward	direct, exact
170	13		per se	essential nature of a thing
170	41		token	characteristic
170	44		lump	add together, make a part of
171	6		entity	being
172	22		metaphorical	a figure of speech in which an idea or thing is used in place of another, simile
172	25		breed	type, kind
172	34		blends	mixture, combination
173	1		overt	observable
173	2		innate	natural, inborn
173	2		branded	labeled
175	1		internment	concentration, confinement
175	7		subservient	subordinate, inferior status, submissive
175	13		subjugation	forcing to submit to control
176	10		scapegoat	someone who bears the blame for others
176	14		brunt	burden, pressures
176	29		annihilate	vanish, physically destroy
177	13		analogous	similar
178	9		barred	banned, stopped, denied
178	16		dismantled	took apart
178	26		antagonism	opposition (active)
178	27		intrusion	interference, intervention
178	40		indigenous	native, original inhabitants
179	13		dwindling	becoming smaller, declining, decreasing
179	20		forcibly	using force, using power
180	8		plight	difficult condition
180	35		inflow	influx, flowing in
181	3		curbing	restraining, slowing down
181	6		volatile	explosive, many erupt into violence
181	18		disparities	differences
181	24		tenuous	weak
181	31		irritant	annoyance
182	12	A	nonperishable	will not spoil or decay
182	13	A	gala	festival
182	20	A	tresses	braids
182	41	A	meningitis	bacterial disease--brain or spinal cord (the membrane which surrounds it)
183	31		hampered	impeded, hindered, restricted
184	11		top-rung	very high position, high prestige
184	32		deep-seated	firmly established
184	35		yellow peril	feeling of danger, hazard of power and influence from Oriental peoples, a form of racism
184	35		rekindled	started again
184	40		erode	destroy
183	12	A	infatuation	love, passion

GLOSSARY OF DIFFICULT-TO-UNDERSTAND WORDS (CONTINUED)

Page	Line	Col.	Term from Text	Explanation
185	17		prevailing	current
185	19		inferiorities	inadequacies, to be inferior, fall short of
185	41		conceptualized	interpreted, explained
185	48		prevalence	being dominant, widely accepted
186	8		incumbent	officeholder, presently holding the position
187	9		hardcore	unemployed--chronic--continual
188	4		per se	essential nature of a thing
188	20		nonsubtle	not refined, very clear
188	38		deteriorate	worsen, decline
189	8		aggravate	intensify, increase
189	18		anecdote	story, account, tale
189	26		unravel	come apart
189	41	B	amalgamation	uniting
190	9	B	bulk	majority, greater part
190	11	B	indigenous	native
190	18	B	taxonomy	classification
190	33	B	bewildering	confusing, variety of
190	48	B	benign	favorable
191	2	B	rubric	heading, title, category
191	31	B	reminiscent	suggestive, remindful, thinking of things past
192	21	A	stigmatized	marked, negative status or social position
192	37	A	entrenched	established
192	39	A	dilemma	plight, condition, choice between equally unsatisfactory alternatives
192	40	A	conceivably	be imagined, understand, cause to begin
192	38	B	contingent	dependent
193	33	A	intrusion	interference
193	19	B	remnants	residual, remainder, what is left
194	38	A	lower-echelon	bottom positions in a bureaucratic organization, unskilled workers in a factory
195	33	A	usury	high rate of interest charged for a loan
195	37	A	pariah	low caste member

KEY TERMS TO DEFINE:

After studying the chapter, define each of the following terms. Then check your work by referring to the answers at the end of Chapter 6 in the Study Guide.

minority group	Melting Pot
majority group	ethnocentrism
stereotype	Anglo-Conformity
prejudice	pluralism
discrimination	legal protection of minorities
Apartheid	population transfer
race	continued subjugation

Caucasoid	de jure racism
Negroid	de facto racism
Mongoloid	scapegoat
amalgamation	extermination/genocide
ethnic group	institutionalized racism
assimilation	Pan-Indian Movement
cultural assimilation	poverty
structural assimilation	relative poverty
marital/physical assimilation	absolute poverty
WASP	poverty line

KEY PEOPLE

State the major theoretical contributions of each of these people.

George Simpson and J. Milton Yinger

Milton Gordon

William J. Wilson

SELF-TEST

After completing this self-test, check your answers against the "Answer Key" at the end of Chapter 6 in this Study Guide and in the text on the page(s) indicated in parentheses.

MULTIPLE CHOICE QUESTIONS

Select the response which best answers the question or completes the statement:

1. A major difference between majority groups and minority groups is: (168)
    a. that majority groups are larger in size
    b. that minority groups are larger in size because of higher birth rates
    c. that majority groups possess physical, cultural, mental, lifestyle, or other characteristics which are negatively-valued in a given society
    d. that minority groups possess physical, cultural, mental, lifestyle, or other characteristics which are negatively-valued in a given society

2. Categorical portrayals of all members of a given group as essentially alike one another, and essentially unlike all members of other groups is known as: (168)
    a. stereotyping
    b. discrimination
    c. amalgamation
    d. genocide

3.   _____ is an irrational, negative feeling or belief about members of a certain group while _____ is unequal and unfair treatment towards members of some specific group. (168)
    a.   Discrimination; prejudice
    b.   Prejudice; discrimination
    c.   Stereotyping; scapegoating
    d.   Scapegoating; stereotyping

4.   The subjugation of blacks by whites in the South African system of racial segregation is: (169)
    a.   amalgamation
    b.   assimilation
    c.   apartheid
    d.   de facto racism

5.   Which of the following refers to a category of people who are distinct because they are culturally different from the dominant societal group: (170)
    a.   social group
    b.   racial group
    c.   ethnic group
    d.   majority group

6.   Assimilation: (171)
    a.   is biological reproduction across different racial group lines
    b.   is the process in which minority groups become absorbed or incorporated into the majority's sociocultural system
    c.   is the voluntary or involuntary movement of minority groups to separate them from the dominant majority group in a given society
    d.   is a system of discriminatory practices that are required or supported by law

7.   The name given for an image of racial and ethnic group relations in the U.S. in which individual immigrant groups each contribute to the creation of a new "American" cultural and physical end product through the process of amalgamation: (172)
    a.   the Melting Pot
    b.   Anglo-Conformity
    c.   ethnocentrism
    d.   pluralism

8.   Modern Switzerland is perhaps the best example of which type of intergroup relationship: (174)
    a.   assimilation
    b.   subjugation
    c.   legal protection of minorities
    d.   pluralism

9.   The conflict theory of social inequality is most compatible with which model of intergroup relations: (175)
    a.   assimilation
    b.   subjugation
    c.   legal protection of minorities
    d.   pluralism

10. Hitler's attempt to exterminate Jews during World War II is the best known example of: (176)
   a. assimilation
   b. legal protection of minorities
   c. pluralism
   d. genocide

11. Which of the following minority groups constitutes the largest racial or ethnic minority in the United States? (177)
   a. African Americans
   b. Native Americans
   c. Hispanic Americans
   d. Asian Americans

12. _____ Americans are the only group in the United States to have been held in slavery. (177-178)
   a. Native
   b. Hispanic
   c. African
   d. Asian

13. Institutional racism: (178)
   a. is an irrational, negative feeling or belief about members of a certain group
   b. has largely been erased in the United States today
   c. was abolished by the Civil Rights Act of 1990
   d. is a discriminatory pattern that has become embedded in prevailing societal structures

14. Which of the following groups migrated to the United States first? (178)
   a. African Americans
   b. Native Americans
   c. Europeans
   d. Hispanic Americans

15. _____ remain the most severely disadvantaged minority group in terms of income, education, occupation, and other quality of life indicators. (180)
   a. African Americans
   b. Native Americans
   c. Hispanic Americans
   d. Asian Americans

16. Which of the following is one of the fastest-growing racial or ethnic minorities in the United States? (180)
   a. African Americans
   b. Native Americans
   c. Hispanic Americans
   d. Asian Americans

17. _____ have been portrayed as a "superminority." (183)
   a. African Americans
   b. Native Americans
   c. Hispanic Americans
   d. Asian Americans

18. _____ poverty refers to the inability to maintain physical survival on a longterm basis. (185)
a.   Absolute
b.   Relative
c.   Total
d.   Partial

19. Compared to the life situation of the middle class, that of the working class may be described as involving _____ poverty. (185)
a.   Absolute
b.   Relative
c.   Total
d.   Partial

20. Sociologist William J. Wilson claims that it is now _____-related factors that keep some people trapped in poverty over the longrun. (187)
a.   race
b.   ethnic
c.   class
d.   bureaucratic

TRUE-FALSE QUESTIONS

T   F   1.   Sociologists today believe there are three pure races of people: Caucasoid, Negroid, and Mongoloid. (169)

T   F   2.   Racial groups consist of people who are genetically and physically different from the majority group. (169)

T   F   3.   Ethnic groups are composed of people culturally different from the dominant societal group. (170)

T   F   4.   Racial minority groups face stereotyping, prejudice and discrimination but ethnic minority groups do not. (169-170)

T   F   5.   Cultural assimilation involves the gradual acceptance and admittance of minority group members into secondary and, later, primary relationships with members of the dominant societal groups. (171-172)

T   F   6.   It is accurate to describe the United States as a Melting Pot in explaining how assimilation occurred in this country. (172)

T   F   7.   Ethnocentrism is the belief in the superiority of one's own way of life, and a corresponding belief in the inferiority of others' ways of life. (172)

T   F   8.   In the United States, the 13th, 14th, and 15th amendments to the Constitution, Civil Rights Laws and Affirmative Action directions are examples of legal protection of minorities. (174)

T   F   9.   Functionalist sociologists find the assimilation model of intergroup relations compatible with their view of the social world. (175)

T   F   10. Symbolic interaction theorists claim that minority group subjugation is based on economic exploitation by powerful social classes. (175-176)

T   F   11.   Death rates among African American men living in Harlem were found to be higher than those for men in Bangladesh. (177)

T   F   12.   African Americans constitute approximately thirty percent of the total U.S. population. (177)

T   F   13.   Institutionalized racist practices having a negative impact on African Americans in the U.S. have been corrected through legislative action. (178)

T   F   14.   Many whites have come to see affirmative action and preferential treatment directives as reverse discrimination against their own group. (178)

T   F   15.   The Native Americans' standard of living was greatly improved when the U. S. Government's Bureau of Indian Affairs provided economic assistance to their reservations. (180)

T   F   16.   Mexican Americans, Cubans, and Puerto Ricans are all in the grouping referred to as "Hispanic Americans." (180)

T   F   17.   Attempts to legislate the use of English as the official language of the United States are directed, at least in part, toward Hispanic Americans who refuse to abandon the Spanish language in favor of English. (180)

T   F   18.   Asian Americans demonstrate the highest levels of median family income of all ethnic groups in the United States. (184)

T   F   19.   Historically, Asian Americans were not subjected to some of the negative responses which they have received in recent years from dominant group members. (184)

T   F   20.   Racial and ethnic minorities are overrepresented among those living in poverty in the United States. (187)

FILL-IN QUESTIONS

Fill in the blank with the word or phrase that best completes the statement.

1.   A _____ group is a recognizable group of people who occupy a subordinate position in a given society. A _____ group is a recognizable group of people who occupy the dominant position in a given society. (167-168)

2.   _____ is the tendency to ignore individual differences among members of a given group and define all members of of the group as alike. (168)

3.   A population that differs from others in the relative frequency of some gene or genes is a _____. (169)

4.   _____ groups consist of people who possess a distinctive, shared culture and a sense of common identification based on that culture. (170)

5.   The process by which minority groups become absorbed or incorporated into the majority's sociocultural systems, thereby eventually losing their individual cultural and/or physical identities is referred to as _____. (171)

6.   _____ assimilation involves changes in behaviors, beliefs, values, and attitudes among minority group members to approximate more closely the patterns of the dominant societal group. _____ assimilation involves the gradual acceptance and admittance of minority group members into secondary and, later, primary relationships with members of the dominant societal group. _____assimilation involves large-scale intermarriage and biological reproduction across majority-minority group lines leading to the gradual blurring of distinctive group differences. (171-172)

7.   Discriminatory practices that are required or supported by law are _____racism; _____ racism is discriminatory actions that exist in practice, though not supported or required by law. (175)

8.   The U.S. Supreme Court's historic 1954 _____ v. _____ decision declared racially-segregated school facilities unconstitutional. (178)

9.   As measured by the U.S. federal government, the _____ _____ is the yearly income needed to provide a nutritionally-adequate diet for the typical non-farm family of four. (185-186)

10.   The American _____ consists of the hardcore poor for whom poverty has become a permanent life situation. (187)

MATCHING QUESTIONS

____ 1. majority group

____ 2. minority group

____ 3. stereotype

____ 4. prejudice

____ 5. discrimination

____ 6. apartheid

____ 7. cultural assimilation

____ 8. structural assimilation

____ 9. marital assimilation

____10. pluralism

____11. genocide

____12. institutional racism

____13. ethnocentrism

A. the belief in the superiority of one's own way of life and the inferiority of others' way of life

B. a recognizable group of people who occupy the dominant position in a given society

C. the legal system of racial segregation in South Africa

D. a categorical portrayal of all members of a given group as essentially like one another, and essentially unlike all members of other groups

E. the attempted physical annihilation of a particular minority group

F. a recognizable group of people who occupy a subordinate position in a given society

G. the giving up of established cultural patterns by a minority group and the acceptance of the majority group's cultural pattern

H. an irrational, negative feeling or belief about members of a certain group, based upon presumed characteristics of that group

I. intermarriage and reproduction across majority-minority group lines

J. the retention of minority group diversities and identities in a given society

K. unequal, unfair treatment towards members of some specific group

L. the acceptance of minority group members into secondary and primary group relationships by members of the majority group

M. a discriminatory pattern that has become embedded in prevailing societal structures

ESSAY QUESTIONS

1.   Distinguish between the concepts of race and ethnicity. Explain why the authors of your text state that the term "ethnic group" has become something of a blanket or umbrella term.

2.   Compare and contrast Functionalist, Conflict and Symbolic Interactionist perspectives on racial and ethnic intergroup relations.

3.   Discuss ways in which the experience of slavery and continued subjugation continue to affect relations between whites and African Americans in the United States.

4.   Briefly outline the intergroup experiences of Native Americans, Hispanic Americans, and Asian Americans with the majority group in the United States. Specify the following: (1) earliest contact between each minority group and the dominant group; (2) legal action(s) affecting the minority group; and (3) current status of each minority group.

5.   Analyze William J. Wilson's claim that class-related factors -- not racial group status -- now keep some people trapped in poverty. Discuss his argument and explain why you agree or disagree with his assertion.

ANSWERS FOR CHAPTER 6

DEFINITION OF KEY TERMS:

minority group: a recognizable group of people who occupy a subordinate position in a given society.

majority group: A recognizable group of people who occupy the dominant position in a given society.

stereotype: a categorical portrayal of all members of a given group as essentially like one another, and essentially unlike all members of other groups.

prejudice: an irrational, negative feeling or belief about members of a certain group, based upon presumed characteristics of that group.

discrimination: unequal, unfair treatment toward members of some specific group.

apartheid: the legal system of racial segregation in South Africa.

race: a population that differs from others in the relative frequency of some gene or genes.

Caucasoid: ethnological term for Indo-European or "white" race.

Negroid: ethnological term for African or "black" race.

Mongoloid: ethnological term for Asian or "yellow" race.

amalgamation: biological reproduction across different racial group lines.

ethnic group: people who possess a distinctive, shared culture and a sense of common identification based on that culture.

assimilation: the process in which minority groups become absorbed or incorporated into the majority group's sociocultural system.

cultural assimilation: the giving up of established cultural patterns by a minority group and the acceptance of the majority group's cultural pattern.

structural assimilation: the acceptance of minority group members into secondary and primary group relationships by members of the majority group.

marital/physical assimilation: intermarriage and reproduction across majority-minority group lines leading to the gradual blurring of distinctive group differences.

WASP: acronym for White Anglo-Saxon Protestant, generally regarded as the majority or dominant group in the United States.

melting pot: name given for an image of racial and ethnic group relations in the U.S. in which individual immigrant groups each contribute to the creation of a new "American" cultural and physical end product through the process of amalgamation.

ethnocentrism: the belief in the superiority of one's own way of life and the inferiority of others' ways of life.

Anglo-conformity: the philosophy and policy that immigrants to the U.S. must abandon their old ways and conform to prevailing Anglo-Saxon cultural patterns.

pluralism: the retention of minority group diversities and identities in a given society.

legal protection of minorities: legislative actions and policies designed to safeguard the rights of minority groups.

population transfer: the voluntary or involuntary movement of minority groups to separate them from the dominant majority group in a given society.

continued subjugation: intergroup pattern in which minority groups are kept in a subordinate social and economic position.

de jure racism: discriminatory practices that are required or supported by law.

de facto racism: discriminatory actions that exist in practice, though not supported or required by law.

scapegoat: an innocent, powerless target for a more powerful individual's or group's frustration and aggression.

extermination/genocide: the attempted physical annihilation of a particular minority group.

institutionalized racism: a discriminatory pattern that has become embedded in prevailing societal structures.

Pan-Indian Movement: an intertribal political coalition united to promote the common interests of Native Americans in the U.S.

poverty: the condition or situation of economic deprivation.

relative poverty: the condition of economic deprivation relative or compared to some other individual or group.

absolute poverty: the inability to maintain physical survival on a long-term basis.

poverty line: as measured by the U.S. federal government, the yearly income needed to provide a nutritionally-adequate diet for a typical non-farm family of four.

KEY PEOPLE:

George Simpson and J. Milton Yinger described six distinctive patterns of majority-minority racial and ethnic group relations: assimilation, pluralism, legal protection of minorities, population transfer, continued subjugation, and extermination/genocide.

Milton Gordon identified several different types or stages of minority group assimilation: cultural assimilation, structural assimilation, and marital or physical assimilation.

William J. Wilson offered the highly-controversial hypothesis that class-related factors of occupational skills and educational levels -- and not racial group status -- now keep some people trapped in poverty over the longrun.

ANSWERS TO MULTIPLE CHOICE QUESTIONS:

1.   d   Minority groups are composed of people who possess traits that are distinctively different from dominant majority societal groups and which are negatively valued in the larger population. Majority and minority groups cannot be distinguished simply in terms of size of the group because, in some situations, "minority" groups may be in the numerical majority in a society. (168)

2.   a   Stereotyping is the categorical portrayal of all members of a given group as essentially like one another, and essentially unlike all members of other groups. (168)

3.   b   Prejudice is an irrational, negative feeling or belief about members of a certain group while discrimination is unequal and unfair treatment towards members of some specific group. (168)

4.   c   Apartheid is the legal system of racial segregation in South Africa. (169)

5.   c   An ethnic group is culturally different from the dominant societal group. Racial groups differ from one another in the relative frequency of some gene or genes. (170)

6.   b   Assimilation is the process in which minority groups become absorbed or incorporated into the majority's sociocultural system. Response "a" is the definition for amalgamation.   Response "c" is the definition for population transfer, and response "d" is the definition for de jure racism. (171)

7.   a   The Melting Pot theory envisioned the assimilation of individual immigrant groups into American society as an amalgamation of cultural and physical traits. (172)

8.   d   Modern Switzerland is perhaps the best example of pluralism because this nation is composed of German, Italian, and French subpopulations who maintain their individual languages and cultural traditions while cooperating with one another on matters or issues of mutual importance. (174)

9. b   The conflict theory of social inequality is most compatible with the subjugation model of intergroup relations because the conflict theory focuses on the differential power resources of various social groups, and the use of power by some groups to exploit and subordinate others. (175)

10. d   Hitler's attempt to exterminate Jews during World War II was an example of genocide or extermination, which refers to attempts to physically destroy or annihilate members of particular minority groups. (176)

11. a   African Americans constitute the largest racial minority group in the United States, making up approximately twelve percent of the total U.S. population. (177)

12. c   African Americans are the only group in the United States to have been held in slavery. They originally were brought to the U.S. involuntarily, as slaves in the Southern plantation economy. (177-178)

13. d   Institutional racism is a discriminatory pattern that has become embedded in prevailing societal structures. Response "a" is the definition for prejudice. Responses "b" and "c" are not true because institutional racism has not been erased in the United States and the Civil Rights Act of 1990 was vetoed by President Bush. (178)

14. b   The ancestors of Native Americans apparently migrated to the North American continent some 30,000 years ago from Asia. They were an indigenous population by the time other groups arrived on the continent. (178)

15. b   Native Americans remain the most severely disadvantaged minority group in the United States in terms of income, education, occupation, and other quality of life indicators. (180)

16. c   Hispanic Americans are the fastest-growing racial or ethnic group, evidencing a growth pattern of 34 percent during the 1980's. (180)

17. d   Asian Americans have been portrayed as a "superminority" because of the economic, educational, and occupational accomplishments of members of the Asian American community. (183)

18. a   Absolute poverty refers to the inability to maintain physical survival on a long-term basis. (185)

19. b   Relative poverty is the situation of being economically deprived compared to some other particular group. Relative to the life situation of the middle class, that of the working class may be described as involving relative poverty or deprivation. (185)

20. c   Sociologist William J. Wilson claims that it is now class-related factors that keep some people trapped in poverty over the longrun. He acknowledges that racial factors may have once been important in originally pushing many minority people into poverty situations, but he argues that class is now more important in this regard than race. (187)

ANSWERS TO TRUE-FALSE QUESTIONS:

1. False -- Although ethnologists often speak of these three major racial groups -- Caucasoid, Negroid, and Mongoloid -- this classification scheme is imprecise and inaccurate. As the text states, the notion that any sort of pure races still exist in the contemporary world is extremely naive. (169)

2. True (169)

3. True (170)

4. False -- Both ethnic and racial minority groups have faced stereotyping, prejudice and discrimination. (169-170)

5. False -- Structural assimilation, rather than cultural assimilation, involves the gradual acceptance and admittance of minority group members into secondary and primary relationships with members of the dominant societal groups. (171-172)

6.   False -- Although the dominant ideology in the United States for many years was the "Melting Pot" -- which envisioned the assimilation of individual immigrant groups into American society as an amalgamation of cultural and physical traits -- Anglo-Conformity became the actual policy in the U.S. instead. (172)
7.   True (172)
8.   True (174)
9.   True (175)
10. False -- Conflict theorists claim that minority group subjugation is based on economic exploitation by powerful social classes. Symbolic Interaction theorists interpret the power struggles that are so characteristic of majority-minority group interactions to be an outgrowth of the differing world views of these groups. (175-176)
11. True (177)
12. False -- African Americans constitute approximately twelve percent of the total U.S. population. (177)
13. False -- Institutionalized racist practices have not been corrected through legislative action. If anything, recent attempts to legislate racial equality through measures designed to deal with the subtle, but persistent, consequences of such institutionalized practices seem to have the opposite effect. (178)
14. True (178)
15. False -- The Native Americans' standard of living became much worse when the Bureau of Indian Affairs became involved in their lives. The Native Americans' way of life was destroyed and their tribal resources squandered or sold away by their so-called guardian. (180)
16. True (180)
17. True (180)
18. True (184)
19. False -- Historically, Asian Americans were subjected to violent attacks, restrictive immigration laws, forced relocation and internment in special camps during World War II, as well as other types of discriminatory treatment. (184)
20. True (187)

ANSWERS TO FILL-IN QUESTIONS:

1.   Minority; majority (167-168)
2.   Stereotyping (168)
3.   Race (169)
4.   Ethnic (170)
5.   Assimilation (171)
6.   Cultural. Structural. Marital. (171-172)
7.   De jure; de facto (175)
8.   Brown v. Board of Education (178)
9.   Poverty line (185-186)
10. Underclass (187)

ANSWERS TO MATCHING:

1.   B   8.   L
2.   F   9.   I
3.   D   10. J
4.   H   11. E
5.   K   12. M
6.   C   13. A
7.   G

126

CHAPTER SEVEN

GENDER AND GENDER ISSUES

Chapter 7 analyzes "sex" and "gender" differences based on biological, psychological and sociological research. "Sex" is defined as a system for classifying people as female or male based upon anatomical, chromosomal, and hormonal differences. "Gender" is a system for classifying people as girl or boy, woman or man, based upon physiological, psychological, and sociocultural characteristics. In a large number of societies, gender stereotypes categorically portray the different sexes as possessing different essential attributes. These stereotypes have led to the creation of gender roles that assign individuals to social positions based upon their sex, and to gender stratification systems in which sex differences become the basis for social inequality hierarchies. The chapter describes traditional gender stereotyping, gender roles, and gender socialization. Major theoretical explanations of gender roles are presented, and the impact of gender stratification on employment, politics, and law is discussed. Functionalist, conflict, and symbolic interactionist perspectives on the gender equality movement are compared.

LEARNING OBJECTIVES:

As you read Chapter 7, use these learning objectives to organize your notes. After completing your reading, briefly state an answer to each of the objectives, and review the text pages in parentheses.

1. Differentiate between "sex" and "gender" as social categories for classifying human beings. (201)

2. State the major biological, psychological, and anthropological findings regarding physical, intellectual, and emotional differences between women and men. (202-204)

3. Describe the process of gender socialization and explain why this phenomenon is such an important factor throughout an individual's life. (204-206)

4. Compare and contrast the views of the classical functionalist and conflict models pertaining to gender roles. Note the major criticisms of each of these explanations of gender differentiation. (206-210)

5. Discuss the gender differences in employment and income of men and women in the United States. Explain what is meant by "the feminization of poverty." (210-215)

6. Describe the impact of gender stratification on the participation of women in the political process in the United States. (217-219)

7. Analyze the ways in which laws have been used to preserve existing gender inequalities and to create new inequalities. (219-221)

8. Differentiate among functionalist, conflict, and symbolic interactionist analyses of the gender equality movement. (221-223)

I.   UNDERSTANDING SEX AND GENDER

    A.   Biological Considerations
        1.   <u>Sex</u> is a system for classifying people as female or male based upon anatomical, chromosomal, and hormonal differences.
        2.   Females and males have different sex organs, chromosomal patterns and proportions of certain hormones.

    B.   Psychological and Sociocultural Considerations
        1.   <u>Gender</u> is a system for classifying people based upon physiological, psychological, and sociocultural characteristics.
        2.   <u>Gender stereotypes</u> categorically portray the different sexes as possessing different essential attributes.
        3.   <u>Gender roles</u> assign individuals to particular tasks specifically because of their sex and the assumed characteristics of that sex.
        4.   <u>Gender stratification</u> -- social inequality hierarchies based upon sex -- occurs when gender roles involve assignment to positions which are categorically subject to unequal rewards for women and men.

II.   TRADITIONAL GENDER STEREOTYPING AND GENDER ROLES

    A.   Sexual Morphology and Gender Differences
        1.   The widespread and continuing human belief in basic intellectual, emotional and other dissimilarities between women and men is premised on the idea that differences in sexual morphology -- anatomical features -- generate differences in rationality and temperament.
        2.   A large body of biological, psychological and anthropological research findings indicates a general absence of significant and consistent intellectual or emotional differences between females and males.

    B.   Biological Findings
        1.   Because men generally are larger and stronger than women, they are assumed to be physically superior to women.
        2.   Although some men may have more immediate strength, women have the advantage over men in terms of long-term physical endurance.
        3.   Evidence that women are not biologically inferior to men can be found in birth and death patterns of females and males.

    C.   Psychological Findings
        1.   According to gender stereotypes, women are more emotional and artistic, while men are more rational and pragmatic.
        2.   Research indicates that the actual range of female/male differences is much smaller than commonly believed.
            a.   Evidence indicates that females and males demonstrate consistent differences in only four major areas: verbal ability, mathematical ability, visual-spatial ability, and aggression.
            b.   However, these differences are not always large or significant.
        3.   Research findings do not support the conclusion that women and men are significantly different in temperament or in intellect.

    D.   Anthropological Findings
        1.   Ethnological data collected by anthropologists point to the variability and elasticity of what some people assume to be natural human biological differences.

2. Margaret Mead's classic study of three tribal groups in New Guinea found very few differences between women and men in terms of psychological patterns or social behaviors.
    a. Among the Arapesh, both men and women displayed essentially feminine traits -- sensitivity, cooperation, and an overall absence of aggression.
    b. Among the Mundugumor, both women and men typically were insensitive, uncooperative, and very aggressive -- traits our culture might define as essentially masculine.
    c. Among the Tchambuli, women were the aggressive, rational, capable sex and men were the emotional, flighty sex.
3. The lesson to be drawn from the work of Mead and other anthropologists is that sex -- like race and age -- may be biological phenomenon, but it also provides certain resources and imposes certain limitations on members of specific groups.
4. Biological sex differences are surrounded and confounded by cultural beliefs and social practices concerning the sexes which manifest themselves in the ways that the two sexes are socialized.

III. BECOMING WOMEN AND MEN: GENDER SOCIALIZATION

A. Infancy and Childhood
    1. Gender assignment -- the categorization of the individual as female or male -- is very important in structuring the infant's relationships to its immediate world, both inside and outside the family.
    2. By the time children are three to four years old, they already have formed an image of themselves as either girl or boy, and a growing knowledge of what being girl or boy means in terms of their own behavior.

B. Adolescence and Early Adulthood
    1. Gender identities and gender roles are consolidated and solidified during adolescence.
        a. For the majority of adolescents, this means accepting gender patterns to which they were exposed during childhood.
        b. Preparation for future adult roles often entails learning about activities deemed appropriate for members of one's sex.
    2. By early adulthood, most individuals have accepted the gender information offered them by the major agents of socialization -- parents, teachers, counselors, and others -- in their society.
        a. For many females, this means their primary emphasis is on nurturing activities, whether for one's own family or for others.
        b. For many males, this means their primary emphasis is on successful careers and occupational achievements.

C. Middle and Late Adulthood
    1. Prevailing beliefs in most societies define certain adult social roles as being the primary responsibility of one sex rather than the other.
        a. The time and energy commitments required by these gender-stereotyped roles lock individuals into a set of structured behaviors and relationships that reiterate and reaffirm their sense of femininity or masculinity.
        b. In later adulthood, women who have defined themselves primarily through roles as mother and wife potentially face a crisis of self-identity and self-worth as children leave home or as they lose their husbands through death.

129

2. In late adulthood, many individuals face retirement, which also produces significant gender role changes.
   a. Jobs provide people with positive social identities and are the primary vehicle for acquiring material resources.
   b. Retirement may cause individuals to believe they no longer are making a productive contribution to society.
3. With advanced age, both women and men face the prospect of having to redefine their conceptions of who and what they are.

IV. THEORETICAL INTERPRETATIONS AND EXPLANATIONS OF GENDER ROLES

A. Gender Roles as Salvation: Classical Functionalism
   1. Functionalism argues that gender roles must be explained in terms of how those roles contribute to societal survival.
   2. The classical statement of this position was offered in the 1950's by Talcott Parsons and Robert Bales, who assumed the critical importance of the family as a basic unit of human social organization:
      a. The family is responsible for producing and raising new societal members.
      b. The family is a unit of consumption in the modern economy.
   3. According to Parsons and Bales, the family must deal with two kinds of relationship problems if it is to persist over time:
      a. Instrumental tasks are goal-directed activities that link the family to the surrounding society in order to acquire necessary material resources for the family.
      b. Expressive tasks are activities carried out on behalf of establishing or maintaining satisfying emotional relationships within the family unit.
   4. Instrumental and expressive tasks could be performed most efficiently if they were undertaken by different individuals. According to Parsons and Bales:
      a. Women were better suited to perform tasks that were people- and relationship-oriented because they were more emotional and empathetic than men (i.e. expressive tasks).
      b. Men were more interested and skilled in performing activities that were task- and production-oriented (i.e. instrumental tasks).
      c. Division of labor by gender is functional for the continued survival of the family unit.

B. Critique of the Functionalist Perspective
   1. The functionalist approach has failed to take into account the fact that throughout history women in many societies frequently played important roles in economic and other productive activities.
   2. Gender identities and gender roles based upon assumptions about differences in female-male abilities and interests tend to misallocate and waste a great deal of potential individual talent.
      a. Women may not consider certain career options because they are prevented from doing so by cultural beliefs and prohibitions that limit the proper female role to the domestic sphere.
      b. Men who otherwise might make superb child-care providers are kept from pursuing this function by prevailing beliefs that emphasize the association of members of their sex with economic, political, and other instrumental roles.
      c. Larger society suffers because well-qualified people are removed from serious consideration for important social roles.

3. The functionalist interpretation fails to explain why social roles differentiated on the basis of gender should be <u>stratified roles</u>.
    a. If both instrumental and expressive tasks are equally important for societal survival, they should receive equal rewards for successful performance.
    b. Expressive roles -- such as mothers and elementary school teachers -- receive a great deal of verbal praise and support, but they do not command the levels of property and prestige awarded to instrumental activities.

C. Gender Roles as Suppression: The Conflict Model
    1. Conflict theorists view traditional gender definitions and gender roles as instruments of oppression in society because they preserve patriarchal systems in which cultural patterns and social practices are structured to ensure the individual and collective advantages of males over females in most aspects of social life.
        a. Gender role differences never have been based solely upon biological considerations.
        b. These differences are a consequence of advances in productive technologies that created economic surpluses, inheritable private property, social class hierarchies, and a structure of patriarchy.
        c. As a result, women were defined as a form of property and came under the possession and control of men.
        d. Males increasingly became involved in economic, political, and military roles, while females increasingly were restricted to domestic, nurturing roles.
    2. Cultural ideologies were established to explain and justify the prevailing social arrangements as male dominance and the role separation of the two sexes increased.
        a. These ideologies stressed the supposed natural physical and intellectual superiority of males over females, and the natural mothering/nurturing instincts of females.
        b. However, the real basis for sex stratification was that patriarchal systems clearly were beneficial to males, who had the physical power to impose their will upon females.
    3. Conflict theorists argue that significant changes in patriarchal patterns are not likely to occur unless women come to recognize their own collective situation and organize collectively to end their exploitation.

D. Critique of the Conflict Perspective
    1. The conflict perspective has been criticized for its overemphasis on the inherent conflicts between women and men, and on the destructive consequences of all existing gender relations.
    2. Marxist versions of conflict theory assert that gender oppression is associated exclusively with capitalism; however, an examination of gender relations in non-capitalist societies demonstrates that this argument is not valid.
        a. For example, in the Soviet Union -- which is based on socialist ideas and principles -- occupational, economic, and other forms of gender inequalities are widespread and significant.
        b. Women in the U.S.S.R. -- like those in such capitalist societies as Japan, Mexico, and the U.S. -- are concentrated in lower-paying occupations and are largely excluded from important political leadership roles.

V.   PATTERNS OF GENDER STRATIFICATION

A.   Gender and Work
    1.   Female participation in the U.S. labor force increased steadily and dramatically in the last half of this century.
        a.   Most women work to help provide their families with basic resources like housing and education, and their labor has become a necessity for family survival.
        b.   Single mothers and divorced or separated women with children often are the sole support of their households.
    2.   Employment prospects are more limited for women than for men.
        a.   Women often are steered into a much narrower range of choices that largely are segregated by sex.
        b.   Many women work in "pink-collar" jobs which tend to be an extension of the traditional female nurturing role -- such as prekindergarten and kindergarten teachers, nurses, dental hygienists, and secretaries.
        c.   A cross-cultural study of work and gender in a dozen modern industrial societies --including the U.S. and Japan -- found striking similarities in employment segregated by sex:
            (1).   Women are concentrated in clerical, sales, and service occupations.
            (2).   Men predominate in administrative and managerial positions, as well as in high and medium prestige production jobs.
    3.   However, some changes have occurred in regard to gender and work roles.
        a.   There has been a dramatic increase in the number of women completing specialized post-graduate training.
        b.   More women are entering law, medicine, and dentistry.

B.   Gender and Income
    1.   Statistics pertaining to earned income in the United States show that women now may be full participants in the labor market, but many have yet to receive a full share of the income rewards from that market.
    2.   Theories that explain income differentials based on gender:
        a.   Human capital factors -- resources such as education, interest, and aptitude that give individuals a better bargaining position to sell their labor in the occupational or job market -- have been used by some theorists to explain the higher salaries received by men.
            (1).   According to this view, men have more interest, training, and previous work experience in occupations that command the highest salaries, and thus, men have more human capital to offer.
            (2).   Conversely, some women chose to invest their time and energy in having and raising children rather than pursuing a career. During the years when women are involved in child rearing, their male counterparts gain job experience and seniority.
        b.   Dual labor market theory argues that there are two distinct tiers or levels of jobs in society.
            (1).   At the top tier of the labor market are those professional, administrative, and technical occupations offering high levels of income and prestige rewards but requiring high levels of skills and training.

(2). At the bottom tier of the market are those service, domestic, and other unskilled jobs that do not require much education or training but do not offer many salary or prestige rewards. The sex-segregated jobs filled primarily by women are those found at the lower tier of the dual-market structure.

c. <u>Gender discrimination</u>: the large gaps between women's and men's salaries can be explained by the fact that women continue to be treated unequally and unfairly in the labor market. There are several forms of gender discrimination:

(1). Systematic exclusion from certain types of occupations on direct grounds -- the fact that they are women -- (e.g., women in the military who are not allowed to serve in direct combat roles)

(2). Systematic exclusion from certain occupations on indirect grounds -- job requirements that are structured to eliminate all (or most) women from consideration -- (e.g., height and weight requirements in employment in police and fire departments).

(3). Job promotion patterns that benefit men more than women. Men are more likely to be on the "fast track," receiving larger and more rapid promotions than women. This problem has been referred to as a "<u>glass ceiling</u>" because even though there are no formal or visible barriers to keep women out of certain elite positions, the beliefs and values that make up the male subculture of the corporate upper class effectively exclude women from real consideration.

3. The feminization of poverty is the increasing association between female and being economically deprived.

a. Throughout the last thirty years, a growing number of women of all ages have been descending into the ranks of individuals whose yearly incomes fall below the minimum poverty line established by the federal government.

b. Much of the growth in female poverty is related to major changes taking place in the composition of the family:

(1). Dramatic increase in single-parent family units headed by women.

(2). A great deal of this poverty is related to the presence of dependent children in these families.

(3) Over two-thirds of African American and Hispanic children live in poverty conditions.

c. The problem is confounded by the fact that women tend to have lower-paying, less-prestigious jobs in a segmented labor market. Often they are unable to find adequate child care arrangements, and they must restrict their employment to meet the needs of their dependent children. In addition, many do not receive child support payments from absentee fathers.

C. Gender and Politics

1. Even though women register and vote in numbers equal to those of men, they remain under-represented in political offices at federal and state levels.

2. Women have begun to move more heavily into political offices at the local (municipal and county) levels.

D. Gender and Law
    1. Historically, the law has been dominated by males and reflects men's belief in the natural physical and intellectual inferiority of women.
    2. Laws concerning rape, abortion, and other sex-related areas contribute to gender inequality.
    3. Rape
        a. The handling of rape cases by the criminal justice system often puts the victim on trial and suggests that women somehow are held at least partially responsible for their own attack.
        b. The rate of rapes in the U.S. is more than 20 times higher than in Japan, and the fear of rape restricts the lives of women in numerous ways.
        c. "Date rape" -- which is committed by an acquaintance or friend of the victim -- is very difficult to document, and victims often are viewed as being at least partially to blame for the situation.
    4. Abortion
        a. Abortion is likely to be the major gender issue of the decade.
        b. State laws are challenging the Supreme Court's 1973 Roe v. Wade decision and attempting to limit or deny women's access to abortion.

E. Gender Equality and Social Theory
    1. Functionalists argue that traditional gender roles promote societal survival and stability:
        a. Gender definitions maximize effective social relations within families, as well as those between family units and the larger society.
        b. Functionalists believe that the feminist movement will encounter strong natural resistance because its challenge will be perceived as a genuine threat to crucial social and cultural patterns.
        c. Changes that are too rapid and too wide-reaching could threaten the society.
    2. For conflict theorists, the key issue is that of strategies for acquiring effective power to overcome the resistance of established elites and bring about necessary fundamental social changes.
        a. Gender equality essentially is a political question whose answer will be based on power considerations rather than on moral or philosophical merit.
        b. There are many subgroup differences -- including racial and ethnic backgrounds, class levels, religions, and sexual orientations -- that are likely to generate different kinds of social realities for individuals and to produce "cross-cutting cleavages."
        c. For significant social change to occur, members of diverse subgroups would have to bind together to demand that changes occur.
    3. For symbolic interactionists, the main consideration is the meaning attached to "male" and "female," as well as the social significance of prevailing cultural views of gender.
        a. Socialization agents and the socialization process itself are critical in producing the individual's impression of the world.
        b. Until and unless the symbolic significance attached to sex and gender is altered, social roles and opportunities will continue to be based on the assumption of the intrinsic inequalities of males and females.

134

GLOSSARY OF DIFFICULT-TO-UNDERSTAND WORDS

Page	Line	Col.	Term from Text	Explanation
199	2		intact	complete, whole
199	5		mold	form, same mother's womb
199	16		bassinets	a baby's basket like bed
201	5		anatomical	human body parts
201	19		infused	instilled, permeated, spread
201	32		temperamentally	physical makeup and elements, emotional response
202	8		morphology	the form and structure of human organisms or any physical or social parts
202	28		notwithstanding	nevertheless, in spite of
203	2		longevity	long period of human life
203	9		pragmatic	practical
203	18		insofar as	to the extent or degree that
203	35		conceptualize	to think about
203	36		elasticity	adaptability, flexibility
204	5		flighty	lightheaded, easily excited
204	18		confounded	wonder struck, dazed, confused
204	21		disentangle	unravel, separate
204	34		enormous	immense, great
205	4		consolidated	united
205	4		solidified	hardened, solid
205	8		entails	requires
206	3		forestalled	prevented
206	25		exploitation	using females for the benefit of males
206	29		compelling	necessary
206	37		viability	functioning
208	4		prosper	succeed, flourish, be strengthened
208	20		misallocate	distribute incorrectly
208	36		praise	approval
209	20		disproportionate	unequal, disparity, an unequal division
209	22		patriarchal	male dominance
209	39		assertion	declartion, declare forcefully
211	6		indulgence	pleasure
212	11		discrepancies	differences
213	14		counterpart	equivalent, with identical function
213	20		encumbered	burdened, loaded down
213	30		tiers	layers
213	36		coincidentally	occuring at the same time
215	1		criterion	standard, yardstick, test
215	5		intrinsic	particular, essential
216	31	A	deficiency	shortage
216	32	A	stunted	shortened, undersized
216	9	B	intact	whole, uncut
216	13	B	accumulate	gather, collect, increase, amass
217	13		mobilize	be put into motion
217	31		intense	strong, concentrated
217	31		sustained	prolonged
217	46		conspicuous	noticeable, marked
218	17		implementation	putting into effect
219	11		perpetrators	one who continues
219	28		inferiority	fall short of, not measure up to
219	40		consenting	saying yes

Page	Line	Col.	Term from Text	Explanation
220	30		affirming	declared
220	40		advocates	supporters
220	44		construed	defined, interpreted
221	2		intervene	interfere, meddle
221	15		ban	deny, stop, not allow
221	39		catastrophic	disastrous, total failure
222	1		entrenched	unmovable, solidly in control
222	34		coalitions	unions, groupings, alliances
223	7		reconceptualization	rethinking, thinking about something in a new or different way
223	22	A	conquistadors	conquerors
223	39	A	trauma	stress
223	23	B	virility	strength, dominance, power
223	39	B	depicting	describing, representing
224	7	A	devotion	loyalty, giving
224	45	A	complicity	collusion, guilt, co-operation
224	41	B	flaws	faults, weakness
225	28	A	carnal	sexual desire
225	29	A	epitomized	illustrated
225	23	B	dichotomy	divide into two parts or groups
225	28	B	receptacle	vessel, container, a receiver
226	15	A	intertwined	crisscrossed, mutually involved
226	21	A	longevity	lifetime, survival
226	29	A	intrinsic	inborn
226	3	B	irrevocably	hopelessly, unalterable, unable to change
227	37	A	docile	submissive, meek, humble
227	20	B	deity	God
228	8	B	subservient	subordinate
228	25	B	irrevocably	unable to change
228	28	B	compulsory	required, enforced
229	37	A	depicted	described, represented
229	25	B	influx	flowing in, moving in
230	49	A	decorative	purely ornamental, to adorn
231	23	A	intangible	not capable of being perceived, not real

KEY TERMS TO DEFINE:

After studying the chapter, define each of the following terms. Then check your work by referring to the answers at the end of Chapter 7 in the Study Guide.

sex

gender

gender stereotypes

gender roles

gender stratification

gender socialization

gender assignment

instrumental tasks

expressive tasks

human capital factors

dual labor market

feminization of poverty

KEY PEOPLE

State the major theoretical contribution of each of these people.

Margaret Mead

Talcott Parsons and Robert Bales

SELF-TEST

After completing this self-test, check your answers against the "Answer Key" at the end of Chapter 7 in this Study Guide and in the text on the page(s) indicated in parentheses.

MULTIPLE CHOICE QUESTIONS

Select the response which best answers the question or completes the statement:

1. _____ is a system for classifying people as girl or boy, woman or man, based upon physiological, psychological, and sociocultural characteristics. (201)
   a. Sex
   b. Gender
   c. Gender stereotypes
   d. Gender stratification

2. When a young girl plays "dress up" by wearing her mother's high heel shoes and lipstick, the girl is going through the process of: (204)
   a. gender stereotyping
   b. gender stratification
   c. gender socialization
   d. gender assignment

3. Based on Margaret Mead's classic study of three tribal groups in New Guinea, the text concludes that: (203-204)
   a. there is virtually no difference in sex role allocation across cultures
   b. biological factors are most important in determining sex role allocation in virtually all societies
   c. men are expected to demonstrate "masculine" behavior, and women are expected to demonstrate "feminine" behavior in virtually all societies
   d. social and cultural factors are very important in determining sex role allocation

4. The categorization of a newborn infant as "female" or "male" is referred to as: (204)
    a. gender assignment
    b. gender stratification
    c. gender assignment
    d. gender stereotyping

5. _____ theorists have attempted to explain gender roles in terms of the contributions of those roles to societal survival. (206)
    a. Symbolic interaction
    b. Role allocation
    c. Functional
    d. Conflict

6. Which of the following is an example of an instrumental task in the family? (206)
    a. helping an unhappy child to get over losing a toy
    b. taking on a full-time occupation to provide more income for the family
    c. encouraging a child before she plays in a soccer match
    d. visiting a sick relative

7. According to Parsons and Bales, women are better suited for what types of tasks? (207)
    a. activities that are goal-oriented
    b. activities that are production-oriented
    c. activities that are people and relationship-oriented
    d. activities that are instrumental in nature

8. Which of the following is not a criticism of the functionalist perspective on gender inequality? (208)
    a. This approach overemphasizes the inherent conflicts between women and men.
    b. This approach fails to take into account the fact that throughout history women in many societies frequently played important roles in economic and other productive activities.
    c. This approach ignores the dysfunctional consequences of the sexual division of labor.
    d. This approach fails to explain why social roles differentiated on the basis of gender should be stratified roles.

9. _____ theorists view traditional gender definitions and gender roles as instruments of oppression in society. (209)
    a. Functional
    b. Conflict
    c. Symbolic interaction
    d. Role allocation

10. Conflict theorists believe that gender role differences primarily are based upon: (209)
    a. biological considerations
    b. psychological considerations
    c. a social construction of reality which defines "masculine" and "feminine" behavior in a given society
    d. advances in productive technologies that created economic surpluses and hierarchies of inequality

The Marxist conflict view that gender oppression is associated exclusively with capitalism is disproved by research pertaining to the experiences of women and men in which of these countries? (209-210)
a. the Soviet Union
b. the United States
c. Japan
d. Mexico

Which of the following is not an example of a "pink-collar" job? (211)
a. nurse
b. waitress
c. dental hygienist
d. elementary school principal

Cross-cultural studies of work and gender demonstrate that: (211)
a. women in the U.S. have a wider range of occupational choices as compared with those in other countries
b. women are concentrated in clerical, sales, and service occupations in many countries
c. women in the U.S. have a narrower range of occupational choices as compared with those in other countries
d. no valid cross-cultural comparison can be made regarding occupational choices by gender

14. The explanation of female-male salary differentials in the U.S. which assesses the resources that individuals bring with them to the labor market is the: (212)
a. human capital perspective
b. symbolic interaction perspective
c. gender discrimination perspective
d. dual labor market perspective

15. The explanation of female-male salary differentials in the U.S. which analyzes the world of work in terms of top tier and bottom tier positions is the: (213)
a. human capital perspective
b. symbolic interaction perspective
c. gender discrimination perspective
d. dual labor market perspective

16. The explanation of female-male salary differentials in the U.S. which focuses on unequal treatment of women in the labor market is the: (213)
a. human capital perspective
b. symbolic interaction perspective
c. gender discrimination perspective
d. dual labor market perspective

17. The fact that a growing number of women of all ages have descended into the ranks of the "official" poor is termed: (215)
a. gender discrimination
b. the feminization of poverty
c. the natural superiority process
d. the poverty line

18. Which of the following contributed significantly to the growth in female poverty over the past three decades? (215)
    a. a dramatic increase in single-parent households
    b. a dramatic increase in the number of families headed by women
    c. the presence of dependent children in female-headed households
    d. all of the above

19. When did women gain the right to vote in the United States? (217)
    a. in the 18th century
    b. in the 19th century
    c. in the 1920's
    d. in the 1950's

20. The U.S. Supreme Court Roe v. Wade decision: (220)
    a. affirmed the Constitutional right of women to decide for themselves whether or not to terminate a pregnancy during the first trimester
    b. limited the availability of abortion services to women in hospitals on military bases and other federally-funded health facilities
    c. limited the types of information about contraception and abortion services that doctors could provide to female patients in federally-funded clinics
    d. none of the above

21. The _____ perspective argues that the feminist movement will encounter strong natural resistance. (221)
    a. human capital
    b. conflict
    c. functional
    d. symbolic interaction

22. Subgroup differences among women -- racial and ethnic backgrounds, class levels, religions, and sexual orientations -- may cause women from a particular group to believe they have more in common with men from their same racial or ethnic background, or social class, than they have with women from different backgrounds. Sociologists refer to this as: (222)
    a. selling out to the dominant group
    b. cross-cutting cleavages
    c. subordinate group cohesion
    d. a pan-minority movement

TRUE-FALSE QUESTIONS

T   F   1. In most societies, sex differences are believed to be responsible for important differences in physical and intellectual abilities of men and women. (200)

T   F   2. Gender represents a classification system based upon anatomical differences among individuals. (201)

T   F   3. Gender roles assign individuals to particular and different tasks specifically because of their sex and the assumed characteristics of that sex. (201)

T   F   4. Men have an advantage over women both in terms of sheer physical strength and of long-term physical endurance. (202)

T   F   5.   Gender socialization is a life-long process. (204)

T   F   6.   By the time most individuals reach adulthood, they have accepted the gender information offered them by the major agents of socialization in their society. (205)

T   F   7.   Conflict theorists divide family-related activities into two types of tasks: instrumental and expressive. (206)

T   F   8.   Conflict theorists argue that the only real function of gender roles is the preservation of patriarchal systems. (209)

T   F   9.   In patriarchal societies, women were defined as a form of property and came under the possession and control of men. (209)

T   F   10. Gender inequalities are identical to class inequalities. (210)

T   F   11. Between 1960 and 1988, the number of working women in the United States more than doubled. (210)

T   F   12. According to the human capital argument, the higher average salaries received by men reflect the fact that men typically possess more human capital resources than women. (212-213)

T   F   13. According to some analysts, woman are a minority group within the larger society. (213)

T   F   14. When women's educational qualifications match or exceed those of men, female-male income differentials disappear. (213)

T   F   15. Because of recent court rulings, women no longer are excluded from any types of occupations. (214)

T   F   16. With more women in the paid workforce, fewer women are descending into the ranks of the "official" poor. (215)

T   F   17. Female-headed families accounted for over half of all poor households in the country. (215)

T   F   18. Women in the U.S. still lag far behind men in terms of political strength. (217)

T   F   19. The presence of some specific number or proportion of women in federal, state, and local governmental offices will guarantee that "the women's view" will be considered and promoted. (218)

T   F   20. For many years, laws defined women as helpless and in need of protection by and from men. (219)

T   F   21. Historically, rape was regarded legally as a crime that could be committed only against women. (219)

T   F   22. Feminists argue that rape is an act motived by passion and sexual desires. (220)

T	F	23.	The incidence of rape in the U.S. is more than 20 times higher than in Japan. (220)
T	F	24.	Abortion promises to become the watershed issue for both proponents and opponents of gender equality. (221)
T	F	25.	For symbolic interactionists, the gender equality movement is essentially a question of the meanings attached to "men" and "women," and the significance of these cultural meanings for societal relations. (222)

FILL-IN QUESTIONS

Fill in the blank with the word or phrase that best completes the statement.

1. _____ is a system for classifying people as female or male based upon anatomical, chromosomal, and hormonal differences. _____ is a system for classifying people as girl or boy, woman or man, based upon physiological, psychological, or sociocultural characteristics. (201)

2. Categorical portrayals of all members of a given sex as being alike in terms of basic nature and specific attributes are _____ _____. (201)

3. Gender _____ refers to the formation of inequality hierarchies based upon sex. (201)

4. The famous anthropological research which studied sex role differences among three tribal groups in New Guinea was conducted by _____ _____ . (203)

5. _____ _____ and _____ _____ issued the classical functionalist statement explaining gender roles in terms of the contribution of those roles to societal survival. (206)

6. Activities carried out in pursuit of some specific group objective or goal are _____ tasks. Activities carried out on behalf of establishing or maintaining satisfying emotional relationships within a group are _____ tasks. (206-207)

7. Critics of the _____ perspective argue that women who otherwise might make world-class engineers or corporate chief executive officers are prevented from even considering these career options by cultural beliefs and prohibitions that limit the proper female role to the domestic sphere. (208)

8. Critics of the _____ perspective state that this perspective overemphasizes the role of capitalism in gender oppression. (209)

9. _____ _____ factors are the resources that individuals bring with them to the labor market. (212-213)

10. The increasing association between being female and being economically deprived is referred to as the _____ of _____. (215)

MATCHING QUESTIONS

____ 1. sex
____ 2. gender
____ 3. gender stereotypes

____ 4. gender roles
____ 5. gender stratification
____ 6. gender socialization
____ 7. gender assignment

____ 8. human capital factors
____ 9. dual labor market
____ 10. feminization of poverty

A. resources that give individuals a better bargaining position to sell their labor in the occupational or job market -- such as education

B. a system of classifying people as girl or boy, woman or man, based upon physiological, psychological, and sociocultural characteristics

C. social inequality hierarchies based upon sex

D. categorical portrayals of all members of a given sex as being alike in terms of basic nature and specific attributes

E. the increasing association between being female and being economically deprived

F. a system of classifying people as female or male based upon anatomical, chromosomal, and hormonal differences

G. a segmented-labor market system which contains two tiers based on the income and prestige rewards allocated to each

H. specific social roles assigned to individuals on the basis of sex

I. social learning process through which individuals acquire and internalize the proper role of female or male as defined by their culture

J. process by which individuals, typically at birth are defined as being either female or male

ESSAY QUESTIONS

1. Explain why the text states that gender identity "represents much more than simply a realization that we are anatomically female or male."

2. Discuss how chronological aging and the movement of people into late adulthood affect their gender identities and behaviors.

3. Describe the impact of gender stratification on employment, income levels, and political participation of women in the United States.

4. Compare and contrast classical functionalist, conflict, and symbolic interaction explanations of gender roles and gender inequality.

5. Explain why laws concerning rape and abortion have been called a "double standard of morality."

ANSWERS FOR CHAPTER 7

DEFINITION OF KEY TERMS:

sex: a system for classifying people as female or male based upon anatomical, chromosomal, and hormonal differences.

gender: a system for classifying people as girl or boy, woman or man, based upon physiological, psychological, and sociocultural characteristics.

gender stereotypes: categorical portrayals of all members of a given sex as being alike in terms of basic nature and specific attributes.

gender roles: specific social roles assigned to individuals on the basis of sex.

gender stratification: social inequality hierarchies based upon sex.

gender socialization: social learning process through which individuals acquire and internalize the proper role of female or male as defined by their culture.

gender assignment: process by which individuals, typically at birth, are defined as being either female or male.

instrumental tasks: activities carried out in pursuit of some specific group objective or goal.

expressive tasks: activities carried out on behalf of establishing or maintaining satisfying emotional relationships within a group.

human capital factors: resources such as education, interest, and aptitude that give individuals a better bargaining position to sell their labor in the occupational or job market.

dual labor market: also referred to as a segmented-labor market system which contains two distinct tiers or levels of jobs. At the top tier are those professional, administrative, and technical occupations offering high levels of income and prestige rewards but requiring high levels of skills and training. At the bottom tier of the market are those service, domestic, and other unskilled jobs that do not require much education or training but do not offer many salary or prestige rewards.

feminization of poverty: the increasing association between being female and being economically deprived.

KEY PEOPLE:

Margaret Mead, an anthropologist, conducted the classic study of three tribal groups in New Guinea: the Arapesh, the Mungudumor, and the Tchambuli. This study demonstrates the variability and elasticity of sex roles and demonstrates that such roles are more than natural human biological differences.

Talcott Parsons and Robert Bales offered the classical functionalist explanation of gender roles in terms of the contribution of those roles to societal survival. They were responsible for coining the terms "instrumental tasks" -- activities carried out in pursuit of some specific group objective or goal -- and "expressive tasks -- activities carried out on behalf of establishing or maintaining satisfying emotional relationships within a group.

1. __b__   __Gender__ is a system for classifying people as girl or boy, woman or man, based upon physiological, psychological, and sociocultural characteristics. __Sex__ is a system for classifying people as female or male based upon anatomical, chromosomal, and hormonal differences. __Gender stereotypes__ are categorical portrayals of all members of a given sex as being alike in terms of basic nature and specific attributes. __Gender stratification__ is a social inequality hierarchy based upon sex. (201)

2. __c__   A young girl imitating her mother by playing "dress up" is going through the process of __gender socialization__ -- the social learning process through which individuals acquire and internalize the proper role of female or male as defined by their culture. (204)

3. __d__   Margaret Mead's study demonstrated that social and cultural factors are very important in determining sex role allocation. (203-204)

4. __a__   __Gender assignment__ is the process by which individuals, typically at birth, are defined as being either female or male. (204)

5. __c__   __Functional__ theorists emphasize the importance of gender roles to the survival of societies. (206)

6. __b__   Taking a full-time occupation to provide more income for the family is an __instrumental task__ because it is an activity carried out in pursuit of some specific group objective or goal -- in this case, providing more income. Responses "a," "c," and "d" are all examples of __expressive tasks__ -- activities carried out on behalf of establishing or maintaining satisfying __emotional__ relationships within a group. (206)

7. __c__   Parsons and Bales argued that women are better suited for activities that are people- and relationship-oriented (i.e. expressive tasks). Responses "a," "b," and "d" are all instrumental tasks, which Parsons and Bales stated were best carried out by men. (207)

8. __a__   Responses "b," "c," and "d" are all criticisms of the functionalist perspective on gender inequality. Response "a" -- the approach that overemphasizes the inherent conflicts between women and men -- is a criticism of conflict theory. (208)

9. __b__   __Conflict__ theorists view traditional gender definitions and gender roles as instruments of oppression in society. These theorists believe that the only real function of gender definitions and gender roles is the preservation of patriarchal systems in which cultural patterns and social practices are structured to ensure the individual and collective advantages of males over females in most aspects of social life. (209)

10. __d__   Conflict theorists believe that gender role differences primarily are based upon advances in productive technologies that created economic surpluses, inheritable private property, social class hierarchies, and a structure of patriarchy in which women were defined as a form of property and came under the possession and control of men. (209)

11. __a__   The Soviet Union tends to disprove the Marxist conflict view that gender oppression is associated __exclusively__ with capitalism. Although the Soviet Union is a society founded on socialist ideas and structured on socialist principles, it is also a society with widespread and significant occupational, economic, and other forms of gender inequalities. (209-210)

12. __d__   The position of elementary school principal is not considered to be a "pink-collar" job. Nurses, waitresses, dental hygienists, prekindergarten and kindergarten teachers would all be considered to be in "pink-collar" positions because well over ninety percent of all persons employed in these occupations are women. Although the vast majority of kindergarten and elementary school teachers are women, most elementary school principals are men. (211)

13. <u>b</u>   Cross-cultural studies of work and gender demonstrate that women are concentrated in clerical, sales, and service occupations in many countries. These studies demonstrate that female occupational patterns in the U.S. are by no means unique when compared with patterns in other modern industrial societies. (211)

14. <u>a</u>   The explanation of female-male salary differentials in the U.S. which assesses the resources that individuals bring with them to the labor market -- including interests and aptitudes, formal education, occupational training, and previous work experience -- is the <u>human</u> <u>capital</u> perspective. (212)

15. <u>d</u>   The explanation of female-male salary differentials in the U.S. which analyzes the world of work in terms of top tier and bottom tier positions is the <u>dual</u> <u>labor</u> <u>market</u> perspective. (213)

16. <u>c</u>   The explanation of female-male salary differentials in the U.S. which focuses on unequal treatment of women in the labor market is the <u>gender</u> <u>discrimination</u> perspective. (213)

17. <u>b</u>   The <u>feminization</u> <u>of</u> <u>poverty</u> is the term used to describe the fact that a growing number of women of all ages have descended into the ranks of the "official" poor. (215)

18. <u>d</u>   Responses "a," "b," and "c" are all factors which have contributed significantly to the growth in female poverty over the past three decades -- including a dramatic increase in single-parent households, a dramatic increase in the number of families headed by women, and the presence of dependent children in female-headed households. (215)

19. <u>c</u>   Women gained the right to vote in the United States in 1920 with the ratification of the Nineteenth Amendment. (217)

20. <u>a</u>   The U.S. Supreme Court <u>Roe</u> <u>v.</u> <u>Wade</u> decision affirmed the Constitutional right of women to decide for themselves whether or not to terminate a pregnancy during the first trimester. (220)

21. <u>c</u>   The <u>functionalist</u> perspective argues that the feminist movement will encounter strong natural resistance -- and this resistance is in the best interest of the social system. (221)

22. <u>b</u>   <u>Cross-cutting</u> <u>cleavages</u> occur because women may identify with a number of important subgroup differences -- such as racial and ethnic groups, class levels, religions, and sexual orientations -- more than with other women from different backgrounds, even though they are all of the same sex. (222)

ANSWERS TO TRUE-FALSE QUESTIONS:

1. True (200)
2. False -- <u>Gender</u> is a system for classifying people based upon physiological, psychological, and sociocultural characteristics. <u>Sex</u> represents a classification system based upon anatomical differences among individuals. (201)
3. True (201)
4. False -- Men have an advantage over women in terms of sheer physical strength; however, women have an advantage over men in regard to long-term physical endurance. (202)
5. True (204)
6. True (205)
7. False -- Functionalist theorists divide family-related activities into instrumental and expressive tasks. (206)
8. True (209)
9. True (209)

146

10. False -- Gender inequalities may be similar to class inequalities in some important respects, but they are not identical to them. Modern stratified societies are multidimensional systems whose individual hierarchies are at least partially independent of one another. (210)
11. True (210)
12. True (212-213)
13. True (213)
14. False -- According to some analysts, even when women's educational qualifications match or exceed those of men, there are large gaps between women's and men's salaries because women continue to be treated unequally and unfairly in the labor market. (213)
15. False -- Women are still excluded from certain types of occupations. Sometimes this occurs on indirect grounds -- such as minimum height and weight standards imposed by some police and fire departments which effectively eliminate virtually all women candidates for the job. There have been very few recent court rulings which have effectively dealt with gender discrimination. (214)
16. False -- A growing number of women of all ages have been descending into the ranks of the "official" poor. Major changes taking place in the composition of the family in the U.S. have contributed to the growth in female poverty. (215)
17. True (215)
18. True (217)
19. False -- Although an increase in the number or proportion of women in federal, state, and local governmental offices would make a difference, it should not be assumed that this increase would guarantee that "the women's view" automatically would be considered and promoted by those polities. (218)
20. True (219)
21. True (219)
22. False -- Feminists do not believe that rape is an act motivated by passion and sexual desires. They argue that rape is an act of power and violence, not of sex. From their perspective, rape is an act of terrorism. (220)
23. True (220)
24. True (221)
25. True (222)

ANSWERS TO FILL-IN QUESTIONS:

1. Sex; gender (201)
2. Gender stereotypes (201)
3. Stratification (201)
4. Margaret Mead (203)
5. Talcott Parsons; Robert Bales (206)
6. Instrumental; expressive (206-207)
7. Functionalist (208)
8. Conflict (209)
9. Human capital (212-213)
10. Feminization of poverty (215)

ANSWERS TO MATCHING:

1.	F	6.	I
2.	B	7.	J
3.	D	8.	A
4.	H	9.	G
5.	C	10.	E

CHAPTER EIGHT

CRIME, DEVIANCE, AND SOCIAL CONTROL

In Chapter 8, sociological and biological views of deviance are presented. Sociologists are especially interested in how certain types of behavior come to be defined as deviant, how norms and rules that define acceptable and unacceptable behavior change over time, and why certain groups of people are more likely to be sanctioned for rule-violating behavior than others. Conversely, biological explanations of deviant behavior tend to emphasize the individual's physical makeup -- such as anatomical or chromosomal differences. The chapter presents several sociological explanations for deviant and criminal behavior, including functionalist, anomie, differential association, labeling, Marxist, and social control theories. Next, the chapter discusses the nature and extent of deviant behavior and crime in the United States in terms of gender, age, race and ethnicity, and social class of offenders. Then, sexual deviance, violence, white collar crime, and drug abuse are examined. Finally, crime in the Third World is discussed. The conclusion is reached that as nations modernize, their rates of crime begin to increase, eventually approaching those of developed nations.

LEARNING OBJECTIVES:

As you read Chapter 8, use these learning objectives to organize your notes. After completing your reading, briefly state an answer to each of the objectives, and review the text pages in parentheses.

1. Define "deviance" and briefly explain the three basic perspectives of deviance. (237-238)

2. State the difference in deviant behavior and criminal behavior and give examples of each. (238)

3. Discuss Emile Durkheim's assertion that criminal behavior is "normal" behavior. (242)

4. Explain how crime might be viewed as "functional" or good for society. (243)

5. Discuss Robert Merton's theory of anomie. List and briefly explain each of the types of deviant behavior produced by anomie. (244-245)

6. Compare and contrast differential association and labeling explanations of how persons become "deviant" or "criminal." (245-248)

7. Analyze the Marxist perspective that argues that prisons in the United States are filled with poor people. (248-251)

8. Explain how social control theories differ from anomie theory and differential association. (251)

9. Indicate why crime statistics may not be an accurate indicator of the actual number and types of crimes committed in the United States. (252-253)

10. Differentiate the two types of white-collar crime. Explain why these crimes may be more costly and hazardous to public well-being than street crime. (260-261)

11. State the "pros" and "cons" of decriminalization of drugs in the United States. (264)

12. Explain why crime rates increase as Third World nations begin to industrialize. (264-265)

<u>OUTLINE</u>

I. DEVIANCE - A SOCIOLOGICAL VIEW

A. <u>Deviance</u> is behavior contrary to a group's or society's norms of conduct and/or social expectations.
    1. Rules of conduct which are thought to be especially important are "codified," or put into the legal code.
    2. Violation of this code (criminal laws) constitutes a crime and is subject to formal punishment by the state.

B. There are three basic perspectives of deviance:
    1. The <u>absolutist</u> perspective argues that deviance resides in the act itself and is wrong at all times (past, present, and future), and in all places.
    2. The <u>normative</u> position sees deviance as the violation of a specific group's or society's rules at a particular time in history.
    3. According to the <u>reactive</u> perspective, behavior is not deviant until it has been recognized and condemned.

C. Deviant behavior, criminal behavior, and deviant <u>and</u> criminal behavior defined:
    1. <u>Deviant behavior</u> is behavior that is a violation of reference group and/or subcultural norms, but is not in violation of the legal code of the larger society.
    2. <u>Criminal behavior</u> occurs when the laws of the larger society are not supported by the norms of an individual's subculture.
    3. <u>Deviant and criminal behavior</u> is behavior that violates both subcultural norms and society's laws.

D. When people violate rules and laws and their transgressions are discovered, they typically will be subject to the disciplinary action of some agent of social control.
    1. Some of these agents are parents, school teachers and administrators.
    2. The state, through the criminal justice system is the one agent of social control empowered to place people on probation, imprison them, and even execute them.
    3. Historically, religious institutions have served as agents of social control by emphasizing atoning for one's sins through penance and/or corporal punishment.
    4. Over the past 100 years and the rise of modern medicine, more and more deviance has been explained and "cured" from a medical perspective.
        a. The deviant is thought of as physically and/or psychologically sick and in need of treatment.
        b. The disease model of deviance took a significant step forward with the formation of Alcoholics Anonymous.

149

E. Sociologists are especially interested in how certain types of behavior come to be defined as deviant, how norms and rules that define acceptable and unacceptable behavior change over time, and why certain groups of people are more likely to be sanctioned for rule-violating behavior than others.

II. THEORIES OF CRIME AND DEVIANCE

A. Biological Explanations
1. Biological theories of deviance are grounded in the idea that deviant and criminal behavior is directly related to, and somehow a result of, an individual's physical makeup.
2. Researchers have attempted various types of documentation of biological differences.
   a. Cesare Lombroso argued that some people are born criminals and destined to a life of crime. The "born criminal" is physiologically distinct from non-criminals and has physical differences that are measurable and predictable.
   More recently, researchers attempted to link biology with crime by focusing on human chromosomes and especially on an abnormal number of chromosomes thought o be present in some violent males.
   c. The latest research focused on identical twins (who share identical genes) and concluded that the criminality of <u>adopted</u> twins is more likely to follow the patterns of criminal behavior of their <u>biological</u> parents than of their adoptive parents. This study focused only on property crime and not violent crime.

B. Sociological Perspective
1. <u>Functionalist</u> Theory
   a. According to functionalist theorists like Emile Durkheim, crime is "<u>normal</u>" for these three reasons:
      (1). Crime and deviance persist in all societies because it is impossible for all members of society to agree on what the rules and norms should be.
      (2). Crime is normal because no society can enforce total conformity to its rules and laws.
      (3). Crime is inevitable because human beings are "normative creatures" who continue to divide the social world into acceptable and unacceptable -- criminal -- behavior.
   b. Durkheim argued that crime is <u>functional</u> for society in four ways:
      (1). There is a vital relation between deviance and progress. The same tolerance that permits creativity and originality also opens the door for undesirable deviant behavior.
      (2). Deviance serves as a visible signal that something is wrong in society and in need of immediate attention.
      (3). Crime helps to clarify boundaries. Every time a rule or law is violated and society reacts to this transgression, it sends a message stating this sanction is important and the law must be obeyed.
      (4). Criminal behavior facilitates "social solidarity" as it draws members of a community together in their revulsion toward the criminal act, and the criminal.

2. Anomie Theory
   a. In his theory of anomie, Robert Merton argues that a significant amount of crime and deviance in societies of the "American type" is caused by the gap between culturally acceptable goals and the culturally acceptable means of achieving these goals.
   b. This "goal-means" gap results in five possible types of behavior:
      (1). Conformity -- Individuals accept both the culturally prescribed goals and means to achieve the goals.
      (2). Innovation -- Individuals accept a societal goal; however, the means to achieve the goal either is not available at all or is available but rejected because it is not expedient and/or may take too much effort.
      (3). Ritualism -- Individuals reject a fundamental value -- such as continually striving for monetary success and upward mobility -- but continue to work hard and meet their economic and social obligations.
      (4). Retreatism -- Individuals reject both the culturally prescribed means as well as the goals of society. Examples include chronic alcoholics and drug addicts.
      (5). Rebellion -- Individuals reject both the culturally prescribed goals and means, and substitute an alternative set of goals and means grounded in a different set of values.
3. Differential Association
   a. Criminologist Edwin Sutherland asserted that criminal behavior is learned in interaction with other people.
      (1). People learn techniques for committing crimes from others.
      (2) They also internalize a series of attitudes which permits them to rationalize their behavior to themselves and others.
   b. From this viewpoint, if definitions favorable to violations of the law are in excess of definitions unfavorable to violation of the law, the individual will engage in criminal behavior.
   c. This perspective has been dismissed as nothing more than a "bad apple" theory; however, this criticism is not valid because the theory does not focus on the person making the definitions favorable or unfavorable to violation of the law but rather focuses on the definitions themselves.
      (1). Thus, law violating behavior can be learned from those who violate the law but have never been caught and punished.
      (2). As a result, criminal behavior can be learned from many people, not just juvenile delinquents, gang members, and "hardened" criminals.
4. Labeling Theory
   a. Labeling theory argues that societies create deviance by making rules and laws whose infraction constitutes deviance, and then applying these rules and laws to certain individuals and labeling them deviant.
      (1). From this perspective, deviant behavior is behavior that people label as "deviant."
      (2). Since there are so many laws and rules governing human conduct, almost everyone engages in deviant and/or criminal behavior.
      (3). The important question is not why people commit certain acts, but rather why only certain people are labeled deviants and criminals.

151

b. The labeling perspective of deviance can be divided into two parts:
   (1). An explanation of how and why some people get labeled; and
   (2). What effect the label has on a person's future behavior.
c. The labeling perspective of deviance is quite compatible with conflict theory because both perspectives assert that rules and laws which define "deviance" are created by the powerful to control the lower classes.
   (1). Moral entrepreneurs campaign to have their values translated into laws designating some behavior as criminal.
   (2). A status degradation ceremony is the process by which people become labeled and recognized as deviants (e.g., the courtroom sentencing process in a criminal trial). As a result of degradation ceremonies, individuals may be forced to live with a master status of "criminal" for many years.
   (3). A master status is a central identifying characteristic of an individual and takes precedence over any other role the person plays.
      (a). Thus, a label such as "ex-con" may become a status which takes precedence over a person's other statuses.
      (b). Labeling theory argues that individuals may find that criminal activity is the only way they can survive in a society which thinks that if a person is "once a deviant, always a deviant."
      (c). A person can also internalize the given label, causing the label to become an important part of that individual's self concept.
   (4). According to labeling theory, deviant behavior can be either primary or secondary deviance.
      (a). Primary deviance is the initial act, or first few episodes of non-conforming/ deviant behavior.
      (b). Secondary deviance is the deviant behavior that occurs as a result of being labeled.

5. Marxist Theory
   a. Marxist theory argues that crime in a capitalist society is the result of the struggle between the bourgeoisie and the proletariat.
      (1). Members of the bourgeoisie (the ruling/ capitalist class) commit crimes of domination and repression, as a result of their economic exploitation and political control of the proletariat (the working class).
      (2). Members of the proletariat commit crimes of accommodation and resistance, as a result of their brutal treatment at the hands of the bourgeoisie and as a economic necessity for the workers' survival.
   b. This perspective asserts that the behavior of rich and powerful people (those who directly or indirectly make the laws) is less likely to be defined as criminal than the behavior of relatively powerless individuals in the lower classes.
   c. For Marxist sociologists, there is only one solution to the crime problem: the end of capitalism.
      (1). The system cannot be salvaged because unequal distribution of wealth and the resulting class struggle are inherent in capitalism.
      (2). Capitalism generates racism, sexism, and a myriad of social injustices, all of which directly or indirectly cause crime.

(3). The solution to the problem of crime would be a socialist-type society that satisfies the needs of all members of society.

6. Social Control Theories
   a. Social control theorists take deviant motivation as given, and attempt to explain why people do not engage in deviant behavior.
   b. For example, Walter Reckless argues in his containment theory that individuals are under pressure to engage in deviant behavior by factors such as poverty, unemployment and economic insecurity, and minority group status:
      (1). They also are pulled or drawn into non-conforming activity by delinquent and criminal subcultures, deviant groups and the portrayal of deviant activity by the mass media.
      (2). Internal psychological pushes such as feelings of hostility, aggressiveness, rebellion, need for immediate gratification, and inferiority contribute to the behavior.
      (3). People avoid rule-violating activity to the extent that these pressures and pulls to deviate are held in check or contained:
         (a). Outer containment consists of supportive family and friends, responsible supervision, and reasonable expectations that can prevent people from engaging in deviant behavior.
         (b). Inner containment consists of factors such as ego-strength, a positive self-image, and high frustration tolerance.
   c. Another control theorist, Travis Hirschi, argues that delinquent behavior is minimized or avoided in those youths who are bonded strongly to society. There are four elements of social bonding:
      (1). Strong attachment to family, teachers, and law-abiding friends are important.
      (2). Commitment to conventional activities such as studying, working hard, and saving money for the future.
      (3). Involvement -- the expenditure of time and energy in conventional behavior.
      (4). Belief in commonly-held values such as respect for the police and respect for the law.
   d. Control theories focus on the clash between deviant motivation and the extent to which this motivation is held in check by an individual's commitment to societal values and norms, and integration into various non-deviant groups.

III. DEVIANT AND CRIMINAL BEHAVIOR

A. How Much Deviance?
   1. The Uniform Crime Report (UCR) is the best known and most widely used source of criminal statistics. The UCR gives detailed information on seven index crimes:
      a. Violent crimes: murder, robbery, rape, and aggravated assault
      b. Property crimes: burglary, larceny-theft, and motor vehicle theft
      c. These crimes are reported in terms of the total number of crimes committed in a particular area (city, state, region, and the nation), and a crime rate.

d. The <u>crime</u> <u>rate</u> is the number of crimes committed per 100,000 population. This rate makes it possible to compare rates of criminal activity in cities and states of varying size and to make comparisons over periods of time.

2. The UCR has been criticized because it is primarily a count of street crimes committed by the lower classes and excludes white collar offenses more likely to be committed by middle and upper class individuals.

   a. As a result, the "crime problem" in the U.S. typically is reported and viewed as being offenses committed by the poor.

   b. The UCR undercounts the incidence of crime in the U.S. because many people do not report crimes when they have been victimized.

3. A <u>victimization</u> <u>survey</u> (the National Crime Survey -- NCS) was developed to learn more about crime victims -- such as who they are, what happened to them, why they don't always contact the police, etc. -- and, based on its findings, projections are made regarding the total number of criminal victimizations for a select number of crimes in the U.S. every year.

   a. Data from a recent NCS indicate that approximately 34 million crimes and attempted crimes occurred in 1986, or 2.57 times as many crimes as reported by the Uniform Crime Report.

   b. NCS data reveal that blacks are more likely to be victimized than whites, and the rates of victimization are higher for unemployed and poor people than for working individuals. Males are much more likely to be victims of violent crimes than women, and the elderly are less likely to be victimized than people of any other age.

4. <u>Self</u>-<u>report</u> <u>studies</u> also are used for gathering information about crime:

   a. People are asked to reveal their involvement in certain types of criminal and deviant activity.

   b. These studies are especially important in addressing questions concerning the relationship between social class and crime.

B. The Offenders

1. Information regarding offenders is incomplete and tends to be limited primarily to those street criminals arrested and/or incarcerated for index crimes (as previously discussed).

2. <u>Gender:</u>

   a. Men commit more crimes than women.

   b. This is true not only in the U.S. but in all countries during all periods of history for which data is available.

   c. Men are much more likely to be arrested for serious crimes such as murder, robbery, assault, and burglary.

   d. Women who commit crimes typically are involved in property offenses such as larceny, forgery, and drug offenses.

   e. Men have a "virtual monopoly" on the commission of organized, corporate, and political crime in the U.S.

3. <u>Age:</u>

   a. Crime is overwhelmingly a youthful activity.

      (1). In 1988, approximately 60 percent of all those arrested in connection with the seven index crimes were under 25 years of age.

      (2). Thirty-one percent of the people arrested for index crimes were under age 18.

b. <u>Aging</u> <u>out</u> is the term used to refer to the fact that the crime rate declines as people age. There are several possible interpretations of why this is true:
  (1). Young people often commit crimes for money, sex, alcohol, and status, whereas adults have access to these things.
  (2). As people age and mature, they become much better at delaying gratification. Older people are less hedonistic than younger individuals.

4. <u>Race</u> and <u>ethnicity</u>:
  a. A disproportionate number of people arrested for street crimes are minority group members.
    (1). Of people arrested in 1988 for all crimes, 30% were black.
    (2). In 1984 blacks made up 40 percent of all jail inmates and 46 percent of the state and federal prison population.
    (3). The percentages of blacks arrested and incarcerated are disproportionately high since blacks account for only 13 percent of the U.S. population.
  b. Samuel Walker argued that blacks have such high rates of arrest and imprisonment because of a bias against crimes committed by people from the lower class:
    (1). Individuals generally commit the types of crimes available to them: street crime is more available to people from the lower class than are corporate (white-collar) crimes.

    (2). The criminal justice system does not measure crime (the UCR) in terms of corporate offenses, nor does it vigorously seek out and prosecute white-collar criminals.

5. <u>Social</u> <u>class</u>
  a. Official statistics (UCR) have reported consistently that rates of crime and arrest are higher in urban ghettos and lower class neighborhoods.
  b. However, there is a controversy among sociologists regarding the class origin of offenders in the United States:
    (1). Based on the research of Charles Tittle and others, it can be argued that researchers should no longer attempt to develop class-based theories of crime because the association between the two variables is so weak.
    (2). On the other hand, John Braithwaite concluded from his studies that it would be a mistake for sociologists to move away from class-based theories of criminality.

C. Sexual Deviance
  1. <u>Prostitution</u> has a very lengthy history, and today, it abounds in both the developed and developing nations of the world.
    a. Prostitution is economically stratified in the U.S.:
      (1). <u>Streetwalkers</u> -- who make contact with customers by walking back and forth over a given territory and soliciting pedestrians or men in cars -- make the least money and have the worst work environment.
      (2). <u>Masseuses</u> -- who work out of massage parlors and make extra money by providing other sexual acts -- are next in the hierarchy.
      (3). <u>Escorts</u> -- who are assigned to a customer through an escort service -- typically work in the customer's home or hotel and make more money because price may be negotiated between the escort and the customer.

(4). <u>Bar girls</u> solicit their own customers in bars.

(5). <u>Call girls</u> -- who make contact with their customers by phone -- are at the top of the prostitution hierarchy because the women are usually well-educated and very attractive and their customers are successful professionals who pay high fees for the services rendered.

b. Prostitutes live in a dangerous world because most are at constant risk of being physically abused by customers, arrested by the police, and infected with sexually transmitted diseases, particularly AIDS.

c. Prostitution rates are growing dramatically in many Third World nations:

(1). Many young women and girls have few employment skills, and there are high rates of unemployment.

(2). These women are both victims, and major transmitters, of AIDS.

d. Several approaches attempt to explain why women become prostitutes:

(1). <u>Psychological approaches</u> typically examine the personality and life histories of these women.

(2). <u>Sociological approaches</u> seek to discover the motivation for becoming a prostitute as well as the process involved in taking on a deviant identity and life-style.

(a). Nannette Davis offers a three stage model in which women drift from promiscuity to occasional exchange of sex for money, and finally to full-fledged prostitution.

(b). Other explanations state that women become prostitutes purely for economic survival reasons. It appears that this is a major explanation for prostitution in Third World nations.

2. <u>Homosexuality</u> has existed in the majority of human cultures throughout history: sometimes it is tolerated and other times it is repressed.

a. In the U.S. it is considered to be deviant behavior because most people do not approve of it and their disapproval takes the form of condemnation, stigmatization and punishment.

b. Kinsey and his associates found that almost one half of American men fell between males who were exclusively heterosexual and those who were exclusively homosexual in sexual orientation and behavior.

c. <u>Situational homosexuality</u> occurs in institutions like the military and prisons where individuals are segregated by sex for extended periods of time.

d. Several explanations have been given for homosexuality:

(1). <u>Biological explanations</u> have focused on chemical or hormonal imbalances; however, studies comparing hormone levels of heterosexuals and homosexuals have been inconclusive, contradictory, and methodologically suspect.

(2). <u>Environmental explanations</u> concentrate on patterns of child-rearing, early sexual experiences, and a variety of other factors that would suggest homosexuality is learned behavior.

e. The homosexual community has been hit especially hard by AIDS, and the association of male homosexuality with AIDS is partially responsible for "gay bashing."

       f.   Lesbians in the U.S. are tolerated more than male homosexuals because different perceptions are held about their behavior and life-style.

D.   Violence
    1.   Approximately 12 percent of crimes known to police in 1989 were crimes of violence:
        a.   Homicide was the leading cause of death for black males 15 to 24 years of age. The southern states have the highest homicide rate in the nation, and murder rates are about twice as high in large cities as in smaller cities and rural areas in the U.S.
        b.   Sociologists David Luckenbill and Daniel Doyle state that a significant number of people in these areas have a life-style characterized by "disputatiousness" -- a culturally-transmitted willingness to settle disputes (especially those perceived as a threat to one's masculinity or status) by using physical force.
    2.   <u>Rape</u> is another serious crime of violence in the U.S. and one which researchers believe is seriously underreported.
        a.   Statistically, 81% of all rape victims are white, but black women were significantly more likely to be raped.
        b.   Two-thirds of the cases involved women between the ages of 16 and 24 years of age.
        c.   More than 90% of the victims reported incomes below $25,000; half of the victims reported family incomes under $10,000.
        d.   <u>Date rape</u> appears to be prevalent in the U.S.:
            (1).   Alex Thio argues that this is true because it is an extension of a traditional culture value of male aggression with regard to females.
            (2).   In addition, the attitude held by a significant number of men and women that date rape is not really rape also exacerbates the problem.
    3.   <u>Gang Violence</u> accounts for a significant amount of all violent crime in the U.S.
        a.   Although there are white street gangs, the vast majority of gang members come from racial and ethnic minority groups.
        b.   In recent years some gangs have become involved in drug-related activities, which has led to a dramatic increase in violence and homicide on city streets.
        c.   One researcher argues that gang members have a distorted version of the American success dream and fit Merton's category of "innovators."
    4.   <u>Family Violence</u> accounts for much more violence than most people realize.
        a.   Research findings indicate there is a high level of child abuse and neglect in the U.S.
        b.   Individuals who have experienced violent and abusive childhoods are more likely to grow up and become child abusers themselves.
        c.   Family violence often follows domestic power relations, although violence in the family may run contrary to traditional power relations, as in the case of "granny bashing."

E.   White Collar Crime: Occupational and Organizational/Corporate
    1.   <u>Occupational crime</u> is law violating behavior committed by individuals or small groups of people in connection with their work. According to Gerald Mars, most of these crimes can be placed into one of the four following categories:

      a.   <u>Hawk</u> <u>Jobs</u> -- provide more freedom concerning how and when people do their work and have less immediate supervision -- are characterized by such deviant acts as padding one's expense account and charging for work which was never performed.

      b.   <u>Donkey</u> <u>Jobs</u> -- workers are not continually watched by management, and they perform repetitive tasks -- such as assembly-line workers or supermarket clerks -- and their criminal behavior often involves stealing small amounts of money or items when they are not being watched.

      c.   <u>Wolfpack</u> <u>Jobs</u> -- workers who operate in teams or crews, such as longshoremen, miners, or garbage collectors -- have access to property or a situation that can be used for their financial benefit.

      d.   <u>Vultures</u> -- positions such as truck and taxi-cab drivers, postal delivery people, and service and sales jobs -- supplement their incomes by participating in illegal activity in addition to their job.

2.   <u>Corporate</u> <u>crime</u> is a form of organizational crime committed by officials for their corporations, and those crimes committed by the organization itself to maximize profits and enhance their position in the marketplace.

      a.   Corporate crime not only costs consumers hundreds of billions of dollars each year, but also

      b.   It also threatens the public's health and safety and may be a form of violent crime.

F.   Drug Abuse

    1.   Drug epidemics occur in the United States in predictable cycles. Drugs are "discovered," widely used, and finally condemned.

    2.   Although research pertaining to why people use drugs has reached diverse conclusions, one important finding has emerged: drug use, at least initially, is learned behavior.

      a.   Individuals learn where to buy drugs, how to use them, and how to rationalize their use.

      b.   Users are from all social classes, racial/ethnic backgrounds, and occupations.

    3.   The causal link between drug use and crime is as yet uncertain; however, the number of people who test positive for drugs at the time of their arrest is high.

    4.   <u>Decriminalization</u> -- the reduction or elimination of penalties for a specific offense -- is being widely discussed in terms of currently illegal drugs in the United States.

      a.   Advocates of decriminalization believe this action would result in reduction of drug-related crimes and violence, as well as cutting opportunities for organized and unorganized criminal activity, and other benefits to society.

      b.   Opponents of decriminalization argue that the fundamental problem with drugs is not their legality or illegality, but the fact that they destroy people.

G.   Crime in the Third World

    1.   As nations modernize, their rates of crime begin to increase, eventually approaching those of developed nations.

      a.   According to Louise Shelley, global/historical patterns of crime indicate that both the <u>process</u> and <u>achievement</u> of development are highly conducive to criminality.

b. Not only will rates of crime in modernizing countries increase and begin to approach those of industrialized nations, but the patterns of criminality in the former will begin to resemble the latter.

2. There are at least four reasons for this upsurge in urban crime in Third World nations:
   a. Rural-to-urban migration has brought about the relocation of millions of high crime risk young males.
   b. Urban areas are centers of wealth -- largely from foreign investment and industrial expansion -- and offer the greatest opportunity for committing property crimes.
   c. There is so much poverty that anything and everything is of value to somebody.
   d. There is an increasing demand for prestige items which motivates people to steal items that enhance their status and "sense of modernization."

3. Marxist criminologists strongly criticize the notion that patterns and rates of criminality in Third World countries follow a universal pattern of development. John Horton and Tony Platt argue that there are numerous roads to modernization and different patterns of criminality:
   (a). Brazil's exceptionally high rate of crime has more to do with multinational corporations keeping labor costs low than that the country is passing through a particular stage of development.
   (b). In Cuba, the low rate of criminality may be a function of a rural, relatively underdeveloped population, or of "socialist construction."

4. Conflict theorists also emphasize that Third World nations are being victimized by developed nations through a process called <u>corporate dumping</u> -- the sale to less developed nations of hazardous products that have been banned or are strictly regulated in the developed world:
   a. Examples include some pharmaceutical products.
   b. In addition, companies in the developed world have been illegally dumping hazardous waste materials in the Third World.

GLOSSARY OF DIFFICULT-TO-UNDERSTAND WORDS

Page	Line	Col.	Term from Text	Explanation
235	3		bystanders	someone who is present but not taking part in the situation, onlooker
236	7		fraud-ridden	excessive misrepresentation, deceit
236	13		intrauterine	used or situated within the uterus
236	19		allegedly	avowed, questionably true, openly declared
237	20		transgression	violating a law, wrong
238	16		condone	overlook, give permission
238	21		rambunctious	unruly, uncontrollable expressions
239	16		empowered	enables, authorized, qualified
239	21		atoning	showing penance, pay the penalty
239	22		penance	a behavioral act to show sorrow or repentance
239	22		corporal	relating to the body, physical
240	1		irreversible	cannot be changed or turned around
240	10		demedicalization	no longer a medical problem
241	32		incarcerated	in prison

GLOSSARY OF DIFFICULT-TO-UNDERSTAND WORDS (CONTINUED)

Page	Line	Col.	Term from Text	Explanation
242	10		prenatal	before birth
242	21		rid	eliminate, free
242	42		inevitable	ultimate, certain
243	1		cloister	monastery
243	7		meditate	ponder, reflect
243	29		probing	investigating, completing
243	44		facilitates	makes easier
243	45		revulsion	disgust
244	9		aspire to	work for, aim at, pursue
244	37		innovators	someone who creates something new, makes changes
244	38		inasmuch	since, in view of the fact that
245	13		abrupt	rushed, hasty, sudden
245	18		innate	inborn
245	26		predisposed	have a tendency
246	13		brag	boast, show off
247	3		facilitating	easing
247	11		infraction	violation
247	20		incarcerated	in prison or jail
247	35		stigmatize	brand, classify, describe
247	45		reintegration	uniting again
248	24		befalls	happens to, occurs to
248	34		abstained	avoid, gone on the wagon, not indulged in
249	4	A	roving	wandering, roaming
249	5	A	cavernous	vast, roomy, spacious
249	9	A	planks	boards
249	38	A	subversive	attempt to overthrow
249	8	B	hooligans	roughneck, outlaw, those who deviate
249	29	B	churned out	produce mechanically, grind out
249	30	B	rapacious	plundering, excessively grasping
250	3	A	surveillance	watching, observing
250	4	A	clandestine	furtive, secretive
250	23		proletariat	workers, laboring class
250	34		anguish	pain, misery, suffering
250	38		inherent	innate, part of, a component of
251	2		affluent	wealthy, rich
251	7		myriad	numberless, uncountable, a large number
251	19		impetus	urge, force
251	32		law-abiding	abiding by the law, not committing deviant acts, accepting the rules of society
251	44		clash	conflict, battle
251	49		amenable	open to influence
252	32		reprisal	retaliation, repayment, revenge
252	32		rectify	cure, correct, remedy
254	9		incarcerated	put in prison or jail
254	33		negligible	unimportant, of little consequence
254	42		plausible	believable
255	1		gratification	giving pleasure
255	2		hedonistic	immediate pleasure in the goal of the person
255	8		disproportionately	distorted, too high
255	43		abounds	prevalent, is everywhere
256	41		prevalence	widespread

160

GLOSSARY OF DIFFICULT-TO-UNDERSTAND WORDS (CONTINUED)

Page	Line	Col.	Term from Text	Explanation
256	44		intravenous	within a vein, entering by way of a vein
257	5		battered	hit
257	10		full-fledged	total
257	17		condemnation	disapproval, criticism
257	17		stigmatization	marked, labeled
257	29		abstinence	avoiding all sexual expression
258	3		promiscuity	random, mixing or mingling
258	16		unabashedly	not embarrassed
258	16		flaunting	parade, display
258	19		salvageable	can be saved
258	46		bystanders	someone present at a situation but not taking part in the event
259	27		exacerbate	make more violent
259	40		lucrative	profitable, producing wealth
260	11		sodomized	oral or anal sex
260	11		berated	scold, condemn
260	11		belittle	to put down a person's self concept, to make a person feel worthless
260	31		typology	classification of types
261	9		fiddling	swindling, thievery
261	24		contrived	devised, planned
261	26		deceptive	misleading
261	35		seeped	leaked, oozed
262	13		negate	disprove, deny
262	18		susceptible	subject, open
263	11		allure	attraction, lure
264	20		permissible	allowable, not prohibited
265	24		intrauterine device	IUD, device inserted and left in the uterus to prevent contraception
265	31		malignant	producing death
265	45		detrimental	harmful
265	46		boomerang	the problem will return
266	20	A	incarceration	putting in prison or jail
266	39	A	banditry	robber, plundering
266	42	A	intrigue	plotting, planning, scheming
266	37	B	intertwined	crisscrossed, mutually involved
267	9	A	hemp	Asiatic herb whose fiber is used for making cord or robe
267	11	A	eradicate	eliminate, do away with
267	38	A	infiltrate	penetrate, get into
267	24	B	diligent	hard-working
267	35	B	viciousness	hostility
268	8	A	indulgence	toleration, permission
268	20	A	effeminate	sissy, unmanly
268	27	A	stigmatized	a mark, branded
268	20	B	abominate	hate, despise
268	24	B	extortion	fraud, being robbed
268	29	B	ubiquitous	widespread
268	43	B	looted	robbed
269	19	B	blatant	visible, glaring
269	21	B	perpetrators	continuation of the abuse of authority
270	13	A	intriguing	captivating, fascinating

GLOSSARY OF DIFFICULT-TO-UNDERSTAND WORDS (CONTINUED)

Page	Line	Col.	Term from Text	Explanation
270	31	A	attributable	characteristic, ascribed
270	13	B	shunned	avoided, kept clear of
270	32	B	chastised	castigate, criticized
270	37	B	proliferation	rapid growth
271	2	B	confiscated	took
271	16	B	lucrative	profitable, producing wealth
272	9	A	resurrected	revived, restored
272	14	A	upsurge	sudden rise
272	26	B	exploiting	taking advantage of, profit by
273	41	A	verge	edge, brink
273	44	A	tarnish	dim, fade, darken
273	46	A	interrogating	questioning on a formal level
273	18	B	irrefutably	impossible to prove wrong
273	39	B	nipped	destroy at the source
273	41	B	precinct	district, subdivision of a town or city

KEY TERMS TO DEFINE:

After studying the chapter, define each of the following terms.   Then check your work
by referring to the answers at the end of Chapter 8 in the Study Guide.

deviance	differential association
absolutist perspective	labeling theory
normative perspective	primary deviance
reactive perspective	secondary deviance
deviant behavior	Marxist theory of deviance
criminal behavior	control theories of deviance
deviant and criminal behavior	occupational crime
biological theories of deviance	corporate crime
anomie	decriminalization
anomie theory	corporate dumping

KEY PEOPLE

State the major theoretical contributions of each of these people.

Cesare Lombroso

Emile Durkheim

Robert Merton

Edwin Sutherland

Howard Becker

Richard Quinney

Walter Reckless

Travis Hirschi

Marshall Clinard

<u>SELF</u>-<u>TEST</u>

After completing this self-test, check your answers against the "Answer Key" at the end of Chapter 8 in this Study Guide and in the text on the page(s) indicated in parentheses.

<u>MULTIPLE CHOICE QUESTIONS</u>

Select the response which best answers the question or completes the statement:

1.   Deviance is: (237)
     a.   behavior contrary to a group's or society's norms of conduct and/or social expectations
     b.   behavior that violates both subcultural norms and society's laws
     c.   behavior in violation of society's laws that is not condemned by the norms of an individual's subculture
     d.   behavior that members of all societies find offensive

2.   Which of the following is <u>not</u> one of the three basic perspectives of deviance? (237-238)
     a.   absolutist
     b.   relativist
     c.   normative
     d.   reactive

3.   According to the text, murder, rape, treason, arson, and child molestation are examples of: (238-239)
     a.   deviant behavior
     b.   criminal behavior
     c.   deviant and criminal behavior
     d.   victimless crimes

4.   Which of the following aspects of deviance is of greatest interest to sociologists? (240)
     a.   how certain types of behavior come to be defined as deviant
     b.   how norms and rules that define acceptable and unacceptable behavior change over time
     c.   why certain groups of people are more likely to be sanctioned for rule-violating behavior than others
     d.   all of the above

163

5. According to Cesare Lombroso: (241)
   a. the struggle between the bourgeoisie and the proletariat produces crime.
   b. a certain amount of crime is functional or "good" for society.
   c. some people are born criminals and destined to a life of crime.
   d. criminal behavior is learned in interaction with other people.

6. According to Emile Durkheim: (243)
   a. the struggle between the bourgeoisie and the proletariat produces crime.
   b. a certain amount of crime is functional or "good" for society.
   c. some people are born criminals and destined to a life of crime.
   d. criminal behavior is learned in interaction with other people.

7. According to Edwin Sutherland: (245)
   a. the struggle between the bourgeoisie and the proletariat produces crime.
   b. a certain amount of crime is functional or "good" for society.
   c. some people are born criminals and destined to a life of crime.
   d. criminal behavior is learned in interaction with other people.

8. According to Marxist criminologists: (248,250)
   a. the struggle between the bourgeoisie and the proletariat produces crime.
   b. a certain amount of crime is functional or "good" for society.
   c. some people are born criminals and destined to a life of crime.
   d. criminal behavior is learned in interaction with other people.

9. The theory of deviance which argues that deviant behavior is caused by the gap between culturally acceptable goals and the culturally acceptable means of achieving them is: (244)
   a. differential association theory
   b. anomie theory
   c. labeling theory
   d. control theory

10. Based on Robert Merton's types of deviant adaptations, homeless people, chronic alcoholics, and drug addicts are: (245)
    a. innovators
    b. ritualists
    c. retreatists
    d. revolutionary

11. Which of the following perspectives argues that if definitions favorable to violations of the law are in excess of definitions unfavorable to violation of the law, the individual will engage in criminal behavior? (245)
    a. differential association theory
    b. anomie theory
    c. labeling theory
    d. control theory

12. The labeling perspective of deviance is quite compatible with the _____ theory. (247-248)
    a. functionalist
    b. anomie
    c. biological
    d. conflict

13. Individuals and organizations who actively campaign to discredit an activity or life-style of another group of people are called: (247)
    a. moral watchdogs
    b. moral entrepreneurs
    c. moral brokers
    d. moral intercessors

14. Which of the following is an example of a status degradation ceremony? (247)
    a. when an individual is convicted and sentenced in criminal court
    b. when a person, on admission to a hospital, is required to wear a hospital gown
    c. when an individual reports to "boot camp" and is given a military haircut
    d. when a student is required to show a current photo ID before being allowed to check out books at the library

15. A master status: (247-248)
    a. is a central identifying characteristic of an individual
    b. is acquired at birth
    c. takes precedence over any other role the person plays
    d. both "a" and "c"

16. According to Quinney and other Marxist criminologists, what type of people are most likely to be defined as "criminal" in a capitalist society? (250)
    a. rich people
    b. powerful people
    c. those who commit street crimes
    d. those who commit corporate and white collar crimes

17. Social control theorists such as Walter Reckless argue that supportive family and friends, responsible supervision, and reasonable expectations serve as a barrier against committing deviant acts. This barrier is a type of: (251)
    a. inner containment
    b. outer containment
    c. ideological social control
    d. direct social control

18. Which of the following is not one of the seven index crimes in the Uniform Crime Report? (252)
    a. burglary
    b. aggravated assault
    c. larceny-theft
    d. occupational crime

19. The crime rate is the number of crimes committed per _____ population. (252)
    a. 10,000
    b. 50,000
    c. 100,000
    d. 1,000,000

20. In 1988, 82 percent of the people arrested in the U.S. were males. What types of crimes were most of them accused of committing? (254)
    a. crimes such as larceny, forgery, and drug offenses
    b. crimes such as murder, robbery, assault, and burglary
    c. crimes such as occupational and corporate offenses
    d. the same types of crimes as women

21. Which of these categories is at the top of the prostitution hierarchy? (256)
    a. call girls
    b. escorts
    c. streetwalkers
    d. masseuses

22. _____ homosexuality occurs in institutions like the military and prisons where individuals are segregated by sex for extended periods of time. (257)
    a. Sporadic
    b. Occasional
    c. Temporary
    d. Situational

23. The leading cause of death for black males between 15 and 24 years of age in the U.S. was: (258)
    a. homicide
    b. drug overdoses
    c. motor vehicle accidents
    d. none of the above

24. Occupational crime is: (260)
    a. committed by individuals or small groups of people in connection with their work.
    b. limited to businessmen and high status professionals.
    c. the same as organizational or corporate crime
    d. engaged in by people who consider themselves to be "professional" criminals

25. The reduction or elimination of penalties for a specific offense is referred to as: (264)
    a. legalization
    b. decriminalization
    c. recriminalization
    d. anticriminalization

TRUE-FALSE QUESTIONS

T   F   1. From the absolutist perspective, deviance resides in the nature of the act itself and is wrong at all times and in all places. (237)

T   F   2. Over the past 100 years, an increasing amount of deviance has been explained and "cured" from a medical perspective. (239-240)

T   F   3. Sociological explanations are based on the idea that "structure determines function;" that is, human action is in some manner the result of an individual's physical makeup. (241)

T   F   4. Recent biological research indicates that the criminality of adopted identical twins is more likely to follow the pattern of criminal behavior of their biological parents than of their adoptive parents. (241-242)

T   F   5. Functional theorists view crime as abnormal and completely dysfunctional for societies. (242-243)

T   F   6. The theory of anomie argues that criminal behavior is learned in interaction with other people. (244)

166

T   F   7.   According to Robert Merton's theory of anomie, "ritualism" occurs when an individual scales down or rejects ambitious goals of financial success, although continuing to work hard and meet one's economic and social obligations. (244-245)

T   F   8.   Labeling theory has been referred to as a "bad apple" theory. (246)

T   F   9.   Labeling theory argues that societies create deviance by making rules and laws whose infraction results in deviance. (247)

T   F   10.   A master status is a central identifying characteristic of an individual and takes precedence over any other role the person plays. (247)

T   F   11.   The initial act, or first few episodes of non-conforming behavior is referred to as secondary deviance. (248)

T   F   12.   According to Marxist theory, crime in a capitalist society is the result of the struggle between the bourgeoisie and the proletariat. (248)

T   F   13.   Marxist sociologists argue that the solution to the problem of crime would be a capitalist-type society in which the workers controlled their own work. (251)

T   F   14.   Social control theories attempt to explain why people do not engage in deviant behavior. (251)

T   F   15.   The Uniform Crime Report is considered to be an accurate measure of all the crime that occurs in the United States annually. (252)

T   F   16.   Victimization surveys indicate that over two and one-half times as many crimes occur in the U.S. each year as are reported in the Uniform Crime Report. (252)

T   F   17.   Crime is overwhelmingly an activity of persons under age 25. (254)

T   F   18.   Of the people arrested in 1988 for all crimes, 69 percent were black and 30 percent were white. (255)

T   F   19.   There is a controversy among sociologists regarding the class origin of offenders in the United States. (255)

T   F   20.   Prostitution rates are decreasing dramatically in the Third World as modernization occurs in the various nations. (256)

T   F   21.   The association of male homosexuality with AIDS is partially responsible for the violent practice of "gay bashing." (258)

T   F   22.   Most rape victims are from families with incomes of over $25,000 a year. (259)

T   F   23.   The vast majority of gang members come from racial and ethnic minority groups. (259)

T   F   24.   According to Gerald Mars, the favorite crimes of workers in "donkey jobs" are padding expense accounts and charging for work never performed. (260)

T   F   25.   Corporate crime not only costs consumers hundreds of billions of dollars each year, but also threatens the public's health and safety. (261)

MATCHING QUESTIONS

Match these individuals with their theoretical contribution:

_____ 1.   Walter Reckless   A.   theory of anomie
_____ 2.   Cesare Lombroso   B.   differential association
_____ 3.   Robert Merton   C.   biological theory of deviance
_____ 4.   Marshall Clinard   D.   containment theory
_____ 5.   Howard Becker   E.   theories about corporate crime
_____ 6.   Richard Quinney   F.   labeling theory
_____ 7.   Edwin Sutherland   G.   crime is "functional"
_____ 8.   Emile Durkheim   H.   Marxist criminology

FILL-IN QUESTIONS:

1.   The _____ perspective argues that deviance resides in the act itself and is wrong at all times (past, present, and future), and in all places. (237)

2.   Behavior that is a violation of referrence group and/or subcultural norms, but is not in violation of the legal code of the larger society is called _____ _____. (238)

3.   _____ _____ is behavior in violation of society's laws but is not condemned by the norms of an individual's subculture. (238)

4.   _____ theories of deviance are grounded in the idea that deviant and criminal behavior is directly related to, and somehow a result of, an individual's physical makeup. (241)

5.   _____ _____ was the functionalist sociologist who perceived that crime is "normal" because all societies have criminal behavior. (242)

6.   The theory of anomie was developed by _____ _____. (244)

7.   _____ _____ theory argues that criminal behavior is learned. (245)

8.   Sociologist Howard Becker is associated with _____ theory. (247)

9.   Non-conforming behavior that occurs as a result of being labeled deviant is _____ _____. (248)

10.   For _____ criminologists the capitalism causes crime. (250)

11.   To learn more about crime victims, the National Crime Survey was started. It is also known as a _____ survey. (252)

12. Crimes committed by physicians, attorneys, and politicians in connection with their work are called _____ crimes. (260)

13. _____ crime is a type of organizational crime committed by officials for their corporations, and also includes the crimes of the corporation itself. (261)

14. Recent discussions of decriminalization have been in regard to the _____ problem. (264)

15. Global-historical patterns of crime indicate that both the process and achievement of _____ are highly conducive to criminality in Third World nations. (264)

ESSAY QUESTIONS:

1. Compare and contrast the functionalist and conflict perspectives regarding deviance in society.

2. Discuss Robert Merton's theory of anomie. Identify each of the modes of adaptation. Explain why this theory fits within the functionalist framework.

3. Analyze the Marxist perspective that argues that prisons in the United States are filled with poor people.

4. Define occupational crime and corporate crime. Give examples of each type. Discuss reasons why the police and courts give these types of crime less attention than street crime.

5. Compare and contrast drug problems and gang problems in the United States, Mexico, and Japan.

ANSWERS FOR CHAPTER 8

DEFINITION OF KEY TERMS:

deviance: behavior contrary to a group's or society's norms of conduct or social expectations.

absolutist perspective: the view that deviance resides in the act itself and is wrong at all times (past, present, and future), and in all places.

normative perspective: the view that deviance is the violation of a specific group's or society's rules at a particular time in history.

reactive perspective: the view that behavior is not deviant until it has been recognized and condemned.

deviant behavior: behavior that is a violation of reference group and/or subcultural norms, but is not in violation of the legal code of the larger society.

criminal behavior: behavior in violation of society's laws but is not condemned by the norms of an individual's subculture.

deviant and criminal behavior: behavior that violates both subcultural norms and society's laws.

biological theories of deviance: theories grounded in the idea that deviant and criminal behavior is directly related to, and somehow a result of, an individual's physical makeup.

anomie: a term used by Emile Durkheim to describe the breakdown of societal rules and norms that regulate human behavior.

anomie theory: According to this theory of deviance by Robert Merton, the gap between culturally acceptable goals and the culturally acceptable means of achieving them leads to deviant behavior. The overemphasis on goals in societies like the United States also contributes to deviance.

differential association: Edwin Sutherland's theory stating that if definitions favorable to violations of the law are in excess of definitions unfavorable to violations of the law, the individual will engage in criminal behavior.

labeling theory: According to this theory, societies create deviance by making rules and laws whose infraction constitutes deviance, and then applying these rules and laws to certain individuals. Labeling theorists are interested in how and why some people get labeled, and how this label affects their future behavior.

primary deviance: the initial act, or first few incidents of deviant behavior.

secondary deviance: non-conforming behavior that occurs as a result of being labeled deviant.

Marxist theory of deviance: Marxists argue that crime in a capitalist society is the result of the struggle between the bourgeoisie and the proletariat. Members of the ruling class commit crimes as a result of their effort to economically exploit and politically control the working class. Workers commit crimes as a result of their brutal treatment at the hands of the bourgeoisie, and the workers' effort to survive economically.

control theories of deviance: These theories take deviant motivation as a given, and attempt to explain why people do not engage in deviant behavior. According to this perspective, deviant motivation is contained by internal factors like a positive self-image and external factors, such as a supportive family and friends.

occupational crime: law violating behavior committed by individuals or small groups of people in connection with their work.

corporate crime: a form of organizational crime committed by officials for their corporations, and those crimes committed by the organization itself to maximize profits and enhance its position in the marketplace.

decriminalization: the reduction or elimination of penalties for a specific offense. For example, some individuals think that the use of currently illegal drugs in the United States should be decriminalized.

corporate dumping: the sale to less developed nations of hazardous products that have been banned or are strictly regulated in the developed world .

170

KEY PEOPLE:

Cesare Lombroso (1835-1909), an Italian physician and criminologist, argued that some people are born criminals and destined to a life of crime. He believed these individuals were biological throwbacks to a "past race" of mankind. Through studying criminal populations, Lombroso attempted to find the root causes of crime. However, his work was not very scientific, and he was never able to conclusively document that criminal tendencies were inherited.

Emile Durkheim, who has been discussed in previous chapters, perceived that crime is "normal" because all societies have criminal behavior. He further argued that a certain amount of crime is functional or "good" for society because it clarifies the social boundaries of society, facilitates group solidarity, serves as a warning light that something is wrong in society, and that tolerance permitting the existence of crime and deviance results in tolerance for the creativity and originality that produces social change.

Robert Merton developed the theory of anomie which argues that a significant amount of crime and deviance in societies is caused by the pressure put on people as a result of the gap between the institutionalized goals of society and the means available for achieving the goals. Deviant adaptations to this pressure are innovation, ritualism, retreatism, and rebellion.

Edwin Sutherland, a criminologist, asserted that criminal behavior is learned in interaction with other people. His theory of differential association states that if individuals have an excess of "definitions favorable to the violation of the law" over definitions favorable to obeying the law, they are likely to be involved in criminal activities.

Howard Becker, a noted sociologist and proponent of labeling theory, states that social groups create deviance by making the rules whose infraction results in deviance, and by applying those rules to particular people and labeling them deviant.

Richard Quinney, a Marxist criminologist, argues that class conflict determines what types of crimes the capitalist (bourgeoisie) and proletariat classes will commit. He asserts that members of the capitalist class commit crimes of "domination and repression," which are motivated by a desire to extract as much money as possible from the lower classes, and to prevent the proletariat from challenging the power and position of the bourgeoisie. On the other hand, the proletariat is seen as engaging in crimes of "accommodation and resistance," which are motivated by a desire to survive in a repressive society, and the frustration, rage, and anguish resulting from this repression.

Walter Reckless states in his "containment theory" that individuals are under pressure to engage in deviant behavior because of factors such as poverty, unemployment and economic insecurity, and minority group status. However, a barrier of outer containment -- consisting of supportive family and friends, responsible supervision, and reasonable expectations -- can prevent people from engaging in deviant behavior. Factors such as ego-strength, a positive self-image, and high frustration tolerance are part of a barrier of inner containment.

Travis Hirschi, also a social control theorist, believes there are four elements of social bonding: attachment to family, teachers, and law-abiding friends; commitment to conventional activities; involvement in conventional behavior; and belief in commonly-held values.

171

Marshall Clinard, one of the foremost authorities in the area of corporate crime, stated that corporate crime is a form of organizational crime committed by officials for their corporations, and the crimes of the corporation itself. He noted that three industries seem especially "ripe" for such crimes: the oil industry, the auto industry, and the pharmaceutical industry.

ANSWERS TO MULTIPLE-CHOICE QUESTIONS:

1. a Deviance is behavior contrary to a group's or society's norms of conduct and/or social expectations. Response "b" is the definition of "deviant and criminal behavior." Response "c" is the definition of "criminal behavior." Response "d" is inaccurate because of the variability of definitions regarding deviance in different societies and/or at different points in time. (237)

2. b The relativist perspective is not one of the three basic perspectives of deviance. The three perspectives are: absolutist, normative, and reactive. (237-238)

3. c Murder, rape, treason, arson, and child molestation are examples of deviant and criminal behavior because those actions violate both subcultural norms and society's laws. (238-239)

4. d In regard to deviance, sociologists are interested in how certain types of behavior come to be defined as deviant, how norms and rules that define acceptable and unacceptable behavior change over time, and why certain groups of people are more likely to be sanctioned for rule-violating behavior than others. As a result, response "d" -- all of the above -- is correct. (240)

5. c According to Cesare Lombroso, some people are born criminals and destined to a life of crime. Response "a" is the view of Marxist criminologists. Response "b" is the perspective of functionalist sociologists. Response "d" is based on the differential association theory by Edwin Sutherland. (241)

6. b According to Emile Durkheim, a certain amount of crime is functional or "good" for society. (243)

7. d According to Edwin Sutherland, criminal behavior is learned in interaction with other people. (245)

8. a According to Marxist criminologists, the struggle between the bourgeoisie and the proletariat produces crime. (248, 250)

9. b The theory of deviance which argues that deviant behavior is caused by the gap between culturally acceptable goals and the culturally acceptable means of achieving them is anomie theory. (244)

10. c Based on Robert Merton's types of adaptations, homeless people, chronic alcoholics, and drug addicts are retreatists. (245)

11. a Differential association theory argues that if definitions favorable to violations of the law are in excess of definitions unfavorable to violations of the law, the individual will engage in criminal behavior. (245)

12. d The labeling perspective of deviance is quite compatible with the conflict theory because both argue that rules are created by the powerful to control the lower classes. (247-248)

13. b Moral entrepreneurs are individuals and organizations who actively campaign to discredit an activity or life-style of another group of people. (247)

14. a When an individual is convicted and sentenced in criminal court, that person has been a part of a status degradation ceremony because this is the process by which people become labeled and recognized as deviants. (247)

15.   <u>d</u>   A master status is a central identifying characteristic of an individual <u>and</u> it takes precedence over any other role the person plays. Responses "a" and "c" both are correct, thus making response "d" -- both "a" and "c" -- the best answer. (247-248)

16.   <u>c</u>   According to Marxist criminologists, those who commit street crimes are the most likely to be defined as "criminal" in a capitalist society. Rich and powerful people, and those who commit corporate and white-collar crimes are the least likely to be defined as "criminal." (250)

17.   <u>d</u>   <u>Inner</u> <u>containment</u>, according to social control theorists such as Walter Reckless, includes supportive family and friends, responsible supervision, and reasonable expectations which serve as a barrier against committing deviant acts. (251)

18.   <u>d</u>   Occupational crime is not one of the seven index crimes in the Uniform Crime Report. The seven index crimes are: murder, robbery, rape, aggravated assault, burglary, larceny-theft, and motor vehicle theft. (252)

19.   <u>c</u>   The crime rate is the number of crimes committed per <u>100,000</u> population. The crime rate makes it possible to compare criminal activity in cities and states of varying size. (252)

20.   <u>b</u>   Men are more likely to be arrested for serious crimes such as murder, robbery, assault, and burglary. Women tend to be involved in property offenses such as larceny, forgery, and drug offenses. Of the males arrested in 1988, most of them were arrested for street crimes and very few were arrested for occupational and corporate offenses. (254)

21.   <u>a</u>   Call girls are at the top of the prostitution hierarchy because these women are usually well-educated and very attractive. Contacts with customers are made by phone, and their customers are successful professionals who can afford to pay high fees for their services. (256)

22.   <u>d</u>   <u>Situational</u> homosexuality occurs in institutions like the military and prisons where individuals are segregated by sex for extended periods of time. This behavior is referred to as "situational" because it is more a function of available alternatives than one's sexual preference. (257)

23.   <u>a</u>   <u>Homicide</u> is the leading cause of death for black males between 15 and 24 years of age in the U.S. (258)

24.   <u>a</u>   Occupational crime is committed by individuals or small groups of people in connection with their work. Response "b" is incorrect because occupational crime is <u>not</u> limited to businessmen and high status professionals: these offenses can be committed by almost any one who is employed. Response "c" is incorrect because occupational crime is <u>not</u> the same as organizational or corporate crime -- committed by officials for their corporations and by the organization itself to maximize profits and enhance their position in the marketplace. (260)

25.   <u>b</u>   <u>Decriminalization</u> is the reduction or elimination of penalties for a specific offense. For example, some individuals think the use of currently illegal drugs in the United States should be decriminalized. (264)

<u>ANSWERS</u> <u>TO</u> <u>TRUE-FALSE</u> <u>QUESTIONS</u>:

1. True (237)
2. True (239-240)
3. False -- Biological explanations -- not sociological explanations -- of deviance are based on the idea that "structure determines function;" that is, human action is in some manner the result of an individual's physical makeup. (241)
4. True (241-242)

5. False -- Functional theorists view crime as "normal" because all societies have criminal behavior. They also believe that a certain amount of crime is functional or "good" for society. (242-243)
6. False -- Differential association theory argues that criminal behavior is learned in interaction with other people. The theory of anomie focuses on the discrepancy between institutionalized goals and the means available for achieving these goals. (244)
7. True (244-245)
8. False -- Differential association theory, not labeling theory, has been referred to as a "bad apple" theory. (246)
9. True (247)
10. True (247)
11. False -- The initial act, or first few episodes of non-conforming behavior is referred to as <u>primary deviance</u>. Deviant behavior that occurs as a result of being labeled is called <u>secondary deviance</u>. (248)
12. True (248)
13. False -- Marxist sociologists argue that there is only one solution to the crime problem: the end of capitalism. (251)
14. True (251)
15. False -- The Uniform Crime Report is not an accurate measure of <u>all</u> the crime that occurs in the United States annually, but rather those crimes <u>known to police</u>. In addition, the Uniform Crime Report has been criticized because it is primarily a count of street crimes committed by the lower classes and excludes white collar offenses more likely to be committed by middle and upper class individuals. (252)
16. True (252)
17. True (254)
18. False -- Of the people arrested in 1988 for all crimes, 69 percent were <u>white</u>, 30 percent were <u>black</u>. (255)
19. True (255)
20. False -- Prostitution rates are increasing dramatically in the Third World as modernization occurs. With high rates of unemployment in many of these areas, young women and girls with few, if any, skills may have little choice but to prostitute themselves. (256)
21. True (258)
22. False -- According to a 1985 report issued by the Bureau of Justice, more than 90 percent of rape victims come from families with incomes below $25,000. (259)
23. True (259)
24. False -- Padding expense accounts and charging for work never performed are the favorite "fiddles" or crimes of those in "hawk jobs" where there is little supervision and a good deal of freedom concerning how and when they do their jobs. (260)
25. True (261)

ANSWERS TO FILL-IN QUESTIONS:

1. Absolutist (237)
2. Deviant behavior (238)
3. Criminal behavior (238)
4. Biological (241)
5. Emile Durkheim (242)
6. Robert Merton (244)
7. Differential association (245)
8. Labeling (247)
9. Secondary deviance (248)

10. Marxist (250)
11. Victimization (252)
12. Occupational (260)
13. Corporate (261)
14. Drug (264)
15. Development (264)

ANSWERS TO MATCHING QUESTIONS:

1. D
2. C
3. A
4. E
5. F
6. H
7. B
8. G

CHAPTER NINE

SOCIAL INSTITUTIONS

Social institutions are orderly, enduring, and established ways of arranging behavior and doing things. In Chapter 9, the social institutions of family, politics and religion are examined. First, marriage and family are analyzed from functional and conflict perspectives. Then, marriage and divorce patterns in the U.S. are discussed. The impact of modernization on the social institution of the family is then assessed. In the second section of the chapter, politics is discussed from the functionalist and conflict perspectives. The U.S. political system is analyzed from pluralist and elitist models of power. Recent changes in world politics are then discussed. In the final section, religion is examined from functional and conflict perspectives. Historical changes in religion from the Puritans to modern televangelists are presented, and the relationship between religion and modernization is explored.

LEARNING OBJECTIVES:

As you read Chapter 9, use these learning objectives to organize your notes. After completing your reading, briefly state an answer to each of the objectives, and review the text pages in parentheses.

1.   State the sociological definition of social institutions. Explain why these institutions are interdependent on one another. (278-279)

2.   Compare and contrast the functionalist and conflict perspectives on the role of the family in society. (280-282)

3.   Discuss the major characteristics of marriages in the United States and explain why most marriages follow a pattern of homogamy. (282-284)

4.   List the major factors associated with divorce in the United States. (286-287)

5.   Describe the relationship between modernization and the family. (289-291)

6.   Compare and contrast the functionalist and conflict perspectives on the role of the state in modern human societies. (293-294)

7.   Differentiate between the power elite and pluralist models of the American political system. (294-297)

8.   Analyze patterns of political participation in the United States in terms of age, socioeconomic status, race, and gender. (297-299)

9.   Discuss the relationship between modernization and political systems. (300-304)

10. Compare and contrast the functionalist and conflict perspectives on the role of religion in societies. (305-306)

11. Based on his analysis of the Protestant Ethic and the rise of capitalism, explain Max Weber's argument that religion can produce social change. (306-307)

12. Identify the historical changes which have occurred in religion from the time of the puritans to the televangelists of today in the United States. (307-308)

13. Specify why it is difficult to determine cause and effect relationships between religion and modernization. (312-316)

OUTLINE

I.   INTRODUCTION

    A.   <u>Social institutions</u> are orderly, enduring, and established ways of arranging behavior and doing things.
        1.   Social relationships in institutions are structured for the purpose of performing some task(s) or accomplishing specific goals.
        2.   These institutions are interdependent and continually affect one another in society.
    B.   This chapter looks at the institutions of marriage and family, politics, and religion, and their interdependent nature.
        1.   For example, the <u>family</u> is the primary source of an individual's <u>religious</u> beliefs.
        2.   Likewise, cults and other <u>religious</u> groups in the United States have become very involved in <u>politics</u>.

II. MARRIAGE AND THE FAMILY

    A.   Theoretical Perspectives
        1.   Functionalist Theory
            a.   According to the functional perspective, the <u>family</u> contributes to the overall functioning of, and therefore, the good of society.
            b.   The family performs six major functions in all societies:
                (1). The family meets the biological and economic needs of its members.
                (2). The family legitimizes some sexual relationships and prohibits others.
                (3). Biological reproduction within the family ensures the group's continuity over time.
                (4). A major portion of childhood socialization takes place in the family.
                (5). The family provides individuals with membership in a larger social structure.
                (6). The family provides people with emotional support and companionship.
        2.   Conflict Theory
            a.   Conflict theorists typically see the family as an institution of domination and exploitation.
                (1). Males exploited by the bourgeoisie in a capitalist society become frustrated and abuse their wives and children.
                (2). The family is the microcosm of the tension, conflict, and oppression that exists in the larger society.

b. From a Marxist perspective, women are victimized twice in a capitalist society:

    (1). As wives and mothers, women are unpaid for their work in the home which helps reproduce "wage slaves" for the capitalist class, and

    (2). If women enter the paid workforce, they usually earn less income than male workers.

c. Sociologist Randall Collins argues that conflict within the family goes beyond capitalist societies.

    (1). Stable family organization is the result of sexual conquest and dominance.

    (2). Since males are physically stronger, they tend to overpower women who become "sexual prizes." In the process, men take permanent possession of the women and, subsequently, the children.

d. Sociologist Jetse Sprey asserts that conflict is anchored in the family as members compete with each other for real and symbolic resources such as money, attention, and power.

B. Love, Marriage, and Divorce American Style

1. <u>Marriage</u> is the socially approved sexual union between a man and a woman that is presumed to be permanent, and is recognized as such both by the couple and others. In the United States most marriages have these characteristics:

a. Most people live in <u>nuclear</u> families which consist of a mother, a father, and their children

b. Most people practice <u>endogamy</u>: selection of marriage mates from within their own tribe, community, social class, nationality, or other grouping.

c. Most people have a <u>neolocal</u> residence in which both marriage partners reside apart from their family of orientation

d. Most people are <u>monogamous</u> -- having only one spouse (at least, only one at a time)

e. Many people are moving toward an <u>egalitarian</u> marriage -- where power and authority are shared equally by husband and wife -- because power in some families is shifting to a more equal form as more women now are bringing home a paycheck.

f. A <u>bilineal</u> <u>descent</u> <u>system</u> is used, in which family membership and inheritance are traced through the lines of both male and female parents to their children.

2. <u>Homogamy</u> -- the tendency of people to marry individuals like themselves physically, psychologically, and/or socially -- is practiced in the U.S.

a. Most marriages occur between two people:

    (1). Of the same social class

    (2). Within the same racial group

    (3). Of the same religion

    (4). With similar levels of education

    (5). With the same physical and psychological characteristics

    (6). Who live within a few miles of each other

b. Homogamy occurs because people are attracted to one another in a system of exchange that could be characterized as a marriage market in which human resources are negotiated and traded, just as goods and services are exchanged in the economic marketplace.

3. Cuber and Harroff constructed a typology of marital relationships:
   a. The Conflict Habituated: characterized by a fair amount of tension and conflict, although it is largely controlled and confined to the home. The couple may stay together because of their children, careers, etc.
   b. The Devitalized: marriages devoid of tension and conflict as well as the original zest that made the relationship alive and enjoyable
   c. The Passive Congenial: characterized by an emotional commitment which initially was weak and, subsequently, the partners drift apart or deliberately pursue their separate interests and careers that are incompatible with those of their mates.
   d. The Vital: the couple derives enormous satisfaction from participating together in shared activities and important life segments involving children and careers.
   e. The Total: total relationships are more multifaceted in that people are completely intertwined and lovingly do everything as a couple.
4. Divorce
   a. In the U.S., the chances that a marriage will end in divorce are associated with the following:
      (1). Age at marriage
      (2). Length of marriage
      (3). Social class of the couple
      (4). Race
      (5). Religion
      (6). Whether one's parents have been divorced
   b. Rates of divorce also have been associated with general economic trends:
      (1). When there are higher rates of unemployment and an uncertain economic future, families may be kept together even if there are internal factors pulling them apart.
      (2). However, Gallaway and Zeller argue that increases in the rate of inflation lead to financial problems and interpersonal tensions, which contribute to a higher divorce rate.
5. Divorce and Children
   a. Research on the effect of divorce on children is inconclusive and sometimes contradictory.
   b. Some investigators report that children adjust to a divorce and their new family situation within two years of the breakup.
   c. Other researchers have found that the negative consequences of divorce can affect children for many years, even after they become adults.
6. The Family and Modernization
   a. Although it would appear that changes in the family over the past 200 years have paralleled the industrialization process in the U.S., sociologist William J. Goode has argued that the relation between Western industrialization and the family is more complex than a simple cause and effect relationship:
      (1). Families in Europe were changing from an extended to a nuclear structure long before the Industrial Revolution, and
      (2). The link between the nuclear family and industrialization is one in which the former met the "demands" of the latter.

b.   Neolocal nuclear families facilitated the geographic and social mobility needed in the industrial society, and significantly more young people were able to develop their talents for the industrialized society because of patterns of bilineal descent.

c.   The Impact of Industrialization on the family was described by Christopher Lasch:

   (1).   Since 19th century educators and social reformers viewed immigrant families as obstacles in the path of the homogenization of the U.S., reformers sought to minimize the impact that parents had on their children by maximizing the influence of the state and school.

   (2).   Families began to lose control of their children as schools were given the task of educating them. Therefore, families did not gradually "lose" child-rearing duties as societies industrialized, but instead, these duties and other aspects of parental influence were taken away by the state.

d.   The Developing World

   (1).   Movement from traditional family structures to nuclear families typically is a function of economic conditions and political philosophies:

      (a).   Families in Third World countries can be changed in large measure as a result of governmental policy in much the same way that U.S. families were changed by social reformers in the 19th century.

      (b).   An example of this is China's introduction of a one child per family policy in the 1970s to slow down population growth.

   (2).   It is impossible to predict how family structures in the developing nations will change as a result of modernization; however, two things are likely to be true:

      (a).   Change will be faster than it has been in the past as many Third World nations attempt to modernize as fast as possible.

      (b).   Both democratic and totalitarian governments will have a growing impact on family size, migration, and control over certain segments of the population (e.g., women).

III. POLITICS AS A SOCIAL INSTITUTION

A.   In all human societies, political institutions regulate the exercise of power -- the ability to carry out one's own will, despite resistance from others -- by various social groups.

   1.   Throughout history, people have agreed to regulate the exercise of power and decision-making through the creation of some sort of political institution.

   2.   In modern or developed societies like the United States and Japan, and in many developing societies like Mexico, final decision-making and other political activities rest with the state -- the social institution which holds a monopoly over the legitimate use of force and exercises governing power in the society.

B. Theoretical Interpretations of Political Institutions
    1. The Functionalist Perspective
       a. For functionalists, the state or polity plays a critical role in "goal-attainment," the process by which important societal objectives are defined, resources are allocated and mobilized toward the realization of these goals, and social control is exercised over individual actions.
       b. The polity decides what, when, where, how, and by whom important societal actions will be carried out and, thus, these political institutions help to ensure that activities necessary for societal maintenance and development will be performed efficiently.

    2. The Conflict Perspective
       a. For conflict theorists like Karl Marx, the state and other political institutions serve as powerful weapons utilized by ruling classes to preserve their own advantaged positions in the economic and social order.
          (1). Laws passed and enforced by the state are seldom neutral; rather, they reflect the power and the interests of the owning classes.
          (2). Examples include tax legislation favoring the ruling class, and state supplied physical force to keep members of the proletariat in their place.
       b. Modern conflict theorists assert that the polity and the economy are intertwined in a symbiotic (mutually supportive) relationship.
C. The U.S. Political System
    1. Freedom and the Constitution
       a. U.S. culture has emphasized individual liberty; however, the extent to which the democratic process has truly worked continues to be debated by political sociologists and other observers.
       b. Two questions are involved:
          (1). The distribution of power within and among population segments; and
          (2). The extent and depth of individuals' involvement in political activities.
    2. The Structure of Political Power
       a. Radical conflict sociologist C. Wright Mills described the "power elite" as a coalition of corporate, political, and military elites who, he believed, secretly controlled most societal activities in the U.S.
       b. Below the power elite are the elected political officials who make up the Congress and other offices of government, and who are believed by the people to have political control.
       c. Below these elected officials is a societal mass consisting of millions of fragmented, alienated individuals who, for the most part, are uninterested and uninvolved in political affairs.
    3. The Pluralist Model
       a. Contrary to Mills' portrayal of the power elite, the pluralist perspective believes that political power in modern societies is dispersed among a variety of competing groups and organizations, with no single unit or combination of units dominating the system.

181

        b.   Veto groups, which shift according to the issues at hand, restrain one another's power and limit each other's influence to specific situations.

        c.   Individuals retain final political power by joining and becoming involved in various organized interest groups.

4.   U.S. Society -- A Power Elite System?

        a.   Recent studies tend to indicate that the power elite interpretation is more valid than the pluralist model.

        b.   Research findings by Thomas Dye indicate a strong concentration of power in the hands of a relatively small number of very influential organizations, and a pattern of common socioeconomic class backgrounds for key office holders.

            (1).   Recent examples include the close working relationship between the federal government and big business during the Reagan Administration.

            (2).   During the decade of the 1980s, the economic position of the wealthiest segment of the U.S. population improved, while that of virtually all other population groups either dropped or remained stagnant.

5.   Patterns of Political Participation

        a.   Existing data indicate a clear pattern of widespread disinterest and noninvolvement in voting, campaign activities, and other forms of political expression.

        b.   <u>Voting</u>:

            (1).   There is a widespread pattern of nonvoting in all types of elections -- including presidential, state and local -- in the U.S.

            (2).   Studies of voting patterns indicate that the likelihood of voting varies with age, with those people between the ages of 30 and 65 more likely to vote than younger or older groups.

        c.   <u>Class</u>, <u>Race</u>, <u>Gender</u>, <u>and</u> <u>Voting</u>:

            (1).   Members of higher socioeconomic status (SES) groups vote with much greater frequency than members of lower SES groups.

            (2).   Formal educational level is the critical class-related factor influencing voter participation.

            (3).   Whites have higher levels of voter participation than either African Americans or Hispanics.

            (4).   Males are more likely to vote than females; however, this particular gap appears to be closing as "gender politics" has become more evident in the past decade.

        d.   A Passive Electorate

            (1).   Other forms of political involvement -- such as volunteering to work for political candidates -- show similar social and demographic patterns to those relating to voting.

            (2).   This disengagement of citizens from the political process has been attributed to everything from contentment with the system to disgust.

D.   Politics in a Changing World

    1.   As modernization and societal development occurred, political rule by physical force was transformed into <u>rule</u> <u>by</u> <u>authority</u> -- political rule based upon a sense of moral obligation, rather than raw power and force.

       a.   As both the rationalization and the secularization of societies grew, <u>charismatic</u> <u>authority</u> -- rule based upon some extraordinary personal quality of the political leader -- and <u>traditional</u> <u>authority</u> -- rule based upon long-standing societal customs -- were replaced by what Max Weber called <u>rational</u>-<u>legal</u> <u>authority</u> -- rule based upon the reasonableness of laws and the acceptability of law-making procedures.

       b.   The growth of these large-scale, legitimate political systems promoted and reflected continuing economic and societal development.

  2.   The Collapse of Communism?

       a.   Capitalism is replacing socialism throughout eastern Europe, and major changes are occurring in the U.S.S.R., perhaps because of the failure of governments in these societies to provide the kinds and levels of economic goods that their citizens need and want.

       b.   If these governments are unable to meet the "rising expectations" of their people in a relatively short period of time, revolutionary changes may once again be demanded by the citizens.

  3.   An End to U.S. Supremacy?

       a.   U.S. world supremacy is being challenged by the emergence of Japan and other countries as economic superpowers.

       b.   Whether or not people in the U.S. can adjust to not being "number one" remains an interesting and significant question.

         (1). The U.S. may experience a growing sense of frustration

         (2). There also may be more hate crimes directed against Asians and Asian Americans in the U.S.

  4.   The Rise of Third World Nationalism

       a.   Some Third World societies like Mexico may be on the rise -- especially if they have control over strategic resources such as supplies of petroleum and other resources vital to the industrial and postindustrial economies of current superpowers.

       b.   Some developing societies have rejected modern social and cultural forms altogether. Others have had growing nationalistic spirit -- an ideology that emphasizes self-governance and the importance of the nation-state.

IV.   RELIGION AS A SOCIAL INSTITUTION

  A. In some form or other, organized religious beliefs and practices have been found in all societies.

     1.   Such religious activity reflects the human being's need to deal with what Emile Durkheim called the "<u>sacred</u>" -- those extraordinary elements of life that inspire a sense of reverence, awe, and fear in people.

     2.   Religious beliefs are matters of faith which, unlike the <u>profane</u> -- commonplace, ordinary elements of everyday life -- cannot be proven or disproven through empirical means.

     3.   Religious statuses and roles were among the first specialized positions to be differentiated in early human society.

  B. Theoretical Perspectives on Religion

     1.   Functionalist Interpretations

       a.   Functionalists like Durkheim argue that religion promotes societal solidarity by uniting members in shared beliefs and values, as well as a common set of rituals.

    b.   Religion also promotes social control by infusing cultural norms and political rules with sacred authority.

    c.   Religion gives societal members a sense of meaning and purpose in life.

2.   Conflict Interpretations

    a.   Conflict theorists view religion as a means of exploitation rather than integration.

    b.   Marx claimed that religion was a powerful tool employed by ruling classes in capitalist societies to maintain their position by deflecting the attention of oppressed classes from real-world concerns to those of an afterlife.

    c.   Contemporary conflict theorists have emphasized the dysfunctional elements of religion:

        (1).   Differences in religious beliefs and values often serve as the basis for the formation of subcultural groups with radically different moral views and policy agendas

        (2).   Particular groups within the society attempt to impose their own religious views and practices on others, resulting in conflicts and power struggles that are divisive to groups and to society at large.

3.   The Protestant Ethnic and the Rise of Capitalism

    a.   Max Weber argued that religion could play a significant role in society -- as a catalyst for social change.

    b.   He examined the role of the Protestant ethic -- the world-view and values associated with the new Protestant religions -- in the rise of modern capitalism. The ethic had two key elements:

        (1).   The concept of predestination -- the belief that one's fate in the afterlife has been decided before or at one's birth, and could not be changed through prayer or good works -- created an uncertainty in people's minds as to their own particular fate.

            (a).   And while this question never could be answered fully, one likely indicator of success or failure in the afterlife was success or failure in this life.

            (b).   Economic prosperity became a fundamental goal for people because such prosperity was a sign that one was among the elect.

        (2).   Worldly asceticism -- denial of material self-indulgence under the belief that frugality was morally superior to concern for worldly pleasures -- was also an important part of this religious ideology. Like prosperity, thrift became a sign of virtue.

    c.   Weber argued that belief in predestination and worldly asceticism encouraged people to try to succeed in their work efforts and led them to activities that translated into capital formation and capital expansion, which were key ingredients for the rise of capitalism.

C.   Religion in the United States: From Puritans to Televangelists

    1.   For most of its history, the U.S. has been both a religious and a religiously-tolerant society.

    2.   Most people have identified with one of three religious traditions -- Protestantism, Catholicism, or Judaism. These religious systems are referred to as denominations -- formal religious organizations that are well integrated into their society and recognize religious pluralism.

3. Folk <u>religions</u> -- interpretations and modifications of more formalized religious traditions to meet the needs of specific population groups -- would include those of Italian Catholic or Polish Catholic immigrants.

4. <u>Popular</u> <u>religions</u> are sets of beliefs that lie outside of, or span the boundaries of, recognized denominations.
    (a). They appeal to large-scale or mass audiences drawn from a variety of backgrounds.
    (b). They typically stand in opposition to the established sociocultural order and offer their members a different vision of what societal life should be like.
    (c). Popular religions resemble <u>sects</u>: religious subcultures or countercultural groups that offer their members a different vision of the social and the spiritual life. Examples include Christian evangelical and Pentecostal movements, and various televangelistic ministries.

5. Religion in the Counterculture Movement
    a. During the 1960's and the decade of the counterculture movement, many people predicted the <u>secularization</u> of society -- the transformation from a religious to a civil and worldly basis -- and a significant decline of religion in everyday life.
    b. However, religion did not disappear. Some conventional religions had declining memberships and, as a result, began to address pressing social issues such as poverty and racial discrimination and to try to reach out to people.

6. The Rise of Fundamentalism
    a. In recent years, Christian fundamentalism, stressing a back-to-basics religious approach and a rejection of secularism and humanism, has become an important and growing social and political force.
        (1). <u>Humanism</u> is the belief that humans, rather than God, are the center of their own destiny.
        (2). Fundamentalists see evidence of creeping "secular humanism" in changing public attitudes and political policies toward abortion, women's proper role in society, homosexuality, etc.
    b. The "new" fundamentalism which has arisen in recent years is not identified with specific and well-defined denominations.
        (1). It appeals to people from a wide variety of socioeconomic classes, residential and geographic backgrounds.
        (2). It is conveyed through television to a dispersed mass audience that numbers in the millions.

7. The Electronic Church
    a. Television has been widely used to convey religious beliefs, but some of the religious programming is more in the nature of an entertainment show, coupled with appeals for financial offerings.
    b. Although fundamentalists are not the only television preachers, most religious programming has these similarities:
        (1). A largely visual appeal and a simple doctrinal message.
        (2). A substantial amount of time is devoted to appeals for financial contributions.
    c. The electronic church generally appeals to older people of lower income and educational levels who already are involved in religion through church membership and participation in religious activities.

185

8. Religion Today
   a. Religion in the U.S. is not likely to become extinct in the foreseeable future. Some predict a return to religion by middle-aged baby boomers.
   b. A high proportion of the U.S. population -- 65 percent in 1988 -- claim membership in a church or synagogue.
   c. Overall, research indicates that a restructuring of existing religious groupings will occur rather than a decline of religious expression per se.

D. Religion and Modernization
   1. The relationship between religion and modernization is complex, with religious beliefs both helping and hindering the development process.
      a. Protestant and Catholic churches in Europe and in the U.S. established systems of formal education long before any schools were funded and controlled by the state.
      b. The umbanda religion of Brazil, which began as a small cult in the 1920's, now has over 30 million members and is a powerful religious and political force in society.
   2. A Force Opposing Modernization
      a. Religion also has been a powerful force against modernization.
         (1). Religious opposition to utilizing artificial birth control as a method for slowing rapid population growth has made modernization increasingly difficult for some poor nations.
         (2) Large-scale, violent clashes between Muslims and Hindus in India clearly indicate that religion will be a major factor in the economic and political development of that nation.
      b. Thus, religion and modernization are involved in a complex web of cause and effect relationships that have both helped and hindered the development process.

GLOSSARY OF DIFFICULT-TO-UNDERSTAND WORDS

Page	Line	Col.	Term from Text	Explanation
277	4		flourished	succeed, was successful
277	8		detached	separated, not connected
277	12		sever	cut
277	14		surrogate	substitute, in place of
278	4		incentive	motive, drive
278	6		agenda	plan, program
278	13		fervently	deep emotion, great feeling, impassioned
279	2		aforementioned	mentioned previously, already talked about
279	19		archbishop	high ranking status in the Catholic church
279	22		suspicious	doubtful, not believing, skeptical
279	25		accord	keeping, conformity, accordance
279	26		disarm	take away weapons
279	29		political arena	a setting of political activity, focus of political influence
279	37		derided	laughed at, ridiculed
279	38		integrity	honor, rightness
279	42		secular	temporal, worldly, opposite of sacred
281	16		buffer	cushion, protection
281	18		degrading	make humble, disgrace, put down, embarrass
281	26		corporate owners	those who own large corporations--factories

GLOSSARY OF DIFFICULT-TO-UNDERSTAND WORDS (CONTINUED)

Page	Line	Col.	Term from Text	Explanation
281	29		brutalize	are not sensitive to the workers needs, cruel or unkind to people
281	33		toil	work
281	42		sanctuary	retreat, shelter
281	45		pervade	spread throughout
282	5		gratification	pleasure
284	10		prospect	outlook, future, chance
284	21		compatibility	working together, being in harmony, being able to relate to each other
284	40		pervasive	diffused, widespread
284	45		devoid	do not have
284	46		zest	pleasure, enjoyment
284	6		endure	last a long time
287	19		contractual	relating to a contract, like a contract
287	38		traumatic	emotional stress which affects behavior
288	2		cognitive	process of knowing
289	1		longitudinal	dealing with the growth and change of an individual or group over time
289	6		reconciling	restore, put back together
290	1		tyranny	control, oppressive power
290	18		homogenization	blending, becoming alike
291	31		ramifications	consequence, outcome
291	34		drastically	radically, harshly, severely
291	41		tacit	unspoken, implied, wordless, suggested
292	23		legitimate	legal, lawful
293	16		attainment	accomplishment, achievement
293	18		enlisted	people in the armed forces who are NOT commissioned officers
293	21		compulsory	required, mandatory
293	24		essence	point, substance, main idea
293	31		coercive	use of force
293	37		oppression	control
294	4		assertion	the forceful statement
294	5		intertwined	mutually involved
294	25		disbursed	spread
294	37		subvert	overthrow, ruin, overturn
295	17		apathy	inaction, no activity, passive
295	32		proponents	those who support
295	32		concede	admit, acknowledge
295	44		coalition	combination, union
296	34		disbanded	done away with, dismissed
296	34		curtailed	limited, shortened, trimmed
296	37		fostering	encouraging
296	40		exuberant	excessive, uncontrolled, unrestrained
296	46		stagnant	still, not moving, not changing
297	5		latter	last, final, second of two groups
297	9		ambiguous	misleading, unclear, can be understood in several different ways
299	17		cynicism	not believing, skepticism
299	38		secularization	transfer from religious control to civil control

GLOSSARY OF DIFFICULT-TO-UNDERSTAND WORDS (CONTINUED)

Page	Line	Col.	Term from Text	Explanation
299	43		ushering	brought, introduced
300	3		inevitable	certain, ultimate, unavoidable
300	29		disenchanted	disillusioned, misled no longer
300	32		resemblance	image, likeness
300	36		forestall	prevent
301	5		destabilization	to make unstable, make shaky, not steady
301	13		leverage	power, effectiveness
301	15		concessions	rights, opportunities
302	6	A	rapids	water in a river rushing quickly over large boulders washed into the river
302	8	A	pristine	in an untouched natural state
302	24	A	sprawling	stretching, spreading
302	31	A	feuding fiefdoms	fighting among feudal land owners (estates), fighting among those who control pieces of land
302	42	A	centrifugal	separatist, believing in separating
302	23	B	filibuster	attempting to delay
302	38	B	fraying	tearing, shredding, coming apart
302	44	B	bungalows	cottage, small house
302	45	B	ostentatious	showoff, put up a front
302	48	B	daggers	knives
303	10	A	defiance	disobedience, opposition
303	9	B	fatalistic shrugs	powerless to do anything, feeling one can do nothing
303	25	B	unanimous	agreeable to everyone
303	35		equate	make equal
303	41		volatile	explosive, changeable
303	43		dissensions	conflict
303	46		unifying	bringing together, uniting
304	3		arbitrarily	without cause, without reason
304	9		deteriorating	to grow worse
304	27		reverence	regard, respect
304	39		entrusted	given
304	43		deities	gods
305	18		infusing	inserting, introducing
305	36		social damnation	to ruin socially, to condemn in this world
305	46		bliss	extreme happiness
306	15		catalyst	to bring about a reaction
306	31		accumulation	collection, piling up, storing
306	40		prosperity	wealth
307	11		tolerance	broad-mindedness, acceptance of differences
307	11		dissenters	those who disagree
307	20		conceived	imagined, thought of
307	29		affiliated	to associate closely with
307	39		chronicled	listed, described
308	6		proliferation	multiplication, to grow in great numbers
309	4		secular	opposite of sacred, everything in this world
309	18		synagogues	Jewish place of worship
309	24		ecumenical	a large body of churches, worldwide influence of churches
309	35		revival	to restore, to renew religious interest

GLOSSARY OF DIFFICULT-TO-UNDERSTAND WORDS (CONTINUED)

Page	Line	Col.	Term from Text	Explanation
309	35		prominence	being well-known, standing out, being noticeable
309	47		spawned	created, brought forth
310	4		antithetical	opposite
310	19		infallibility	correctness, no errors, perfect
310	23		atonement	redeem, absolve, pay the penalty
310	25		resurrection	rising, rallying, bring back
311	1		pictorial	visual, pictures, graphic
311	15		devotion	giving, allotting, assigning
311	19		brethren	members of a sect
312	3		jettisoned	throw away, discard
312	7		infused	instilled, filled, saturated
312	14		avowed	openly declared, acknowledged
312	15		sporadic	occasional, infrequent
312	42		hinder	get in the way of, interfere with, hamper
313	21		incarnation	another bodily form
313	21		commensurate	equal in measure, corresponded
314	8		encyclical	a papal letter to the bishops of the church
315	8		fatalistic	humans are powerless to change events which are fixed in advance
315	25		abdicate	give up, retire, quit
315	45		hindered	got in the way, interfered with, hampered
315	47		intricate	complex, involved, complicated
316	11	A	decimated	destroyed
316	14	B	stability	support
316	38	B	unprecedented	unheard of, exceptional
317	10	A	affluent	wealthy, rich
317	27	A	oligarchy	rule by the few
317	13	B	deteriorated	worsened
317	31	B	inescapable	not hidden, not concealed, highly visible
318	32	A	allegations	not supported charges
318	32	A	dispel	drive away, dismiss
318	36	A	faltering	not steady, shaking
319	14	A	indigenous	native
319	22	A	superseded	take the place of, to set aside
319	13	B	multifaceted	several distinct parts
319	34	B	waned	decreased, faded
319	34	B	cosmos	order, harmony of the universe
319	35	B	woefully	regretfully, sorrowfully
321	4	A	abrupt halt	quick stop
321	8	A	banished	exiled, cast out
321	12	A	eradicated	eliminated, weeded out
321	49	A	proliferation	multiplication, to grow in great numbers
321	3	B	bizarre	strange, unusual
321	22	B	affront	insult, outrage
321	27	B	secularization	transfer from religious control to civil control
321	44	B	deterioration	decay, decline
321	51	B	deviant	people who violate norms (rules)

KEY TERMS TO DEFINE:

After studying the chapter, define each of the following terms. Then check your work by referring to the answers at the end of Chapter 9 in the Study Guide.

social institutions	charismatic authority
nuclear family	traditional authority
extended family	rational-legal authority
endogamy	sacred
neolocal residence	profane
monogamy	Protestant ethic
egalitarian marriage	predestination
bilineal descent	worldly asceticism
homogamy	denominations
power	folk religions
state	popular religions
polity	sects
power elite	cults
mass (society)	secularization
pluralism	humanism
rule by authority	

KEY PEOPLE

State the major theoretical contribution(s) of each of these people to the study of family, politics, and/or religion:

William J. Goode

Christopher Lasch

Karl Marx

C. Wright Mills

Thomas Dye

Max Weber

Emile Durkheim

190

After completing this self-test, check your answers against the "Answer Key" at the end of Chapter 9 in this Study Guide and in the text on the page(s) indicated in parentheses.

MULTIPLE CHOICE QUESTIONS

Select the response which best answers the question or completes the statement:

1. Which of the following statements is **not** true regarding social institutions? (278-279)
    a. Social institutions are orderly, enduring, and established ways of arranging behavior and doing things.
    b. Social relationships in institutions are structured for the purpose of performing some task(s) or accomplishing specific goals.
    c. Social institutions largely are independent from one another in society.
    d. Social institutions include the family, politics, and religion.

2. According to the functionalist perspective, the major functions of the family include: (280-281)
    a. Legitimizing all sexual relationships.
    b. Meeting family members' biological and economic needs.
    c. Helping family members who migrate from other countries to maintain their own language patterns and cultural diversity.
    d. Promoting societal solidarity and strengthening social control.
    e. All of the above.

3. According to conflict theorists: (281-282)
    a. The family is a sanctuary of love, companionship, and emotional support.
    b. The family meets the biological and economic needs of its members.
    c. Biological reproduction within the family ensures the group's continuity over time.
    d. The family is a microcosm of the tension, conflict, and exploitation existing in the larger society.
    e. All of the above.

4. A family consisting of a mother, a father, and their two children, is called a(n): (282-283)
    a. nuclear family
    b. extended family
    c. blended family
    d. model family

5. The tendency for people to marry individuals like themselves physically, psychologically, and/or socially is called: (283)
    a. monogamy
    b. matriarchy
    c. exogamy
    d. homogamy

6. Most marriages in the U.S. occur between two people of the same: (283-284)
    a. social class
    b. racial group
    c. religion
    d. level of education
    e. all of the above

7. According to Cuber and Harroff, which type of marital relationship is characterized by a fair amount of tension and conflict, which marital partners usually confine to the home? (284-285)
    a. the conflict habituated
    b. the devitalized
    c. the passive congenial
    d. the total
    e. none of the above

8. Which of the following is <u>correct</u> regarding divorce rates in the U.S.? (286-287)
    a. Divorce rates are highest for those who have been married for over seven years.
    b. Divorce rates are higher in the lower class than in the middle and upper classes.
    c. Divorce rates for whites tends to be higher than for blacks.
    d. Divorce rates are highest for marriages in which both the bride and groom are over 30 years of age when they marry.

9. Sociologist _____ argues that the relation between Western industrialization and the family is much more complex than a simple cause and effect phenomenon because families in Europe were changing in structure before the arrival of the Industrial Revolution. (289)
    a. Christopher Lasch
    b. Karl Marx
    c. William J. Goode
    d. Emile Durkheim

10. According to the text, China's introduction of a one child per family policy is an example of: (291)
    a. the way in which changes in governmental policy can have a long-term impact on the size and structure of families.
    b. the way in which governmental resistance to change can produce dramatic population growth in a society.
    c. the way in which birth control technology cannot overcome ideological resistance in a society.
    d. the exploitation of women in a society.

11. The ability to carry out one's own will despite resistance from others is: (292)
    a. authority
    b. polity
    c. power
    d. force

12. The _____ perspective claims that the state plays a critical societal role in "goal-attainment" activities. (293)
    a.   conflict
    b.   symbolic interaction
    c.   pluralist
    d.   rational-legal authority
    e.   functionalist

13. The _____ perspective focuses on the state and other political institutions as an important resource employed by some groups to gain and maintain control over other groups in society. (293)
    a.   conflict
    b.   symbolic interaction
    c.   pluralist
    d.   rational-legal authority
    e.   functionalist

14. Which of these sociologists first described the "power elite"? (294)
    a.   Emile Durkheim
    b.   Karl Marx
    c.   C. Wright Mills
    d.   William J. Goode
    e.   Christopher Lasch

15. The power elite has members from all of the following, except: (294-295)
    a.   the executive branch of the federal government
    b.   chancellors and presidents of Ivy League universities
    c.   high-ranking officials from the largest corporations
    d.   "top brass" from branches of the military services

16. Pluralists believe that _____ prevent any single group or coalition from becoming dominant. (295)
    a.   lobbyists
    b.   political leaders
    c.   members of the power elites
    d.   veto groups

17. Which of the following is true regarding voting patterns in the U.S.? (297-299)
    a.   In recent years, a substantial increase has occurred in the percentage of the voting age population turning out to vote in presidential elections in the U.S.
    b.   The likelihood of voting is greatest between the ages of 30 and 65.
    c.   Members of lower socioeconomic status groups vote with greater frequency than members of higher socioeconomic groups.
    d.   Formal education level does not appear to have much influence on whether or not a person votes.

18. According to Max Weber, rule by authority: (299)
    a.   occurs when political power in modern societies is dispersed among a variety of competing groups and organizations
    b.   occurs when a few elites control the State
    c.   occurs when political rule is based upon a sense of moral obligation, rather than raw power and force
    d.   occurs when political rule is based upon raw power and force, rather than a sense of moral obligation

19. Political rule based upon some extraordinary personal quality of the political leader is: (299)
    a.   charismatic authority
    b.   traditional authority
    c.   rational-legal authority
    d.   sacred authority

20. According to the text, which of the following political developments is most likely to occur in the future? (300-304)
    a.   Socialism will replace capitalism in the U.S.
    b.   Capitalism will replace socialism throughout eastern Europe and parts of the U.S.S.R.
    c.   Communism will grow stronger as the U.S.S.R. becomes better able to provide citizens with the economic goods they desire.
    d.   The U.S. will maintain its "number one" position in the world because of its economic and military successes.

21. The extraordinary elements of life that inspire a sense of reverence, awe, and fear in people were called _____ by Emile Durkheim. (304)
    a.   holy
    b.   religious
    c.   profane
    d.   sacred
    e.   none of the above

22. Which of these sociologists argued that religion provides a basis for social cohesion by uniting the members of the societal population in shared beliefs and values, as well as a common set of rituals? (305)
    a.   Robert Merton
    b.   Karl Marx
    c.   C. Wright Mills
    d.   Max Weber
    e.   Emile Durkheim

23. Which of these sociologists claimed that religion is "the opium of the people?" (305)
    a.   Robert Merton
    b.   Karl Marx
    c.   C. Wright Mills
    d.   Max Weber
    e.   Emile Durkheim

24. Which of these sociologists examined the role of the Protestant ethic in the rise of modern capitalism? (306)
    a.   Robert Merton
    b.   Karl Marx
    c.   C. Wright Mills
    d.   Max Weber
    e.   Emile Durkheim

25. The Protestant ethic was based on which of these beliefs? (306)
    a.   predestination
    b.   indulgence
    c.   worldly asceticism
    d.   all of the above
    e.   only "a" and "c"

26. Denominations are: (307)
    a. formal religious organizations that are well integrated into their society and recognize religious pluralism.
    b. new and distinctive religious organizations that exist in a state of high tension with the established religions in society.
    c. religious subcultural or countercultural groups that offer their members a different vision of the social and the spiritual life.
    d. interpretations and modifications of more formalized religious traditions to meet the needs of specific population groups.

27. Folk religions are: (307)
    a. formal religious organizations that are well integrated into their society and recognize religious pluralism.
    b. new and distinctive religious organizations that exist in a state of high tension with the established religions in society.
    c. religious subcultural or countercultural groups that offer their members a different vision of the social and the spiritual life.
    d. interpretations and modifications of more formalized religious traditions to meet the needs of specific population groups.

28. Fundamentalists believe that the rise of _____ is a great threat. (309-310)
    a. communism
    b. Catholicism
    c. Protestantism
    d. socialism
    e. humanism

29. Which of the following statements is <u>not</u> true regarding the electronic church? (311)
    a. Religious programming often is more in the nature of an entertainment show than a doctrinal presentation.
    b. Fundamentalists are the only prime-time preachers.
    c. Religious broadcasts all tend to have a largely visual appeal and simple doctrinal message.
    d. Many of the viewers are older people of lower income and educational levels.

30. According to the U.S. Census Bureau, in 1988 what percentage of the U.S. population claimed membership in a church or synagogue? (311)
    a. 25%
    b. 45%
    c. 65%
    d. 85%

TRUE-FALSE QUESTIONS

T   F   1. Functionalists are primarily concerned with how the family contributes to the overall well-being of individual family members. (280)

T   F   2. In every known society incest taboos regulate the sexual behavior of people related within certain degrees of kinship. (281)

T   F   3. Conflict theorists argue that there is a hidden conservative view built into the functionalist interpretation of the family. (281)

T   F   4.   According to the Marxist perspective, women are victimized in the workforce but not in their roles as wives and mothers. (281)

T   F   5.   In the United States most people live in nuclear families, practice endogamy, have a neolocal residence, are monogamous, are moving toward or are in an egalitarian marriage, and have a bilineal descent system. (282)

T   F   6.   Divorce rates are highest in young marriages. (286)

T   F   7.   There is a relationship between rates of divorce in the U.S. and general economic trends. (287)

T   F   8.   Conclusive evidence exists to demonstrate that marital dissolution has a very negative impact on children's emotional well-being. (287)

T   F   9.   Sociologist William Goode argues that neolocal nuclear families facilitated the geographic and social mobility needed for the industrialization of society. (289)

T   F   10.   Christopher Lasch claims that reformers sought to minimize the impact that parents had on their children by maximizing the influence of state and schools. (290-291)

T   F   11.   Power is defined as "the ability to carry out one's own will with the assistance of others." (292)

T   F   12.   Courts are the social institution which hold a monopoly over the legitimate use of force and exercise governing power in the society. (292-293)

T   F   13.   Functionalists believe that the state and other political institutions serve as power weapons utilized by the ruling classes to preserve their own advantaged positions. (293)

T   F   14.   Karl Marx regarded the political apparatus in capitalist societies as the ultimate instrument of class oppression. (293)

T   F   15.   Modern conflict theorists argue that a political economy exists which supports and furthers existing social inequality arrangements. (294)

T   F   16.   According to C. Wright Mills' power elite theory, the masses largely were powerless. (295)

T   F   17.   Based on the power elite perspective, even though elites run the political system, they still are accountable to the public and to governmental checks and balances. (295)

T   F   18.   The pluralist perspective states that veto groups shift according to the issues at hand and limit each other's influence to specific situations. (295)

T   F   19.   According to your text, recent studies of the U.S. power structure provide evidence that the pluralist model may have greater validity than the power elite interpretation. (296)

T   F   20.   During the decade of the 1980's, the economic position of virtually all economic segments of the U.S. population improved. (296)

T   F   21.   The United States ranks close to the top in terms of its citizens' participation in electoral politics. (297)

T   F   22.   Minorities, the young, and members of lower socioeconomic status groups have the lowest rates of political participation in the U.S. (297-298)

T   F   23.   Evidence points to a growing cynicism in people's perceptions of how politics works in the U.S. (299)

T   F   24.   As modernization occurred, political rule by physical force was transformed into rule by authority. (299)

T   F   25.   According to Max Weber, rational-legal authority is based upon long-standing societal customs. (299)

T   F   26.   Third World societies like Mexico with control over supplies of petroleum and other vital resources may be on the rise as some First World societies experience decline. (301)

T	F	27.	Religious statuses and roles were among the first specialized positions to be differentiated in early human society. (304)
T	F	28.	Functionalists argue that religion promotes societal solidarity, promotes social control, and provides people with a sense of meaning and purpose in life. (305)
T	F	29.	Conflict theorists believe that focusing workers' attention on the "sweet by and by" of the afterlife perpetuates the workers' misery in the present life. (305)
T	F	30.	Religious beliefs both help and hinder the development process in many societies. (312)

FILL-IN QUESTIONS

Fill in the blank with the word or phrase that best completes the statement.

1. _____ _____ are orderly, enduring, and established ways of arranging behavior and doing things. (278)

2. The tendency for people to marry individuals like themselves physically, psychologically, and/or socially is called _____. (283)

3. The _____ is the social institution that holds a monopoly over the legitimate use of force and exercises governing power in a given society. (292-293)

4. The term _____ _____ was used by C. Wright Mills to describe a coalition of corporate, political, and military elites who, according to Mills, secretly controlled the State in the U.S. (294)

5. According to Max Weber, _____ authority was rule based upon some extraordinary personal quality of the political leader. _____authority was rule based upon long-standing societal customs. Rule based upon the reasonableness of laws and the acceptability of law-making procedures was _____ authority. (299)

6. Commonplace or ordinary elements of everyday life are referred to as _____ while those extraordinary elements of life that inspire a sense of reverence, awe, and fear in people are referred to as _____. (304)

7. Max Weber's term for the world-view and values associated with the Protestant Christian religions that developed in Western Europe during the 16th and 17th centuries was _____ _____. (306)

8. _____ are formal religious organizations that are well integrated into their society and recognize religious pluralism. (307)

9. _____ religions represent particular interpretations and modifications of more formalized religious traditions to meet the needs of specific population groups. (307)

10. _____ religions are sets of beliefs that lie outside of or span the boundaries of recognized denominations and appeal to mass audiences drawn from a variety of backgrounds. (307)

197

MATCHING

Match these individuals with their theoretical contributions.

_____1. William J. Goode
_____2. Karl Marx
_____3. C. Wright Mills
_____4. Max Weber
_____5. Emile Durkheim
_____6. Christopher Lasch
_____7. Thomas Dye

A. believed that the state took child-rearing duties away from the family

B. claimed that neolocal nuclear familie helped facilitate Western industrialization

C. his research findings indicate a strong concentration of power in the hands of relatively few people in very influential organizations

D. argued that religion and politics both contributed to oppression in capitalist societies

E. coined the term "power elite"

F. stated that religion could produce social change in societies

G. dealt with the issue of what was sacred and what was profane in society

ESSAY QUESTIONS

1. Compare and contrast functional and conflict perspectives on the role of the family in society.

2. Discuss the factors which are associated with a successful marriage and the factors associated with divorce in the U.S.

3. Explain what is meant by the term "power elite" and note who (or what) is included in this category.

4. Indicate why some form of religion is found in every human society.

5. Differentiate between functional and conflict views on the primary role or consequence of religion in modern societies.

ANSWERS FOR CHAPTER 9

DEFINITION OF KEY TERMS:

social institutions: orderly, enduring, and established ways of arranging behavior and doing things.

nuclear family: a family group consisting of a mother, a father, and their children.

extended family: a family group that extends beyond the immediate relationship of husband, wife, and their children and includes several generations.

endogamy: custom that requires individuals to choose marriage mates from within their own tribe, community, social class, nationality or other grouping.

neolocal residence: system in which both marriage partners reside apart from their family of orientation.

monogamy: marriage form permitting each person to have only one spouse.

egalitarian marriage: a system where power and authority are shared equally by husband and wife.

bilineal descent: family membership and inheritance traced through the lines of both male and female parents to their children.

homogamy: the tendency for people to marry individuals like themselves physically, psychologically, and/or socially.

power: the ability to carry out one's own will, despite resistance from others.

state: the social institution that holds a monopoly over the legitimate use of force and exercises governing power in a given society.

polity: in functionalist terminology, another name for the state.

power elite: term used by C. Wright Mills to describe a coalition of corporate, political, and military elites which, according to Mills, secretly controlled the state in the U.S.

mass (society): societal population consisting of millions of fragmented, alienated individuals who are uninterested and uninvolved in political affairs.

pluralism: the view that political power in modern societies is dispersed among a variety of competing groups and organizations, with no single unit or combination of units dominating the system.

rule by authority: political rule based upon a sense of moral obligation, rather than raw power and force.

charismatic authority: in Max Weber's terminology, political rule based upon some extraordinary personal quality of the political leader.

traditional authority: in Max Weber's terminology, political rule based upon long-standing societal customs.

rational-legal authority: in Max Weber's terminology, political rule based upon the reasonableness of laws and the acceptability of law-making procedures.

sacred: those extraordinary elements of life that inspire a sense of reverence, awe, and fear in people.

profane: the commonplace, ordinary elements of everyday life.

Protestant ethic: Max Weber's term for the world-view and values associated with the Protestant Christian religions that developed in Western Europe during the 16th and 17th centuries.

predestination: as part of the Protestant ethic, the belief that one's fate in the afterlife had been decided before or at one's birth, and could not be changed through prayer or good works.

worldly asceticism: as part of the Protestant ethic, the denial of material self-indulgence under the belief that frugality was morally superior to concern for worldly pleasures.

denominations: formal religious organizations that are well integrated into their society and recognize religious pluralism.

folk religions: interpretations and modification of more formalized religious traditions to meet the needs of specific population groups.

popular religions: sets of beliefs that lie outside of or span the boundaries of recognized denominations and appeal to mass audiences drawn from a variety of backgrounds.

sects: religious subcultural or countercultural groups that offer their members a different vision of the social and the spiritual life.

cults: new and distinctive religious organization that exist in a state of high tension with the established religions in society.

secularization: societal transformation from a religious to a civil and worldly basis, with a significant decline of religion in people's everyday lives.

humanism: the belief that humans, rather than God, are the center of their own destiny.

KEY PEOPLE:

William J. Goode, a contemporary sociologist, argued against the assumption that industrialization has been the principal, if not sole factor responsible for changes in the family over the past 200 years in the U.S. He asserted that the link between the nuclear family and industrialization is one in which the former met the "demands" of the latter: neolocal nuclear families allowed for the social and geographic mobility needed for Western industrialization to occur.

Christopher Lasch, also a contemporary sociologist, focused his research on how industrialization affected the family in the U.S. He believes that the family did not gradually lose child-rearing duties as societies industrialized, but rather that these duties and other aspects of parental influence were taken away by the state in a rather short period of time.

As discussed in previous chapters, Karl Marx regarded the political apparatus in capitalist societies -- the state -- as the ultimate instrument of class oppression. He argued that the state plays a direct and active role in maintaining bourgeoisie dominance and proletarian subordination. Likewise, Marx claimed that organized religion is a reflection of the underlying mode of economic production whose basic structure is responsible for shaping all other facets of human social life. He stated that religion is "the opium of the people" because he believed that religion focused workers' attention on an afterlife with its promise of eternal bliss, thereby deflecting their attention from their misery in the present life.

C. Wright Mills coined the term "power elite" to describe a coalition of high-ranking officials from the largest corporations, the branches of the military services, and the executive branch of the federal government, which formed an "inner circle of power" that secretly controlled the state in the U.S. Below the "power elite," were

200

the elected political officials in Congress and other offices of government, and below that was a societal mass consisting of millions of individuals who, for the most part, were uninterested and uninvolved in political affairs.

Thomas Dye conducted extensive research to examine the institutionalized centers of power in the U.S., and his findings indicate a strong concentration of power in the hands of a relatively small number of very influential organizations, and a pattern of common socioeconomic class backgrounds for key office holders across the different institutional sectors.

Max Weber explained the process by which political rule by physical force was transformed, as modernization occurred, into rule by authority. He divided authority into three types: charismatic (based upon some extraordinary personal quality of the political leader), traditional (based upon long-standing societal customs), and rational-legal (based upon the reasonableness of laws and the acceptability of law-making procedures). Weber also examined the ways in which religion can serve as a catalyst for social change. He argued that the Protestant ethic -- the world-view and values (such as predestination and worldly asceticism) associated with the new Protestant religions -- contributed significantly to the rise of modern capitalism.

Emile Durkheim provided the classic functionalist argument that religion promotes societal solidarity, strengthens social control, and gives societal members a sense of meaning and purpose in life. His analysis of religion attempted to explain the universal presence of religious activity throughout history. Durkheim believed that religion reflects humans' needs to deal with the "sacred" -- those elements that inspire a sense of reverence, awe, and fear.

ANSWERS TO MULTIPLE CHOICE QUESTIONS:

1. c Responses "a," "b," and "d" are correct statements regarding social institutions. To be a correct statement, response "c" should state that "Social institutions largely are interdependent upon one another in society. (278-279)

2. b Only response "b" is a major function of the family as defined by the functionalist perspective. Response "a" is incorrect because the family legitimizes some sexual relationships while at the same time prohibiting others. Response "c" is not part of the functionalist view, and response "d" is a major function of religion, not the family, in society. (280-281)

3. d Responses "a," "b," and "c" are all functionalist views of the family. Only response "d" (the family is a microcosm of the tension, conflict, and exploitation existing in the larger society) is stated by conflict theorists. (281-282)

4. a Nuclear families are made up of a mother, a father, and their children. Extended families extend beyond these relationships to include several generations. Blended families are created by remarriage and include step-children and half brothers/sisters. (282-283)

5. d Homogamy is the tendency for people to marry individuals like themselves physically, psychologically, and/or socially. Monogamy is a marriage form permitting each person to have only one spouse. Matriarchy is a system where power and authority are vested in females. Exogamy is a custom that requires individuals to choose marriage mates from outside certain groups. (283)

6. e Most marriages in the U.S. occur between two people of the same social class, racial group, religion, and level of education, thus making "e" -- all of the above -- the correct response. (283-284)

7.	a	The conflict habituated marriage is characterized by a fair amount of tension and conflict, which marital partners usually confine to the home. (284-285)
8.	b	Only response "b" -- divorce rates are higher in the lower class than in the middle and upper classes in the U.S. -- is correct. Response "a" is incorrect because divorce rates are highest within the first seven years of marriage. Response "c" is not correct because divorce rates for blacks tend to be higher than for whites. Response "c" is wrong because divorce rates are highest in young marriages rather those in which both the bride and groom are over 30 years of age when they marry. (286-287)
9.	c	William J. Goode argues that the relation between Western industrialization and the family is much more complex than a simple cause and effect phenomenon. He does not believe that industrialization has been the principal, if not sole factor responsible for changes in the family in the U.S. (289)
10.	a	The text uses China's introduction of a one child per family policy as an example of the way in which changes in governmental policy can have a long-term impact on the size and structure of families. (291)
11.	c	Power is defined as the ability to carry out one's own will despite resistance from others. (292)
12.	e	The functionalist perspective claims that the state plays a critical societal role in "goal-attainment" activities. (293)
13.	a	The conflict perspective focuses on the state and other political institutions as an important resource employed by some groups to gain and maintain control over other groups in society. (293)
14.	c	C. Wright Mills first described the "power elite." (294)
15.	b	Chancellors and presidents of Ivy League universities were not described by C. Wright Mills as being part of the power elite. The executive branch of the federal government, high-ranking officials from the largest corporations, and "top brass" from branches of the military services constituted the power elite. (294-295)
16.	d	Pluralists believe that veto groups prevent any single group or coalition from becoming dominant. (295)
17.	b	Only response "b" is true -- that the likelihood of voting is greatest between the ages of 30 and 65. All other responses are false. (297-299)
18.	c	Weber indicated that rule by authority occurs when political rule is based upon a sense of moral obligation, rather than raw power and force. (299)
19.	a	Charismatic authority is political rule based upon some extraordinary personal quality of the political leader. Traditional authority is based upon long-standing societal customs. Rational-legal authority is based upon the reasonableness of laws and the acceptability of law-making procedures. (299)
20.	b	Only response "b" is a possibility discussed in the text -- that capitalism will replace socialism throughout eastern Europe and parts of the U.S.S.R. (300-304)
21.	d	The extraordinary elements of life that inspire a sense of reverence, awe, and fear in people were called sacred by Emile Durkheim. (304)
22.	e	Emile Durkheim argued that religion provides a basis for social cohesion by uniting the members of the societal population in shared beliefs and values, as well as a common set of rituals. (305)
23.	b	Karl Marx claimed that religion is "the opium of the people." (305)
24.	d	Max Weber examined the role of the Protestant ethic in the rise of modern capitalism. (306)
25.	e	Only "a" -- predestination -- and "c" -- worldly asceticism -- are correct. Response "b" -- indulgence -- was not a basic belief of the Protestant ethic. (306)

26. <u>a</u>   Denominations are formal religious organizations that are well integrated into their society and recognize religious pluralism. Response "b" defines "cult." Response "c" defines "sects." Response "d" defines "folk religions." (307)

27. <u>d</u>   Folk religions are interpretations and modifications of more formalized religious traditions to meet the needs of specific population groups. (307)

28. <u>e</u>   Fundamentalists believe that the rise of <u>humanism</u> is a great threat. (Humanism is the belief that humans, rather than God, are the center of their own destiny.) (309-310)

29. <u>b</u>   Based on the text, responses "a," "c," and "d" are true statements. Since the question asks which statement is <u>not</u> true - only response "b" is correct. Fundamentalists are not the only prime-time preachers. A large number of evangelical Christian ministers who do not hold a conservative, back to basics doctrinal view also carry on much of their work over the television airways. (311)

30. <u>c</u>   According to the U.S. Census Bureau, <u>65</u>% of the U.S. population claimed membership in a church or synagogue. (311)

ANSWERS TO TRUE-FALSE QUESTIONS:

1. False -- Functionalists are primarily concerned with how the family contributes to the overall functioning of and, therefore, the <u>good</u> <u>of</u> <u>society</u> -- not the overall well-being of individual family members. (280)

2. True (281)

3. True (281)

4. False -- According to the Marxist perspective, women are victimized in both the workforce and in their roles as wives and mothers. (281)

5. True (282)

6. True (286)

7. True (287)

8. False -- There is conflicting evidence on both the short and long term consequences of marital dissolution on the emotional well-being and behavior of children. (287)

9. True (289)

10. True (290-291)

11. False -- Power is defined as the ability to carry out one's own will, <u>despite resistance from others,</u> not "with the assistance of others." (292)

12. False -- The <u>state</u> is the social institution which holds a monopoly over the legitimate use of force and exercise governing power in the society. (292-293)

13. False -- <u>Conflict theorists,</u> not functionalists, believe that the state and other political institutions serve as power weapons utilized by the ruling classes to preserve their own advantaged positions. (293)

14. True (293)

15. True (294)

16. True (295)

17. False -- According to the power elite perspective, elites run the political system and largely are unaccountable to the public and to governmental checks and balances. (295)

18. True (295)

19. False -- According to the text, recent studies -- especially those conducted by Thomas Dye -- of the U.S. power structure provide evidence that the <u>power elite</u> model, not the pluralist model, may have greater validity. (296)

20. False -- During the decade of the 1980's, the economic position of the wealthiest segment of the U.S. population improved, while that of virtually all other population groups either dropped or remained stagnant. (296)

21. False -- The United States ranks close to the <u>bottom</u> in terms of its citizens' participation in electoral politics. (297)
22. True (297-298)
23. True (299)
24. True (299)
25. False -- According to Max Weber, rational-legal authority is based upon the reasonableness of laws and the acceptability of law-making procedures. By contrast, traditional authority is upon long-standing societal customs. (299)
26. True (301)
27. True (304)
28. True (305)
29. True (305)
30. True (312)

<u>ANSWERS</u> <u>TO</u> <u>FILL</u>-<u>IN</u> <u>QUESTIONS</u>

1. Social institutions (278)
2. Homogamy (283)
3. State (292-293)
4. Power elite (294)
5. Charismatic; traditional; rational-legal (299)
6. Profane; sacred (304)
7. Protestant ethic (306)
8. Denominations (307)
9. Folk (307)
10. Popular (307)

<u>ANSWERS</u> <u>TO</u> <u>MATCHING</u>:

1. B
2. D
3. E
4. F
5. G
6. A
7. C

CHAPTER TEN

POPULATION

Chapter 10 explores the field of demography -- the scientific study of population. Demography is an interdisciplinary subject with ties to sociology, the other social sciences, business, and medicine. The aspects of demography that sociologists primarily are interested in are: (1) population processes (fertility, mortality, and migration), (2) the size and distribution of a population, and (3) the structure and characteristics of a population. The chapter analyzes the major variables influencing fertility, mortality, and migration rates in First World countries, such as the U.S., and in Third World countries. Population composition is discussed in terms of sex ratios and age/sex or population pyramids. The population of the U.S. is examined in terms of its size, composition, and distribution. The views of Thomas Malthus and Karl Marx on the causes of population growth and its consequences are analyzed. The chapter next presents the theory of demographic transition, the problems of underpopulation in some societies, and the problems of overpopulation pressures in others. These problems include pressure on cities, societies, human health, ecologies, economies, international security, political institutions, and the international banking system. Finally, the chapter discusses the population crisis in Africa, perspectives on controlling fertility, and the politics of food.

LEARNING OBJECTIVES:

As you read Chapter 10, use these learning objectives to organize your notes. After completing your reading, briefly state an answer to each of the objectives, and review the text pages in parentheses.

1. Indicate why the field of demography is so important to social scientists, business people and governmental officials. (325-326)

2. Discuss the major variables that can affect the birth rate, and specify how demographers use the "crude birth rate" and the "total fertility rate." (327-329)

3. State the three major reasons why people die in any society. Note the major causes of death in First World and in Third World countries. (329-331)

4. Explain the concept of "life expectancy," and state the major reasons why people in Japan live much longer than people in Ethiopia. (332)

5. Describe the "push" and "pull" factors of migration. (333-335)

6. Discuss the Malthusian theory of population growth, and indicate whether or not the theory was correct. (343-344)

7. Outline the theory of demographic transition and note the stage of the transition in which most Third World countries are "stuck." (344-345)

8. List and briefly discuss the major problems resulting from overpopulation in less developed countries. (347-351)

9. Describe ways in which population growth can be slowed. (353-354)

10. Explain how political, economic and religious variables all are linked to issues of reproduction, contraception, and food distribution. (353-356)

OUTLINE

I. INTRODUCTION

   A. Demography is the scientific study of population. Demographers are especially interested in population growth and how this growth is affected by birth, death and migration rates.
       1. Businesses need such information to determine what range of products to sell to a given population and how to market these products.
       2. Governments need this information to determine the needs of a given segment of the population and the proper allocation of tax dollars.
   B. Sociologists are most interested in these aspects of demography:
       1. Population processes (fertility, mortality, and migration)
       2. The size and distribution of a population
       3. The structure and characteristics of a population

II. FERTILITY

   A. Fertility refers to the number of children born to women in a given population. The fertility rate is a function of two factors:
       1. Fecundity (the biological component) is the physical ability to conceive and bear children. For most women, this is between the ages of 12 and 45.
       2. Social and psychological factors in a woman's environment:
           a. Intercourse variables refer to the commencement of and frequency of sexual activity over a given period of time.
               (1). The more time spent in marriage the more likely a woman will become pregnant.
               (2). The longer marriage is postponed, the fewer children a woman is likely to have. The term biological clock refers to the upper limits of fecundity (approximately 45 years of age) when women are physically able to conceive a child.
           b. Conception variables are those factors that determine if a woman will become pregnant or not. These include:
               (1). The use of contraceptives, and
               (2). The presence (and duration) or absence of breast feeding.
           c. Gestation variables (miscarriage and stillbirth, induced abortion) are those factors that determine if a fetus will come to term resulting in a live birth.

   B. Fertility Measures
       1. The crude birth rate (CBR) is the number of births per year for every 1,000 members of the population. This statistic is "crude" because the age structure or distribution of the population is not considered.
       2. The total fertility rate (TFR) is a measure of completed fertility, or the total number of children born per 1,000 women.

III. MORTALITY

A. There are three major reasons why people die in any society: they degenerate, they are killed by communicable diseases, and they are killed by social and environmentally-related diseases.

    1. Degeneration refers to the biological deterioration of the body. In modern societies the primary degenerative diseases are: cardiovascular or heart disease, cancer, and stroke.

    2. Communicable diseases are those maladies contracted from another human being.

        a. These diseases are especially deadly where medical facilities and treatment are poor and population density is high.

        b. Smallpox, chicken pox, cholera, diptheria, and malaria are major problems in Third World Countries.

        c. The AIDS virus is a communicable disease contracted directly from another person through sexual contact and directly by contact with infected blood (usually a transfusion or intravenous drug use). Pregnant women infected with the AIDS virus also can transmit the disease to their babies.

    3. Social and Environmentally-Related Diseases

        a. Deaths related to the social and economic environment include those resulting from unsafe products, hazardous working conditions and pollution.

        b. Occupationally-caused diseases account for as many as 100,000 deaths annually in the U.S.

        c. It has been argued that between 75-90 percent of all cancers in the U.S. are environmentally related.

        d. Both industrialized and developing nations have industrial pollution and have spent relatively little money on environmental safeguards.

B. Mortality Measures

    1. The crude death rate (CDR) is the number of deaths per year for every 1,000 members of the population. This is a "crude" measure of mortality inasmuch as it does not take into account the age distribution of a population.

        a. CDR's in developed countries like the U.S., Japan, and France are relatively low, even though these nations have older populations. These countries have quality medical care, few deaths resulting from nutritional deficiencies, and a greater ability to control most communicable diseases.

        b. The CDR in some Third World nations is higher than the CDR in First World countries. Other Third World nations have a CDR which is lower than that of First World countries. Low CDR's in developing countries are the result of two factors:

            (1). They have very young populations, with as many as 50 percent of their citizens under 15 years of age. Young people die at a much lower rate than older individuals.

            (2). Communicable diseases have been effectively controlled in much of the Third World.

    2. The infant mortality rate is the number of deaths during the first year of life per 1,000 live births.

        a. This rate is often used as a measure of a country's economic well-being.

        b. Developed nations typically have low infant mortality rates, while poor nations have much higher rates.

3. The <u>maternal mortality rate</u> is the number of women who die per 10,000 live births.
   a. In developed nations the maternal mortality rate is extremely low (two or three).
   b. In developing countries complications and death during childbirth are still common.

C. Social Correlates of Mortality
   1. Social correlates of death in the U.S. are as follows:
      a. As a group's occupational prestige goes up, death rates go down.
      b. As income and education go up, mortality goes down.
      c. Nonwhite mortality is higher than white mortality by at least 10 percent in every group up to age 80.
      d. People (especially men) who are married have lower rates of mortality than single people.
      e. As a group, women live approximately seven years longer than men in the United States.
   2. <u>Life expectancy</u> is the statistical average length of time a person in a given population can expect to live.
      a. In the developed world, life expectancy is 73 years; while in developing nations it is 60 years.
      b. Differences is life expectancy can be seen in a comparison of Japan and Ethiopia:
         (1). A person born in Japan in 1988 can expect to live 79 years, while someone born in Ethiopia has a life expectancy of 41 years of age.
         (2). In Ethiopia, the <u>average</u> life span is dramatically reduced because of the number of children who die in the first year of life. Once an individual makes it through the first year, that person's chance of living past age 41 increase dramatically.
         (3). The Japanese as a <u>group</u> can expect to live almosttwice as long as people in Ethiopia because of the high levels of income, technology, nutrition, education, and health care in Japan.
      c. Research indicates that even in developed countries human beings may be reaching the upper limits of <u>average</u> life expectancy, about 85 years.

IV. MIGRATION

A. <u>Migration</u> is the relatively permanent movement of people from one place to another. Migration is usually the result of social, political, or economic conditions that may <u>push</u> or <u>pull</u> individuals and groups, resulting in "streams" of migrants moving within or across national boundaries.
   1. <u>Push factors</u> -- such as little economic opportunity or racial, religious, and political persecution -- serve to drive off or send a stream of migrants from a particular geographical location.
   2. <u>Pull factors</u> -- such as increased opportunity for employment or better living conditions -- serve as socioeconomic magnets and draw migrants to a given geographical location.

B. Internal vs. International Migration
   1. <u>Internal migration</u> refers to the movement of people within a political state. The U.S. has been experienced three major internal shifts in population.

a. The movement of people from rural to urban areas in the U.S., starting in the 1800s.

b. In the last 25 years, the most significant movement of people has been from the northeastern and Midwestern "frostbelt" to the "sunbelt" stretching from Florida to California.

c. In the 1970s, nonmetropolitan areas began growing faster than cities as people moved from urban areas to the countryside.

2. International migration is the movement of people across political states.

a. This type of migration is a relatively recent phenomenon, occurring, for the most part, over the past four hundred years.

b. Most international migration is voluntary; however, some of the largest movements of people either were forced or were the result of fear and political pressure.

c. With the exception of the slave experience, migration to the United States has been voluntary. At some points in time, restrictive immigration laws have limited the number of immigrants from various parts of the world.

3. Illegal Immigration has been a highly controversial topic in the U.S.

a. The U.S. Census Bureau recognizes three groups of illegal immigrants:

(1). Settlers come to the U.S. on a "more or less" permanent basis;

(2). Sojourners -- such as farm laborers -- do seasonal work and then return to their country of origin; and

(3). Commuters cross the border daily.

b. The impact illegal aliens have on the U.S. economy has been debated:

(1). Some researchers argue that these workers take the lowest paid jobs, displacing American-born laborers who then move up the economic ladder.

(2). Others believe that these workers have helped the economy in the U.S. by providing low-wage workers to industries.

(3). Still others argue that illegal aliens take thousands of jobs from some U.S. citizens and depress wages of other citizens.

V. POPULATION COMPOSITION

A. The sex ratio is the number of males per 100 females in a given population.

1. In the U.S. in 1986, the sex ratio had declined to 95.2, indicating a surplus of females and the fact that women live longer than men in the U.S., as they do in most societies.

2. The sex ratio and growth rate are indicators of people's chances of getting married in a given population:

a. More males are born than females; but because males also have a higher mortality rate, by the age of 20-24, the sex ratio is balanced (100).

b. From the age of 25 and up, there is a surplus of females; and, because American women on an average marry men two or three years older than themselves, there are not enough men to go around.

c. Other researchers believe that the trend will go the other way for females born between 1960 and 1975, and that they will find a surplus of husbands.

209

B.   An <u>age</u>/<u>sex</u> or <u>population</u> <u>pyramid</u> summarizes the age and sex characteristics of a given population by five-year cohorts or groups.
  1.   Age/sex pyramids for Mexico, Japan and the U.S. look quite different:
    a.   The Mexican pyramid is called a "true pyramid" and indicates a rapidly-growing population with each age cohort (group) larger than the preceding one. Societies with this type of pyramid will continue to grow for the foreseeable future.
    b.   The pyramids of Japan and the U.S. illustrate populations that are aging and have a slow rate of growth.
  2.   The U.S. population is characterized by a low fertility rate and an aging population, as well as a changing racial and ethnic composition of the country:
    a.   Blacks are the largest minority group in the U.S.
    b.   The Hispanic population is growing rapidly because of high birth rates and international migration.

VI.   POPULATION OF THE UNITED STATES

A.   Preliminary statistics from the 1990 census indicate these three population trends in the U.S.:
  1.   The continuing movement of people to the western and southern regions of the country;
  2.   A population shift from the cities to surrounding suburbs; and
  3.   A rapidly increasing minority population in some areas of the country.
B.   The majority of people who migrated within the U.S. in the last decade relocated for economic reasons:
  1.   People were "pushed" from the northeast and Midwest as a result of a perceived or real downturn in the economy.
  2.   People were "pulled" to the west and south because of perceived or real economic opportunity in those regions.
C.   The migration of people will have significant political ramifications in regard to congressional seats and social ramifications in terms of composition of the population:
  1.   <u>Sluburbs</u> -- residential areas which are part slum and part suburb -- are developing because suburbs are becoming "ports of entry" for new immigrants to the U.S.
  2.   Immigrants no longer are living in central cities first, and then moving to suburbs, as was typical in the past. They are moving directly to suburbs and putting a tremendous strain on social services, especially schools.

VII.   WORLD POPULATION

A.   The history of world population growth can be divided into three periods:
  1.   The first encompasses almost all of human existence and lasted until the 18th century.
  2.   The second period began in the 1800s with the Industrial Revolution when the population grew rapidly in Europe and America because of a significant decline in mortality.
  3.   The third phase is the "population explosion" currently taking place in the developing world, where mortality rates have dropped rapidly as a result of technology, but fertility rates have declined only slightly.

B.   Thomas Malthus (1766-1834), an English economist and clergyman, attempted to explain and project population growth.
      1.   Malthus' theory was based on what he considered to be a natural law:
            a.   Since food supply increased arithmetically (1-2-3-4, etc.), while population increased geometrically (2-4-8-16, etc.), it was only a matter of time before human population outstripped the ability of the environment to sustain the population.
            b.   When this "carrying capacity" was reached, positive checks -- such as disease, war, and vice -- would create growth limits.
            c.   However, this suffering could be avoided if people used preventive checks to control their fertility.   From Mathus' perspective, the only acceptable solution -- preventive checks -- to limiting births was delayed marriage and/or moral restraint (celibacy).
      2.   The Malthusian theory has several major shortcomings:
            a.   The idea that food production could not keep up with the population was wrong, as demonstrated by the Industrial Revolution.   Today, the problem is not one of production, but rather one of distribution.
            b.   The belief that delayed marriage and/or moral restraint were the only ways to reduce fertility was a moral position and not a scientific one.
            c.   His conclusion that poverty is the inevitable result of population growth is false.
      3.   Karl Marx was a major critic of Malthusian theory:
            a.   Marx argued that problems like poverty resulting from overpopulation were not the result of any natural laws (arithmetic and geometric progressions of food and people), but were the result of an oppressive, exploitative capitalist system.
            b.   For Marx, the solution was not "moral restraint" but socialism, an economic system that would outproduce capitalism and insure an equitable distribution of food, material goods, and services.

C.   The demographic transition theory is the perspective that explains population changes in the modern world.   The theory divides change into three stages:
      1.   Stage One (high growth potential) has high rates of birth and death, and slow growth.
      2.   Stage Two (transitional growth) has a high birth rate and a low death rate resulting in explosive population growth.
      3.   Stage Three (incipient decline) has both low fertility and mortality and, therefore, slow population growth.

D.   Underpopulation
      1.   Population decrease may occur in many industrialized countries before the end of this century:
            a.   The average family size in most of these nations is less than the 2.1 children per couple necessary for a population to remain stable over the long run.
            b.   For example, couples in Australia, New Zealand, Canada, the United States and Japan have decided to limit the size of their families.   As a result, they increasingly are using effective birth control devices and/or abortion to do this.

211

2. Kingsley Davis argues that several factors contribute to declining fertility:
    a. High divorce rates contribute to declining fertility because:
        (1). Divorce reduces the time men and women spend in marriage; and
        (2). A high divorce rate is indicative of marital instability -- thus, people with marital problems often postpone having children.
    b. As more women have entered the labor force in recent years, a "chilling effect on fertility" has occurred:
        (1). Single women often postpone marriage in favor of continuing their education so they can get better paying, more prestigious jobs.
        (2). Men now face more competition from increasingly better-educated women, and so the men also opt to delay marriage and stay in school.
        (3). When two working people marry, the husband is in no position to demand that his wife quit her job.
        (4). The employment of married women contributes to marital instability and to the need for women to play "Superwoman" in their attempts to meet the duties and responsibilities of being a wife, mother, and full-time employee. As a result, some choose to have only one child or to forego a family altogether in favor of the rewards of a successful career.
3. Other researchers state that the current desire to lead the "good life," plus the financial ability to do so when both husband and wife work, has contributed to the growing number of "DINK'S" (double income, no kids) in the developed world.
4. Positive aspects of below-replacement level fertility:
    a. An older society will have less crime and less need for criminal justice personnel and facilities.
    b. An older population will result in a more experienced work force, less job turnover, and lower unemployment.
    c. Homes can be smaller and more energy efficient.
5. Negative aspects of population declines:
    a. An older population will tend to be more conservative and less innovative.
    b. Medical costs will increase dramatically.

E. Problems of Overpopulation
    1. The world's population is increasing at an alarming rate. For example, Africa, has a <u>doubling time</u> -- the number of years it takes a given population to double in size -- of only 24 years.
    2. Population pressure triggers a range of economic, social, political, and environmental problems:
        a. <u>Pressure on cities</u>:
            (1). As people in Third World countries attempt to escape from the poverty and hopelessness of the countryside, they move to Third World cities (<u>rural-to-urban migration</u>) which already are growing rapidly because of <u>natural increase</u> (births over deaths).
            (2). This movement results in major problems of congestion, housing, and pollution.

b. <u>Pressure on societies</u>:
   (1). In Latin America, Asia, Africa, and other developing nations, tremendous population increases put extreme pressure on the already inadequate infrastructure (health, education, transportation, communication, etc.).
   (2). The lack of jobs and high rates of unemployment create major problems for developing nations.
   (3). As a result of the lack of education necessary for a growing number of jobs in modernized societies, people in many developing nations are likely to remain in or retreat to the agricultural sector which already is "hopelessly inefficient."

c. <u>Pressure on human health</u>:
   (1). Life chances of people in poor, overcrowded nations, are very limited.
   (2). Problems include high infant mortality rates and children with low birth weight who, if they survive, may suffer mental retardation.
   (3). People are living longer in developing nations, which do not have the resources to provide for the health care needs of the aged.

d. <u>Pressure on ecologies</u>:
   (1). Fossil fuels and other renewable resources are being depleted
   (2). Rain forests are being destroyed as people search for firewood and farmland.
   (3). Deforestation leads to a reduction of rainfall which, in turn, facilitates soil erosion.
   (4). Soil erosion eventually causes the land to lose the ability to sustain vegetation, and agricultural productivity declines.

e. <u>Pressure on economies</u>:
   (1). Overpopulation is a major factor retarding economic growth in the developing world.
   (2). Demand for products and services is low in societies where the majority of people are poor and/or unemployed.
   (3). Manufacturers can produce only what the domestic population can afford to buy.
   (4). High rates of population growth mean that any increase in economic prosperity is likely to be nullified by the addition of new members to the society.
   (5). Many Third World economies cannot keep up with population growth, and the modernization process has stopped, or even reversed. As a result, millions of people have lost hope of ever improving their economic "lot" in life.

f. <u>Pressure on international security</u>:
   (1). Third World countries could engage in "wars of distribution" against the developing world.
   (2). Terrorist threats and attacks have become all the more possible because of new technology.
   (3). Regional conflicts have erupted in the Third World as poor nations compete with one another for raw materials, markets, and political dominance.
   (4). Young, Third World people residing in poverty with little or no hope of prosperity in their homeland are cognizant of the wealth on the other side of the border -- as is the case

with Mexico and the nations of Central America and their proximity to the U.S. -- and cross the frontier in search of a better life.

g. Pressure on political institutions:
   (1). Overpopulation can be related to problems of food, water, power and housing shortages, as well as high levels of communal violence among rival ethnic groups competing for scarce resources.
   (2). The threat of political unrest and revolution often leads to totalitarian regimes intent on preserving order and maintaining power.

h. Pressure on the international banking system:
   (1). Loans made in the past two decades by banks to Third World nations now have become a major problem because the world economy slid into a serious recession and the price of raw materials produced by developing nations dropped.
   (2). The banking community had little choice but to restructure the loans and to impose "austerity measures" on developing nations, thus making it even harder for these countries to modernize their societies and meet the demands of rapidly-growing populations.

VIII. CRISIS IN AFRICA

A. While population-related problems exist throughout the Third World, they are at their most dangerous level in Africa.
   1. With 661 million people in 1990 and a crude birth rate of 31 per 1,000, Africa has a population doubling time of 24 years.
   2. Because so many people will reach reproductive age in the next generation, the population would continue to increase even if fertility were to drop to replacement level.

B. Along with the problem of runaway population growth, most African economies are in shambles, and environmental and political problems are making the situation even worse:
   1. Nine of the ten countries with the lowest life expectancies in the world are in Africa;
   2. Nine of the ten countries with the highest infant mortality rate are in Africa; and
   3. Six of the ten countries with the lowest literacy rate, and eight of the ten countries with the lowest rate of access to safe water are also in Sub-Saharan Africa.

C. To solve Africa's many problems would require extensive internal and external solutions.

IX. CONTROLLING FERTILITY

A. Controlling fertility is the only acceptable way of reducing the rate of population increases; however, many countries only recently have acknowledged that they have a population problem.

B. Many attempts by governments to control fertility have been controversial.
   1. The Chinese government was successful in reducing Chinese fertility by using a system of rewards and punishments to limit families to only one child.
   2. Some other developing nations have been able to limit fertility through use of less controversial strategies.

214

C.   The theory of demographic transition argues that fertility should drop as a nation industrializes.
D.   If fertility is to be reduced voluntarily, the motivation to have a large family must be lowered:
1.   People in developing countries may have children for financial security -- someone to take care of them in their old age -- or for a variety of social and religious reasons;
2.   Thus, to get people to limit fertility which occurs for these reasons, it is necessary to have economic changes, such as old-age pensions and education which alerts people to the dangers of overpopulation.
E.   New birth control devices like Norplant and Capronor may prove effective in lowering fertility in the poor nations of the world.

X.   THE POLITICS OF FOOD

A.   While as many as 2 percent of the world's people may be starving at one time, the real problem is chronic malnutrition.
1.   At least 25 percent of the Third World population does not have a daily minimal intake of proteins or calories.
2.   Production and distribution of food are variables in why people do not get enough to eat:
a.   Ecological-related causes of food shortages -- including weather conditions, poor soil and soil erosion, and pests -- determine how much food can be produced.
b.   Political and economic variables exist that are not related to how much food is produced, but how it is distributed.

B.   Experts tend to agree that world food shortage is primarily a function of political and economic conditions.
1.   Political and economic decisions made by leaders of developing countries significantly affect both the production and the distribution of food.
2.   Some of the poorest countries in the world do not allocate sufficient monies to feed their rapidly-growing population but spend the money on defense instead.   For example, Ethiopia allocates 42 percent of its annual budget for military purposes.

GLOSSARY OF DIFFICULT-TO-UNDERSTAND WORDS

Page	Line	Col.	Term from Text	Explanation
325	4		secure	acquire, get
325	5		potential	possible, latent
325	6		establishment	organization, place of business
325	8		disposable	remaining after bills and taxes have been paid
326	10		allocation	distribution, assignment
326	13		replete	filled
326	13		utmost	extreme, highest
326	14		necessity	requirement, need
326	15		interdisciplinary	across and between academic disciplines
326	20		crucial	critical, of great importance
326	21		unprecedented	exceptional, having no precedent (an earlier occurrence)
327	4		conceive	to be pregnant

215

GLOSSARY OF DIFFICULT-TO-UNDERSTAND WORDS (CONTINUED)

Page	Line	Col.	Term from Text	Explanation
327	14		contraception	techniques used to prevent pregnancy
327	16		schema	diagram, presentation
327	17		commencement	starting, beginning
328	3		postponed	put off, delayed
328	4		pursued	worked for
328	29		fetus	unborn child
329	10		cohort group	a group within a specific age category
329	21		degenerate	decline in function
329	24		primary	key, most important
329	34		ravaged	destroyed, devastated
329	41		vulnerable	exposed, open to attack
329	44		intravenous	within or entering byu way of the veins
330	18		disposed of	eliminated, thrown away
331	7		jeopardizing	putting in danger, putting at risk
331	18		deficiencies	shortages
331	27		epidemics	diseases which spread through a population
332	1		susceptible	subject, prone, have a tendency
332	1		maternal	mother
332	11		correlates	interrelationships
332	12		random	determined by accident rather than design, casual
332	12		phenomenon	thing
332	16		prestige	reputation, standing or estimation in the eyes of the people
332	34		drastically	severely, to a great degree
333	13		mobility	movement
333	21		magnets	attractions
334	9		desperate	bold, death-defying
335	4		influx	rush in, flow in, pour in
335	5		tremendous	huge, immense
335	8		quotas	numbers, ratios, allowances
336	16		disproportionate	unequal, large difference in
336	22	A	plight	difficulty, condition
336	32	A	discrepancy	difference
336	30	B	deputy chairman	second in command
337	4		surplus	excess, large number
340	3		census	population count
340	27		spurts	quick increase
340	27		nullified	invalidated, of no consequence
340	32		famine	extreme hunger, starvation
340	43		meager	slight, slim
340	43		infusion	introduction
340	44		antibiotics	a substance produced by a microorganism and able to kill another microorganism
340	45		sanitation	hygiene, cleanness
341	27	A	ominous	hopeless
343	5		per annum	for each year
343	19		celibacy	no sex, abstinence
343	29		abortion	expulsion of the human fetus during the first 12 weeks of gestation
343	30		inevitable	certain, sure, unavoidable
344	2		"Parson of Doom"	preacher of fate or judgement

GLOSSARY OF DIFFICULT-TO-UNDERSTAND WORDS (CONTINUED)

Page	Line	Col.	Term from Text	Explanation
345	1		commodity	thing, article
345	30		incipient	starting, commencing, beginning
345	36		irreversible	cannot change
346	6		ramifications	consequence, result
346	30		marital instability	problems in the marriage
347	5		pursuing	seeking, following
347	5		affordable	able to pay for
348	7		slums	densely populated urban areas with crowding, dirt, poverty, and usually a high crime rate
348	7		pavement dwellers	people who live on the sidewalks
348	15		infrastructure	basic framework of the society or government
348	20		adage	saying, statement
348	39		debilitating	weakening, makes someone weak or tired
348	43		circumstances	situations, conditions
349	2		commodity	thing, article
349	8		burgeoning	growing rapidly, flourishing
349	18		deforestation	cutting all the trees and plants in a forest or jungle
349	21		sustain	support, provide for
349	22		ecologist	one who studies the relationship between living things and their environment
349	32		prosperity	wealth
349	39		per capita	with respect to each unit of population
350	6		accommodation	adapting, adjustment
350	9		proliferation	spread, rapid growth
350	26		cognizant	aware
350	36		heterogeneity	mixed, many subcultures and/or ethnic groups
350	38		communal	community, group
350	48		regimes	administration, government
351	26		austerity	control, severe
351	38		ubiquitous	widespread
352	19		tragic	unfortunate, misfortune, sad
352	26		retrogression	reversal in development
352	32		fluctuating	variable, swings
352	41		paltry	inferior, trivial, very small
352	47		squandered	wasted
353	10		boon	benefit
353	12		tantamount	equal to, same as
353	19		campaign	action, crusade
353	25		causality	relation between cause and effect
353	27		egalitarian	equal, removal of unequal access to resources
353	35		sparse	few
353	37		pensions	money paid by the government to the elderly
353	43		abstinence	avoidance, not doing something
354	14		compulsory	required, enforced
354	14		sterilization	to take away the power to bear offspring (children)
354	43		emaciated	waste away physically, very thin people caused by extreme hunger
355	1		malnutrition	inadequate food
355	12		malnourished	not enough food
355	15		albeit	though

Page	Line	Col.	Term from Text	Explanation
356	3		disincentive	deterrent, prevent from taking place
356	37	A	flaunt	parade
356	41	A	virile	being a real man, vigorous, capable of having frequent sexual intercourse
357	24	A	epidemic	disease
357	5	B	campaign	action, crusade
357	8	B	enthusiastic	happy, whole hearted
358	27	A	cultivation	farming
358	28	B	deploy	to spread over the country
359	20	B	dilemma	a choice between equally unsatisfactory alternatives
360	8	B	deficit	shortage
360	12	B	alleviate	relieve, decrease

KEY TERMS TO DEFINE:

After studying the chapter, define each of the following terms. Then check your work by referring to the answers at the end of Chapter 10 in the Study Guide.

fertility	migration
fecundity	push factors
intercourse variables	pull factors
biological clock	internal migration
conception variables	international migration
gestation variables	sex ratio
crude birth rate (CBR)	age/sex or population pyramid
total fertility rate (TFR)	sluburb
crude death rate (CDR)	demographic transition theory
infant mortality rate	doubling time
maternal mortality rate	

KEY PEOPLE

State the major theoretical contribution of each of these people to the study of demography:

Kingsley Davis

Thomas Malthus

Karl Marx

After completing this self-test, check your answers against the "Answer Key" at the end of Chapter 10 in this Study Guide and in the text on the page(s) indicated in parentheses.

MULTIPLE CHOICE QUESTIONS

Select the response which best answers or completes the statement:

1. Demographers in the field of sociology are interested in: (326)
    a. population processes such as fertility, mortality, and migration.
    b. the size and spatial distribution of a population.
    c. the structure and characteristics of a population.
    d. all of the above

2. _____ refers to the number of children born to women in a given population. (327)
    a. Fertility
    b. Fecundity
    c. The crude birth rate
    d. The natural birth rate

3. The upper limits of fecundity when women are physically able to conceive a child is called: (328)
    a. the gestation variable
    b. the biological clock
    c. the conception variable
    d. the fertility factor

4. Which of the following is not one of the three major reasons why people die in any society? (329)
    a. people degenerate
    b. people are killed by communicable disease
    c. people are killed in wars
    d. people are killed by products of the social and economic environment

5. Which of the following statements about the mortality rate in Third World nations is true: (332)
    a. Third World nations may have either lower or higher mortality rates than the developed nations.
    b. Third World nations have been able to significantly lower their infant mortality rates.
    c. Third World nations have been unable to control many communicable diseases.
    d. Third World nations have an aging population, with up to 50 percent of their citizens over 20 years of age.

6. In the United States, mortality rates are higher for: (332)
    a. people who are married as compared with those who are single.
    b. people in high prestige, high stress professions as compared with those in low stress positions such as laborers.
    c. people with lower levels of education and income as compared with those with higher levels of education and income.
    d. people who are white as compared with those who are nonwhite.

7. The statistical average length of time a person in a given population can expect to live is called: (332)
    a. life span
    b. life expectancy
    c. mortality rate
    d. actuarial factor

8. In regard to migration, increased opportunity for employment and better living conditions would be examples of: (333)
    a. opportunity factors
    b. migration motivators
    c. push factors
    d. pull factors

9. According to the U.S. Census Bureau, illegal immigrants who do seasonal work and then return to their country of origin are categorized as: (335-336)
    a. commuters
    b. settlers
    c. sojourners
    d. documented workers

10. A sex ratio of 95.2 means that there are: (336)
    a. 95.2 males per 100 females in the population
    b. 95.2 females per 100 males in the population
    c. 95.2 male babies born per 100 female babies
    d. 95.2 female babies born per 100 males babies

11. The U.S. population is characterized by a _____ fertility rate and a(n) _____ population. (337)
    a. high; aging
    b. low; aging
    c. high; young
    d. low; young

12. The majority of people who migrated in the U.S. in the last decade primarily relocated for: (339)
    a. lower taxes in other countries.
    b. political and social reasons.
    c. better weather conditions.
    d. economic reasons.

13. A sluburb is: (340)
    a. an area of the city previously occupied by businesses but is now used for low-income housing.
    b. a residential area that is part slum and part suburb.
    c. a residential area that is being gentrified by upper-income individuals.
    d. an inner city slum in which homeless people congregate.

14. Which of the following predicted that food supply would not increase sufficiently to keep up with population growth, thus leading to the need for preventive checks on fertility? (343)
    a. Kingsley Davis
    b. Karl Marx
    c. Thomas Malthus
    d. Nathan Keyfitz

15. Karl Marx argued that problems such as poverty resulting from overpopulation were caused by: (344)
    a. natural laws.
    b. unnatural laws.
    c. arithmetic and geometric progressions of food and people.
    d. oppressive, exploitative capitalism.

16. The _____ theory explains population changes in the modern world in terms of three stages. (344-345)
    a. demographic transition
    b. demographic regeneration
    c. Malthusian
    d. doubling time

17. Underpopulation is most likely to occur in: (346)
    a. undeveloped nations
    b. developing nations
    c. Third World nations
    d. industrialized nations

18. According to Kingsley Davis, all of these factors contribute to declining fertility in the U.S., except: (346)
    a. the high divorce rates.
    b. the increasing percentage of married women who are gainfully employed.
    c. the increasing number of husbands who demand that their wives quit their jobs to start families.
    d. the conflicting and time-consuming demands of the "Superwoman" role.

19. While population-related problems exist throughout the Third World, they are at their most dangerous level in: (351)
    a. Mexico
    b. Africa
    c. India
    d. Central America

20. Which of the following countries established a one child per family policy in order to limit fertility? (353)
    a. China
    b. Japan
    c. India
    d. Canada

21. The world's food shortage is related to: (355-356)
    a. bad weather conditions
    b. poor soil and soil erosion
    c. political and economic variables
    d. all of the above

22. Some of the poorest countries in the world allocate large portions of their annual budgets for: (355)
    a. agriculture
    b. military expenditures
    c. health care
    d. imported food

221

TRUE-FALSE QUESTIONS

T   F   1. Fertility is the physical ability of women to conceive and bear children. (327)

T   F   2. Birth control pills are the most frequently used form of birth control. (328)

T   F   3. The crude birth rate is the number of births per year for every 1,000 members of the population. (328)

T   F   4. Degenerative diseases accounted for 68 percent of all deaths in the U.S. in 1982. (329)

T   F   5. Deaths relating to industrial pollution typically are limited to the rich, First World nations. (330)

T   F   6. Communicable diseases have been effectively controlled in much of the Third World. (331)

T   F   7. In developed nations the maternal mortality rate is extremely low, while in poor countries deaths during childbirth are still common. (331-332)

T   F   8. The Japanese as a group can expect to live almost twice as long as people in Ethiopia. (332)

T   F   9. Research indicates that even in developed countries human beings may be reaching the upper limits of average life expectancy, about 85 years. (332)

T   F   10. In the last 25 years in the U.S., the most significant movement of people has been from the sunbelt to the frostbelt. (333)

T   F   11. Throughout history, all migration to the United States has been voluntary. (335)

T   F   12. Most social scientists agree that illegal aliens have taken thousands of jobs from U.S. citizens. (336)

T   F   13. Age/sex pyramids of Japan and the U.S. illustrate populations that are aging and have a slow rate of growth. (337)

T   F   14. Thomas Malthus predicted that if people did not utilize preventive checks to control their fertility, positive checks would occur. (343)

T   F   15. Malthus believed that preventive checks included the use of all of the following: contraception, abortion, delayed marriage, and/or celibacy. (343)

T   F   16. Stage Two of the demographic transition occurred as a result of the Industrial Revolution. (345)

T   F   17. Many developing nations are "stuck" in Stage Two of the demographic transition. (345)

T   F   18. Third World cities are growing rapidly because of natural increases and rural-to-urban migration. (347)

T   F   19. According to the text, the threat of nuclear war in developing nations is the biggest danger to international security in First World countries. (350)

T   F   20. At least 25 percent of the Third World population does not have a daily minimal intake of proteins or calories. (354-356)

FILL-IN QUESTIONS

Fill in the blank with the word or phrase that best completes the statement.

1.   _____ is the scientific study of population. (325)

2.   The number of children born to women in a given population is _____ while the physical ability of women to conceive and bear children is _____. (327)

3.   _____ variables refer to the commencement of and frequency of sexual activity over a given period of time. _____ variables are those factors that determine if a woman will become pregnant or not. _____ variables are those factors that determine if a fetus will come to term resulting in a live birth. (327-328)

4.   The _____ _____ rate is a measure of completed fertility, or the total number of children born per 1,000 women. (329)

5.   The infant mortality rate is the number of deaths during the first year of life per _____ live births. The maternal mortality rate is a measure of the number of women who die per _____ live births. (331)

6.   _____ factors serve to drive off or send a stream of migrants from a particular locale. _____ factors serve as a socioeconomic magnet and draw migrants to a given geographic area. (333)

7.   Movement of people within a political state is referred to as _____ migration. Movement of people across political states is called _____ migration. (333-334)

8.   The _____ ratio is the number of males per 100 females in the population. (336)

9.   Thomas Malthus argued that food supply increased _____, while population increased _____. (343)

10. According to the theory of demographic transition, fertility should drop as a nation _____. (353)

ESSAY QUESTIONS

1.   Define demography and explain some of its major uses in the social sciences, business, and government.

2.   Discuss the relationship of fertility, mortality, and migration in population growth or decline.

3.   Compare and contrast the population composition of the United States and other First World countries with those of developing nations in the Third World.

4.   Outline the major problems created by overpopulation pressures on cities, societies, human health, ecologies, economies, international security, political institutions, and the international banking system.

5.   Explain why the "politics of food" includes both the production and the distribution of food.

DEFINITION OF KEY TERMS:

fertility: the number of children born to women in a given population.

fecundity: the physical ability of women to conceive and bear children.

intercourse variables: the commencement of and frequency of sexual activity over a given period of time.

biological clock: the upper limits of fecundity (approximately 45 years of age) when women are physically able to conceive a child.

conception variables: factors that determine if a woman will become pregnant or not (such as the use of contraceptives).

gestation variables: factors that determine if a fetus will come to term resulting in a live birth (such as miscarriage and stillbirth, or induced abortion).

crude birth rate (CBR): the number of births per year for every 1,000 members of the population.

total fertility rate (TFR): the measure of completed fertility, or the total number of children born per 1,000 women.

crude death rate (CDR): the number of deaths per year for every 1,000 members of the population.

infant mortality rate: the number of deaths during the first year of life per 1,000 live births.

maternal mortality rate: the number of women who die per 10,000 live births.

migration: the relatively permanent movement of people from one place to another.

push factors: serve to drive off or send a stream of migrants from a particular locale (such as little economic opportunity; racial, religious, and political persecution; etc.).

pull factors: serve as a socioeconomic magnet and draw migrants to a given geographical location (such as increased opportunity for employment or better living conditions).

internal migration: the movement of people within a political state.

international migration: the movement of people across political states.

sex ratio: the number of males per 100 females in a given population.

age/sex or population pyramid: a device for summarizing the age and sex characteristics of a given society by five-year cohorts or groups.

sluburb: a residential area which is part slum and part suburb.

demographic transition theory: the perspective that explains population changes in the modern world.   The theory divides this change into three stages: (1) Stage One (high growth potential) has high rates of birth and death, and slow population growth; (2) Stage Two (transitional growth) has a high birth rate and a low death rate resulting in explosive population growth; and (3) Stage Three (incipient decline) has both low fertility and mortality, and, therefore, slow population growth.

doubling time: the number of years it takes a given population to double in size.

KEY PEOPLE:

Kingsley Davis analyzed social factors which he believed had a powerful influence on fertility.   He argued that such factors as high divorce rates, women entering the labor force in increasing numbers, the employment of married women, and the need of "Superwomen" to juggle their multiple roles all contributed to lower levels of fertility in industrialized countries.

Thomas Malthus (1766-1834), an English economist and clergyman, predicted that human populations would outstrip "carrying capacity," the point at which the environment could no longer sustain the population.   He believed that when this point was reached, there would be positive checks -- such as disease, war, and vice -- on population. The only way to avoid the problem was to utilize preventive checks to control fertility.   The only acceptable preventive checks to Malthus were delaying marriage and/or moral restraint (celibacy).

Karl Marx   was a critic of the Malthusian theory.   Marx thought that problems like poverty resulting from overpopulation were not the result of any natural laws (arithmetic and geometric progressions of food and people), but were the result of an oppressive, exploitative capitalist system.   Thus, the solution was not "moral restraint" but socialism, an economic system that would outproduce capitalism and insure an equitable distribution of food, material goods and services.

ANSWERS TO MULTIPLE CHOICE QUESTIONS:

1.   d   Demographers in the field of sociology are interested in population processes such as fertility, mortality, and migration; the size and spatial distribution of a population; and the structure and characteristics of a population. Response "d" -- all of the above -- is correct. (326)

2.   a   Fertility refers to the number of children born to women in a given population.   Fecundity is the physical ability of women to conceive and bear children.   The crude birth rate is the number of births per year for every 1,000 members of the population.   The natural birth rate is not a concept used by demographers. (327)

3.   b   The upper limits of fecundity when women are physically able to conceive a child is called the biological clock. (328)

4.   c   The text does not indicate that people being killed in wars is one of the three major reasons why people die.   The text does mention all of the other responses: they degenerate, they are killed by communicable diseases, and they are killed by products of the social and economic environment. (329)

5.   a   Only response "a" is correct about the mortality rate in Third World nations: Third World nations may have either lower or higher mortality rates than developed nations.   The other responses are incorrect.   Third World nations have been unable to significantly lower their infant mortality rates, but a number of the nations have been able to control many

communicable diseases. Third World nations do not have aging populations; they have very young populations with up to 50 percent of their citizens below 15 years of age. (332)

6.   c   In the United States, mortality rates are higher for people with lower levels of education and income as compared with those with higher levels of education and income. Response "a" is incorrect because people who are single have higher mortality rates than those who are married. Response "b" is incorrect because people in low prestige jobs, such as laborers, have a higher mortality rate than people in prestigious professions. Response "d" is incorrect because nonwhite people have higher mortality rates than white people. (332)

7.   b   The statistical average length of time a person in a given population can expect to live is called life expectancy. (332)

8.   d   Increased opportunity for employment or better living conditions are examples of the pull factors of migration. (333)

9.   c   The U.S. Census Bureau refers to illegal immigrants who do seasonal work and then return to their country of origin as sojourners. Response "a" -- commuters -- cross the border on a daily basis. Response "b" -- settlers -- arrive on a more or less permanent basis. Response "d" is not a term used by the Census Bureau. If anything, the illegal immigrants would be referred to as "undocumented workers." (335-336)

10.   a   A sex ratio of 95.2 means that there are 95.2 males per 100 females in the population. The sex ratio is the number of males per 100 females in a given population. (336)

11.   b   The U.S. population is characterized by a low fertility rate and an aging population. (337)

12.   d   The majority of people who migrated in the U.S. in the last decade primarily relocated for economic reasons. (16) Response "a" is incorrect because most of the moves were internal, not international, migration. Although some may have moved for political and social reasons or for better weather conditions, the text indicates that the majority were leaving areas that were economically depressed and moving to areas in which they hoped to find economic opportunity. (339)

13.   b   A sluburb is a residential area that is part slum and part suburb. (340)

14.   c   Thomas Malthus predicted that food supply would not increase sufficiently to keep up with population growth, thus leading to the need for preventive checks on fertility. (343)

15.   d   Karl Marx argued that problems like poverty resulting from overpopulation were caused by oppressive, exploitative capitalism. (344)

16.   a   The demographic transition theory explains population changes in the modern world in terms of three stages. (344-345)

17.   d   Underpopulation is most likely to occur in industrialized nations. (346)

18.   c   Kingsley Davis discussed all of the factors listed except "the increasing number of husbands who demand that their wives quit their jobs to start families." He noted that when two working people marry, the husband is in no position to demand that his wife quit her job. (346)

19.   b   Population-related problems are at their most dangerous level in Africa because that nation has a population doubling time of 24 years. Many of the economies on that continent are in shambles, and environmental and political problems are making the situation even worse. The problems are confounded by the presence of AIDS in some African nations. (351)

20.   a   China established a one child per family policy in order to limit fertility. (353)

21.   d   The world's food shortage is related to bad weather conditions, poor soil and soil erosion, and political and economic variables, thus making response "d" -- all of the above -- correct. (355-356)

22.   b   Some of the poorest countries in the world allocate large portions of their annual budgets for military expenditures. (355)

1.   False -- Fertility refers to the number of children born to women in a given population. Fecundity is the physical ability of women to conceive and bear children. (327)
2.   False -- Abortion is the most frequently used form of birth control. (328)
3.   True (328)
4.   True (329)
5.   False -- Deaths relating to industrial pollution are found in Third World, as well as First World, nations. (330)
6.   True (331)
7.   True (331-332)
8.   True (332)
9.   True (332)
10.   False -- The most significant movement of people in the U.S. has been from the frostbelt to the sunbelt. (333)
11.   False -- Although most migration to the U.S. has been voluntary, slavery was not a voluntary process. (335)
12.   False -- Social scientists disagree about the impact of illegal aliens in the U.S. Some believe these individuals have helped the economy and others believe they have harmed the economy and U.S. citizens. (336)
13.   True (337)
14.   True (343)
15.   False -- Malthus believed that the only acceptable preventive checks on fertility were delayed marriage and/or celibacy. (343)
16.   True (345)
17.   True (345)
18.   True (347)
19.   False -- Although the threat of nuclear war is an ever present danger, the "Aspiration Bomb" may prove to be the biggest threat facing the developed world. This bomb is made up of young, Third World people residing in poverty with little or no hope of prosperity in their homeland. Living close to affluent nations, these individuals are cognizant of the riches that lie on the other side of the border, and cross the frontier in search of a better life. (350)
20.   True (354-356)

1.   Demography (325)
2.   Fertility; fecundity (327)
3.   Intercourse; conception; gestation (327-328)
4.   Total fertility (329)
5.   1,000; 10,000 (331)
6.   Push; pull (333)
7.   Internal; international (333-334)
8.   Sex (336)
9.   Arithmetically; geometrically (343)
10.   Industrializes (353)

CHAPTER ELEVEN

URBANIZATION

Chapter 11 begins with a discussion of the historical development of cities. The relationship between urbanization and industrialization is explored. Three theories -- the concentric zone model, the sector model, and the multiple nuclei model -- developed by human ecologists to explain the relationship between humans and cities are presented. The chapter examines the processes of suburbanization, gentrification, and exurbanization. Next, the growth of sunbelt cities and the decline of winter cities in the United States are analyzed. Different perspectives on why large numbers of people left urban areas and moved to rural and semi-rural towns also are analyzed. American cities are beset with a wide range of serious problems: (1) cities have the largest concentration of poor people in the country; (2) cities have high rates of unemployment and poverty as a result of the flight of business and industry to the suburbs and the sunbelt, and (3) inner city residents often lack education and technical skills necessary for employment. Finally, the chapter presents the problems faced by desperately poor Third World cities with unprecedented rates of population growth.

LEARNING OBJECTIVES:

As you read Chapter 11, use these learning objectives to organize your notes. After completing your reading, briefly state an answer to each of the objectives, and review the text pages in parentheses.

1. Discuss the historical development of cities. Indicate when and under what circumstances human beings first lived in permanent settlements. (365-366)

2. Analyze the relationship between urbanization and industrialization. (366-368)

3. Outline the three major theories of the human ecology school and state the major criticism of each of the models. (368-370)

4. Explain the processes of suburbanization, gentrification, and exurbanization in the United States. (371-374)

5. Describe the rise of sunbelt cities and the decline of frostbelt cities over the past 25 years. (374-379)

6. Compare the composition of large urban areas with those of smaller towns and villages, and explain how social theorists have viewed the rural/urban (Gemeinschaft/Gesellschaft) dichotomy. (380-382)

7. Discuss the major problems facing cities in the United States. (383-392)

8. Identify the problems associated with urban explosion in developing nations. (386-392)

<u>OUTLINE</u>

I.   INTRODUCTION

    A.   Currently the world's great urban centers are breeding grounds for a long and growing list of social and environmental problems. Nowhere is the unequal distribution of wealth and life chances more evident than in the cities.

    B.   Problems in the urban United States express larger patterns of gender and racial inequality, poverty, and political dominance and corruption.

    C.   Cities in the developing world face even greater challenges than those in wealthy, industrial nations because Third World nations do not have the economic resources necessary to solve the tremendous problems associated with burgeoning urban populations.

II. EARLY CITIES

    A.   The first permanent human settlements appeared about 8,000 B.C. There are three principle explanations of how cities emerged:
        1.   The <u>agricultural surplus theory</u> states that cities came into being as a result of a surplus of basic foodstuffs that allowed some people to develop occupations outside of agriculture.
        2.   The <u>central place theory</u> asserts that cities emerged because farmers needed a central market to exchange and distribute their produce.
        3.   The <u>trading theory</u> states that specialists were responsible for producing the surplus food vital for the growth of cities.
            a.   Traders introduced new seeds and livestock that resulted in improved crops and a successful agricultural revolution.
            b.   This revolution in turn permitted people to develop occupations other than farming.

    B.   The importance of cities in the evolution of human societies cannot be overstated:
        1.   As cities developed, the division of labor became more complex as specialists in war, religion, politics, trade, art, and an assortment of crafts emerged.
            a.   This increased the types and forms of human interaction.
            b.   Human existence no longer revolved around hunting and gathering.
        2.   Stratification of society occurred as a result of the occupational specialization which developed in cities.

III. PRE-INDUSTRIAL CITIES

    A.   By the beginning of the modern era and the birth of Christ, cities located on trade routes and important waterways were thriving in many parts of the world.

    B.   Some of these cities had large populations even by today's standards.
        1.   In the second century A.D. Rome had approximately one million people.
        2.   After a long period of decline known as the Dark Ages, cities once again prospered in Europe during the Renaissance.
        3.   Cities prospered as a result of the Industrial Revolution and, in turn, the "industrial urbanization" of Europe was possible because of the cities.

IV. CITIES IN THE MODERN WORLD

   A. The Industrial Revolution significantly changed the size, structure, and composition of cities in the United States and Europe:
      1. People flowed into urban areas from the countryside.
      2. They typically lived in hastily built, overcrowded, unsanitary apartments.

   B. In the United States, problems in the cities were exacerbated by the arrival of large numbers of immigrants from Poland, Germany, Italy, and Ireland in the middle of the nineteenth century:
      1. They crowded together in the slums of the city.
      2. Political corruption and incompetence were rampant.
      3. However, many people prospered in spite of the problems.

   C. Over the past 100 years the world has become increasingly urban.
      1. The proportion of people living in cities in developed nations is greater than in urban areas in less developed nations.
      2. Cities in developing nations have been growing at an incredible rate and have a doubling time of less than 20 years.

V. HUMAN ECOLOGY AND THE CITY

   A. Human ecology is the area of sociology concerned with the study of the spatial distribution and aspects of human life.

   B. Human ecologists constructed three major theories which attempt to explain the relationship between humans and cities:
      1. The concentric zone model views the city as a series of zones emanating from the center, with each zone characterized by a different group of people and activity.
         a. This model assumes that cities have one center and are comprised of a heterogeneous population.
         b. Expansion occurred through the process of invasion and succession when newly-arrived immigrants settled in the "zone of transition" (invasion), and they took the place of those more upwardly-mobile residents who were moving to the next zone (succession).
         c. This theory has been criticized for being simplistic, over generalized, and inaccurate; however, it still is considered to be a classical theory of urban development.
      2. The sector model sees urban zones as wedge-shaped sectors radiating out from the center, or Central Business District (the major shopping and commercial area of a city).
         a. The sector model has the advantage of taking into account the existence of hills, mountain ridges, and rivers that exist in so many cities as well as the significance of shipping and transportation lines.
         b. However, this model has been criticized for placing too much emphasis on the role of the upper classes in determining spatial organization and neglects the part played by other socioeconomic groups in the distribution of city space.
      3. The multiple nuclei model views the city as comprised of multiple centers or nuclei.
         a. In some cases these nuclei have existed since the origin of the city, while in other instances, the nuclei increased as the city grew and diversified.

230

b. This model has been criticized because most cities really have only one center, the other nuclei are merely sub-centers.

VI. FROM JAMESTOWN TO MANHATTAN AND BACK

A. The settlement of Jamestown, Virginia, by the British in 1607 was the initial step leading to the eventual urbanization of the U.S.
1. By the end of the 17th century, New York, Boston, and Philadelphia were relatively small, prosperous cities.
2. Until the early 1800s, most U.S. cities were free of congested areas and serious social problems.

B. The Civil War was a landmark period in the evolution of American cities:
1. Prior to the war, most cities were commercial centers.
2. After the war and with the shift toward manufacturing, the U.S. entered the Industrial Age and the urban population rose dramatically.

C. Suburbanization initially was a direct result of the prosperity and technological advancements of the 1920s.
1. Automobile ownership provided access to outlying areas.
2. Affordable tract homes made this exodus from cities possible.
3. Suburban growth rates slowed dramatically from the Great Depression in the 1930s to the end of World War II, at which point in time suburbanization of the country resumed.
    a. Construction of relatively low-cost tract housing and the availability of federally-insured loans opened up the suburbs to working-class families.
    b. Housing discrimination and lack of buying power kept blacks out of the suburbs until the 1970s.
4. Suburbanization of the U.S. since 1945 is an example of the process of "invasion" and "succession" based on the concentric-zone model.

D. Gentrification and Exurbanization
1. Gentrification is the return of middle and upper-class people to deteriorating central city neighborhoods for the purpose of buying run down apartments and homes and converting them into expensive, fashionable dwellings.
    a. Gentrification helps raise the urban tax base and preserve buildings that would otherwise be vandalized and/or torn down.
    b. However, the poor who previously lived in these areas are displaced by upscale shops and boutiques, as well as housing they cannot afford.
2. Exurbanization is the movement of people to towns beyond the ring of big city suburbs. This process has been referred to as the "suburbanization of the suburbs."

VII. SUNBELT CITIES

A. In the early 1970s the sunbelt began to grow for at least five reasons:
1. Wage rates -- conservative legislation and illegal workers from Mexico and Central America kept the cost of labor down, making the region attractive to business.
2. Avoiding unionization -- industries began leaving the northeast to escape the relatively high cost of union labor in that region.
3. Tax incentives -- local governments started subsidizing new industries by giving them generous tax breaks.

4.   Federal expenditure patterns -- influential sunbelt politicians were successful in winning big military contracts and physical improvements such as highway projects from the federal government.
5.   Changing structure of the economy -- the region benefited as the economy changed from heavy industry and manufacturing to high technology and information processing.

B.   The growth of sunbelt cities is not limited to monetary concerns only:
1.   Warm weather is important to people with more leisure time.
2.   Some individuals assume they are leaving behind crime, pollution, and congestion of old industrial cities.

C.   Problems in sunbelt cities:
1.   Crime is on the rise.
2.   Levels of pollution and traffic congestion are on the rise.
3.   Not everyone has shared in the economic prosperity of the sunbelt; Sunbelt poverty has been fostered by low wages in the region.
4.   Oil revenues have dried up.
5.   The most serious problem is the lack of water.

VIII. WINTER CITIES

A.   According to one interpretation, the success of sunbelt cities and the corresponding decline of winter cities is a temporary rather than permanent shift in the U.S. economy. Eventually the economic fortunes of these areas will converge and even out.

B.   Another point of view is that economic development is always uneven with each region of the country developing in a different manner.
1.   The U.S. is now in a period of growth that favors the sunbelt because of the move into the post-industrial era which emphasizes high-technology and light industry.
2.   If the winter cities are to be successful again, they will have to cultivate new economic activities.

C.   Winter cities now face global competition from Japan, Germany, and a number of rapidly-developing Third World nations, as well as from sunbelt cities.

IX.   THE METROPOLITAN TRANSITION

A.   Not only did people move from winter states to sunbelt cities, thousands of others left urban areas and moved to rural and semi-rural towns.

B.   Sociologist Fred Williams offers explanations for this migration pattern:
1.   Period explanation -- the slowdown and reversal of urban growth that began in the 1970s is a unique and, therefore, temporary distortion of ongoing metropolitan expansion resulting from the convergence of economic and demographic factors.
2.   Regional restructuring -- the deindustrialization of the 1970s that hit the winter cities is a component of a new geography of urban growth.   Cities will expand in different geographic regions of the country for reasons unrelated to past growth.
3.   The deconcentration explanation -- the slow down and reversal of population growth in many of the country's largest cities is a fundamental break with past trends.   Most people are deciding to live in smaller cities and semi-rural areas.

232

X. URBAN COMPOSITION AND LIFESTYLE
   A. Cities are not only larger than towns and villages but differ in their composition in at least three dimensions:
      1. Urban residents typically are younger than non-urban persons, and urban residents are less likely to be married than their rural counterparts of the same age.
      2. As city size increases, the number of racial, ethnic, and religious minorities increases because minority group members are attracted to, and usually concentrated in cities.
      3. The larger the community the higher the mean educational, occupational and income levels of the population.

   B. Early Theorists
      1. Georg Simmel (1858-1918) argued that life in the city forced people to selectively respond to the almost overwhelming amount of stimuli they are bombarded with in a rapidly changing, culturally-diverse environment.
         a. Because of this overstimulation, people interact with one another on a more superficial level.
         b. The result is a nation of detached, self-serving urban residents.
      2. Louis Wirth (1857-1952) noted that the greater size, heterogeneity, and density of city life led to numerous, impersonal, "secondary" type relations as opposed to "primary" -- warm, intimate, personal -- contacts.
         a. Having fewer primary relations leads to a variety of individual maladies including anomie, alienation, and psychological stress.
         b. These individual problems, in turn, are responsible for urban problems such as crime, alcoholism, drug abuse, broken families, and mental illness.
      3. This anti-urban bias, coupled with a nostalgia for unspoiled rural life, has a long tradition in American thought.
         a. It appears that small towns and rural areas have been romanticized by many people.
         b. The rural/urban (Gemeinschaft/Gesellschaft) typology is at best only partially true: urban residents often live in "ethnic enclaves" or are bound together by some common trait or interest with which they can create a "quasi-Gemeinschaft" community.

   C. Contemporary Theorists
      1. Contemporary urban investigations have observed patterns of interaction on city streets:
         a. Dabbs and Stokes observed that pedestrians give more room to people who are beautiful, because "beautiful people" have social power.
         b. William Whyte's research on pedestrians -- especially those from different countries -- led him to the conclusion that large cities may have a homogenizing or leveling affect on certain aspects of people's lives.
      2. Herbert Gans constructed a typology of inner city residents:
         a. Cosmopolites are intellectuals and professionals as well as students, writers, and artists who live in the inner city to be near special cultural facilities.
         b. The unmarried or childless are made up of two subgroups, those who move to the outer city when they can afford to, and those permanent, low-income individuals who live in this "zone of transition" for the rest of their lives.

       c.   Ethnic villagers are those people residing in quasi-Gemeinschaft neighborhoods who successfully isolate themselves from the anonymity of big city life, and find a good deal of satisfaction in intra-ethnic primary group relations.

       d.   The deprived, and the trapped and downwardly mobile are the very poor, emotionally disturbed and handicapped residents of the city. This primarily non-white population makes up the growing underclass in urban America.

   3.   William Whyte examined a group of trapped and downwardly mobile city dwellers, street people:

       a.   Shopping bag ladies are the toughest, hardiest individuals among the street people.

          (1).   Many of them come from middle-class backgrounds and some are well educated.

          (2).   They have no ties to social service agencies, are totally outside the system, and have no desire to be reintegrated into normal patterns of life.

       b.   Beggars range from professional blind beggars to "Bowery bums" who lack the skills to be gainfully employed.

       c.   Three-card monte dealers often work with a "shill" (a companion in on the fix) and typically let people win a few bets so they will increase their wagers, and the dealer ultimately can win.

   4.   Conflict theorists believe that street people are victims of a capitalist society that cannot provide employment for those who want to work and that refuses to finance social support systems to care for those individuals who are unable to work.

       a.   For example, the deinstitutionalization of patients who were in mental hospitals;

       b.   Lacking basic interaction skills and having few possibilities for employment, these individuals often roam the streets in a frightened and confused state of mind.

XI.   URBAN PROBLEMS

  A.   Urban Poverty

     1.   Although there is more rural than urban poverty, people living in urban ghettos make up the largest concentration of poor in the United States.

       a.   This is especially true in winter cities.

       b.   In 1987, 32 million people in the U.S. lived in poverty.

          (1)   About 1/3 were elderly or disabled;

          (2).   Another 1/3 were temporarily poor because of personal misfortune; and

          (3).   The final 1/3 were chronically poor, although able-bodied: this group makes up the nation's underclass.

     2.   In the past 20 years the number of desperately poor people -- especially African Americans -- living in cities has increased tremendously.

       a.   By 1980 approximately 38 percent of all poor black people in the nation's 10 largest cities lived in census tracts classified as "extreme-poverty" areas.

       b.   A decade earlier, this figure was 22 percent instead of 38 percent.

     3.   John Dilulio argues that "the truly disadvantaged" (urban underclass) exist mainly because they are consistently victimized by "the truly deviant" -- a large number of predatory street criminals.

4. Crime is not the only cause of chronic poverty: loss of manufacturing jobs in U.S. cities has created high rates of unemployment.
5. Bernard Friedan asserts that even when jobs are available in central cities, poor people have difficulty finding employment:
   a. Many jobs are filled by word of mouth, and poor people do not have friends or relatives employed where they might find out about jobs for which they are qualified.
   b. Inner city residents often lack the education necessary for even relatively low paying entry level jobs.
   c. Many poor people (especially single women with children) are not looking for work because they cannot find and/or afford day care for their children and have given up hope of finding jobs.

B. The Homeless
   1. Poverty and the deinstitutionalization policies of psychiatric facilities have produced a large number of homeless people.
      a. One study found that 29% of the homeless are mentally ill and that a significant number of people without shelter are Vietnam veterans.
      b. Other studies indicate that between 25 and 45 percent of homeless individuals are alcoholics.
   2. The homeless have become a more diverse population:
      a. At the beginning of the 1980s, they were mostly single men and women; however, a significant number now are intact families and women with children.
      b. Some of the homeless have employment; some are graduates of vocational schools or universities.

C. What Causes Poverty?
   1. Some writers argue that the poor have no one to blame for their problems but themselves:
      a. According to Edward Banfield, the poor cause their own problems because they are lazy, dirty, apathetic, etc. and their only interests in life are sex and a good time.
      b. Banfield argues that the poor possess a distinct set of values, attitudes and patterns of behavior that makes economic success next to impossible and, as a result, the poor live in a self-perpetuating "culture of poverty."
   2. Other explanations are based on the idea that inner city poverty is a function of "domestic colonialism."
      a. Based on a Marxist view, Savitch argues that the inner cities were systematically exploited by the bourgeoisie in the same way that African and Asian countries were exploited by the colonial powers beginning in the 19th century.
         (1). Savitch argues that suburbanites drive to work each day, use the cities' resources -- such as water, power, streets, police, etc. -- and then drive back home in the evening while the poor foot their bill.
         (2). According to this perspective, the minority work force in the inner city is exploited by the wealthy and paid low wages. When the labor force in winter cities demanded higher wages, the capitalist class moved their factories to the sunbelt and found a new class of workers to exploit.
      b. Sternlieb rejects this interpretation, arguing that it is not exploitation, but indifference and abandonment that brought bad economic times to inner cities.

3. Still other researchers state that the deplorable conditions in which inner city residents live will not improve until those in power begin looking at the urban underclass from a different perspective.
   a. Wacquant and Wilson note that conservative political ideology has defined the problems of ghetto dwellers in "individualistic and moral terms."
   b. This individualistic perspective ignores the ways in which structural changes in the society, economy, and state have caused wholesale urban poverty.
   c. Politicians need to look at the problem using what C. Wright Mills called the "sociological imagination" -- the ability to recognize that maladies such as poverty which afflict a significant number of people cannot be explained at the individual level of analysis ("the unemployed are sick, lame, lazy, etc."), but rather that these problems are rooted in the social structure of society, which much change in order to resolve those problems.

XII. URBAN EXPLOSION IN DEVELOPING NATIONS

A. The process of modernization in the Third World is being accompanied by high rates of urban growth.
   1. Many Third World nations such as Mexico, Bangladesh, and Egypt have primate cities -- one giant metropolitan area at least twice as big as the nation's second largest city -- that serve as the country's economic, political, and cultural center.
      a. Some observers believe that primate cities are good for a nation's urban development because they believe a "trickle down" effect occurs which benefits the entire nation.
      b. This is disputed by others who believe the concentration of resources in primate cities slows down the development of other urban areas.
   2. Rapid population growth in Third World cities is the result of two factors:
      a. Natural increase (births over deaths), and the overall high rate of population increase in developing nations.
      b. Rural-to-urban migration may account for up to 75 percent of urban growth in poor countries.

B. "Hell is a city," according to Paul Harrison, in his book Inside the Third World
   1. Urban slums in developing nations are densely-packed areas of human misery and suffering. The lack of housing is the most serious problem, as these examples demonstrate:
      a. In India's four largest metropolitan areas approximately 1/4 to 1/3 of the population lives in dwellings considered unfit for human habitation.
      b. In Mexico City over 400,000 migrants per year end up in central city slums or squatter settlements called los villas miserias -- "cities of the miserable" -- and 42% of Mexico City's residents lived in slums in 1990.
      c. The poorest 25% of the population in most African and low-income Asian countries cannot afford the least expensive permanent housing.

2. Children <u>suffer</u> <u>disproportionately</u> in many Third World cities:
    a. Many are abandoned by their parents who are too poor to house, feed and clothe them.
    b. Children roam the streets, often travel in packs, and do anything they can to survive:
        (1). In Bogota, Columbia, gangs of 10-25 members armed with knives and razors steal what they can and fight with each other and the police.
        (2). In Brazil, there are as many as 20 million abandoned children.
        (3). In India, tens of thousands of children beg in the streets.
3. The potential for collective <u>violence</u> is the greatest political threat:
    a. When the masses begin comparing themselves to their more affluent urban neighbors, they often demand a share of the wealth.
    b. In Africa and Asia, a disproportionate number of migrants are young (between 15-30), single males with a higher-than-average education (than non-migrants) who are cut off from the stabilizing influence of family and friends, and these individuals are the most likely to engage in urban violence.
4. A growing number of Third World cities are powder kegs just waiting to explode.

GLOSSARY OF DIFFICULT-TO-UNDERSTAND WORDS

Page	Line	Col.	Term from Text	Explanation
363	6		grandiose	splendid, grand, ambitious
363	14		social conscience	sensitive regard for fairness or justice
364	4		diversity	differences, variety
364	8		inasmuch	since
364	14		burgeoning	exploding, rapidly growing
364	15		ominous	threatening
365	6		deplete	use up, consume
365	6		heretofore	up to this time
365	14		surplus	excess, over supply
365	17		clustering	grouping
365	30		assortment	variety
365	32		hierarchical	arranged by ranks by authority
366	10		hydrants	a pipe from which water may be drawn to run over or around an object such as a dam
366	15		spillways	to run over or around an object such as a dam
366	19		dwindled	became smaller
366	21		stagnation	standing still, no development
366	27		culminated	climaxed
367	1		squalor	dirt and poverty
367	7		disrupted	broken down
367	14		rampant	widespread
368	39		emanating	emerging, coming out
369	5		tenements	apartments with minimum standards of sanitation, safety, comfort, and occupied by poor families
370	18		spatial	relating to space
370	31		neglects	disregards, overlooks, omits

GLOSSARY OF DIFFICULT-TO-UNDERSTAND WORDS (CONTINUED)

Page	Line	Col.	Term from Text	Explanation
370	36		discrete	separate
370	37		diversified	producing variety
371	7		congested	high density, concentrated in a small space, crowded
371	22		catapulted	thrown, launched
371	29		decentralization	movement from urban center to outlying areas
371	34		affordable	able to pay for
372	23		deteriorated	decayed, degraded
376	1		inasmuch	since
376	5		unionization	the act of becoming a member of a labor union (collective action in the workplace)
376	12		incentives	motivations, drives
376	16		subsidy	aid, payment
377	12		postindustrial	after industrialization
378	23		frostbelt	areas in the north and midwest which receive frost in the wintertime
378	23		bastards	those who are inferior
378	23		taunting	insult, sarcastic challenge
378	37		heyday	period of greatest prosperity
378	41		convergence	coming together, uniting
378	45		revitalize	give new life to
379	14		flourish	succeed, prosper, thrive
379	18		innovative	creative
379	26		envisioned	saw in the future, imagined
379	34		viability	development
380	27		stagnation	standing still, not moving
381	9		heterogeneity	mixed groups of people--socially, economically, and ethnic background
381	19		sentiment	feeling, judgment, opinion
381	19		nostalgic	homesickness, looking back to a time that probably never existed
381	22		alienating	turn against, hostile
381	47		deferring	submitting, yielding
382	14		intellectuals	rational thinkers, wisdom
382	30		disheveled	untidy
383	9		affliction	trouble
383	11		ghettos	high density, low income, high poverty areas of the city, usually populated by minority groups
383	21		tremendously	immensely, extreme size
384	12		deinstitionalization	to remove the status of an institution, closing down
386	10		maladies	unwholesome condition
386	27		referendum	vote
386	35		astonishing	surprising
387	11		impeded	hindrance, interfered with
388	32	A	dustbins	trash cans
388	18	B	unwittingly	not knowingly, unaware
388	36	B	dismantled	taken apart, taken to pieces
389	7	A	meager	small, insufficient
389	10	A	scavenging	salvaging usable material from trash cans
389	10	A	prostitution	selling sex for money

389	11	B	shrewdest	sharpest, most clever
390	2		unabated	full force
390	4		catastrophic	disaster, utter failure
390	16		melancholia	extreme depression
390	17		malodorous	not smelling well, ill-smelling
391	19		slums	crowded, dirty, run-down housing, and poverty found in the inner city
391	36		thugs	criminals
392	19		commensurate	equal
392	29	B	conquistadors	Spanish explorers and conquerors in the 16th century
392	32	B	ubiquitous	widespread, constantly encountered
392	41	B	protracted	drawn out
393	11	A	deteriorating	becoming worse
393	15	A	influx	flowing in
394	3	A	mind boggling	too much to think about, overwhelming
394	8	A	uninhabitable	cannot be occupied or lived in
394	21	A	summoned	called
394	26	A	resettlement	take up residence again
394	29	A	formidable	overwhelming, overpowering
394	50	A	fleas	wingless bloodsucking insect, often found on dogs and cats
394	28	B	hermetically	airtight
394	32	B	kiosks	small structure with one or more open sides
394	37	B	dissuaded	to advise against something
396	26	A	megalopolis	densely populated area centering on the largest city
396	31	A	topography	geographical features of the land
396	36	B	geriatric	problems and diseases of old age
397	17	A	accumulation	collecting, gathering
398	1	B	remedy	cure, solution

KEY TERMS TO DEFINE:

After studying the chapter, define the following terms. Then check your work by referring to the answers at the end of Chapter 11 in the Study Guide.

agricultural surplus theory

central place theory

trading theory

urbanization

human ecology

concentric zone model

sector model

Central Business District

multiple nuclei model

gentrification

exurbanization

period explanation

regional restructuring

deindustrialization

deconcentration

domestic colonialism

primate cities

Robert Park and E. W. Burgess

Homer Hoyt

Fred Williams

Georg Simmel

Louis Wirth

Herbert Gans

William H. Whyte

Edward Banfield

C. Wright Mills

Paul Harrison

SELF-TEST

After completing this self-test, check your answers against the "Answer Key" at the end of Chapter 11 in this Study Guide and in the text on the page(s) indicated in parentheses.

MULTIPLE CHOICE QUESTIONS

Select the response which best answers the question or completes the statement:

1. The agricultural surplus theory states that cities came into being as a result of: (365)
    a. the need for a central market in which farmers could exchange and distribute their produce.
    b. specialists and traders who produced the food surplus vital for the growth of cities.
    c. a surplus of basic foodstuffs that allowed some people to develop occupations outside of agriculture.
    d. people becoming tired of performing hunting and gathering activities.

2. As cities developed, the division of labor: (365)
    a. became more complex
    b. increased the types and forms of human interaction
    c. no longer revolved around hunting and gathering
    d. all of the above

3. The first cities were located: (365-366)
    a. on trade routes
    b. on important waterways
    c. near major highways
    d. all of the above
    e. only "a" and "b"

4.   Cities prospered as a result of: (366)
     a.   the fall of the Roman Empire
     b.   the Dark Ages
     c.   the Industrial Revolution
     d.   the Great Depression

5.   The area of sociology concerned with the form and development of the community in human populations is: (368)
     a.   demography
     b.   human ecology
     c.   human geography
     d.   social anthropology

6.   Which model of city growth views the city as a series of zones emanating from the center, with each zone characterized by a different group of people and activity? (368)
     a.   concentric zone model
     b.   sector model
     c.   Central Business District model
     d.   multiple nuclei model

7.   Cities such as Los Angeles and Chicago have numerous centers of activity based on manufacturing, retailing, wholesaling, and education. As these cities have grown, they also have incorporated a host of smaller cities. This pattern of urban development can best be described by: (370)
     a.   the concentric zone model.
     b.   the sector model.
     c.   the Central Business District model.
     d.   the multiple nuclei model.

8.   Suburbanization in the United States was the result of: (371-372)
     a.   prosperity and technological advancements
     b.   increased ownership of automobiles
     c.   affordable tract housing and federally-insured loans
     d.   all of the above
     e.   only "a" and "b"

9.   Sociologists refer to the return of middle and upper-class people to deteriorated central city neighborhoods as: (372-373)
     a.   reurbanization
     b.   gentrification
     c.   exurbanization
     d.   desuburbanization

10. The movement of people to towns beyond the ring of big city suburbs is called: (373)
     a.   reurbanization
     b.   gentrification
     c.   exurbanization
     d.   desuburbanization

11. Which region of the United States has grown the most rapidly since the mid-1970s? (374-375)
    a. Sunbelt cities
    b. Winter cities
    c. Midwestern cities
    d. Pacific Northwestern cities

12. Low wage rates, lack of unionization, and tax incentives for corporations have all contributed to the growth of: (375-376)
    a. Sunbelt cities
    b. Winter cities
    c. Midwestern cities
    d. Pacific Northwestern cities

13. Which of these perspectives sees the slowdown and reversal of urban growth that began in the 1970s as a unique, temporary distortion of ongoing metropolitan expansion resulting from the convergence of economic and demographic factors? (379)
    a. the regional restructuring position
    b. the period explanation
    c. the deconcentration explanation
    d. the urban distortion explanation

14. _____ argued that life in the city forced people to selectively respond to the almost overwhelming amount of stimuli they are bombarded with in a rapidly changing, culturally-diverse environment. (381)
    a. Louis Wirth
    b. Emile Durkheim
    c. Georg Simmel
    d. Max Weber

15. Which of the following is not included in Herbert Gan's typology of inner city residents? (382)
    a. cosmopolites
    b. the unmarried or childless
    c. ethnic villagers
    d. the deprived
    e. the homeless

16. From a conflict perspective, street people are: (382)
    a. lazy, dirty and apathetic.
    b. not making use of opportunities for education and vocational training which are available to them.
    c. victims of a capitalist society that cannot provide employment for everyone who wants to work.
    d. in need of reinstitutionalization.

17. The theory of "domestic colonialism" argues that: (384)
    a. the inner cities are systematically exploited by the wealthy.
    b. suburbanites who work in the central city but live in the suburbs do not pay their fair share of the costs of maintaining the city.
    c. the wealthy take advantage of the inner city's minority work force by paying them low wages.
    d. all of the above.

242

18. Primate cities: (387)
    a. exist in developed countries such as the U.S. and Japan.
    b. exist in Third World nations such as Mexico and Bangladesh.
    c. are one giant metropolitan area at least twice as big as the nation's second largest city.
    d. all of the above.
    e. only "b" and "c".

19. According to the text, which of the following is the most serious and debilitating problem facing Third World cities? (391)
    a. lack of housing
    b. water, air and noise pollution
    c. high rates of unemployment
    d. food and power shortages
    e. none of the above

20. In Africa and Asia, a disproportionate number of migrants are: (392)
    a. women and children.
    b. young, single males.
    c. families of men, women and children.
    d. affluent individuals fleeing problems in the Persian Gulf.

TRUE-FALSE QUESTIONS:

T F 1. The first permanent human settlements began to appear at about 8,000 B.C. (365)

T F 2. Stratification of society occurred as a result of the occupational specialization which developed in cities. (365)

T F 3. London was the first city ever to have a population of one million people. (366)

T F 4. Cities in Europe and the U.S. which developed during the Industrial Revolution did not develop problems of overcrowding, poverty, and disease for a number of years. (366-367)

T F 5. The proportion of people living in cities in developed nations is greater than the proportion of people residing in urban areas in less developed nations. (368)

T F 6. Robert Park and E. W. Burgess coined the term "human ecology." (368)

T F 7. The sector model of urban growth is based on the idea that urban zones are pie or wedge-shaped sections radiating outward from the Central Business District. (370)

T F 8. The Civil War was a landmark period in the evolution of U.S. cities. (371)

T F 9. Since the 1920s, suburban growth rates in the U.S. have never slowed down. (371)

T F 10. Exurbanization is the return of middle and upper-class people to deteriorated central city neighborhoods. (372-373)

T F 11. According to some theorists, the winter cities have benefited more than the sunbelt cities from federal expenditure patterns. (377)

T F 12. Over the last two decades, tens of thousands of people have moved from rural and semi-rural towns to major urban areas in the U.S. (379)

T F 13. Urban residents tend to be younger than non-urban persons. (380)

T F 14. Racial, ethnic, and religious minorities are concentrated in smaller, semi-rural areas in the U.S. (380)

T F 15. Many researchers hold an anti-urban bias and a nostalgia for rural life. (381)

243

T	F	16.	William Whyte argued that the toughest, hardiest individuals among the street people were the shopping bag ladies. (382)
T	F	17.	People living in urban ghettos make up the largest concentration of poor in the U.S. (383)
T	F	18.	Deinstitutionalization policies of psychiatric facilities have contributed significantly to the number of homeless people in the U.S. (384)
T	F	19.	Virtually all of the rapid urban growth in Third World nations is the result of high birth rates. (384)
T	F	20.	According to the text, violence in Third World nations is unlikely because the masses have accepted their fate. (391-392)

MATCHING

Match these individuals with their theoretical contributions.

_____ 1. Homer Hoyt
_____ 2. Robert Park
           and E.W. Burgess
_____ 3. Fred Williams
_____ 4. Georg Simmel
_____ 5. Louis Wirth
_____ 6. Herbert Gans
_____ 7. Edward Banfield
_____ 8. William H. Whyte
_____ 9. C. Wright Mills
_____10. Paul Harrison

A. coined the term "human ecology" and developed, with others, the concentric zone model of urban development

B. encouraged people to use the "sociological imagination" to look at social problems

C. wrote that urban poverty is caused by the laziness and sloth of the poor

D. developed the sector model of urban development

E. studied the movement from urban areas to rural and semi-rural towns and offered the period explanation, the regional restructuring position, and the deconcentration explanation

F. wrote Inside the Third World and stated that "hell is a city"

G. believed that people became "overstimulated" by life in the city and were forced to interact with one another on a superficial level

H. developed a typology of inner city residents which included cosmopolites and ethnic villagers

I. emphasized the effect of size, heterogeneity and density of cities on primary and secondary relations of people

J. conducted research on street people, including shopping bag ladies, beggars, and three-card monte dealers

ESSAY QUESTIONS

1. Discuss the statement in the text that the development of cities is inextricably linked to the stratification of society.

2. Explain how suburbanization, gentrification, and exurbanization can have both positive and negative impact on society. Note which socioeconomic groups tend to benefit or to be harmed by the various processes.

3.   Describe the population shift which has occurred from winter cities to sunbelt cities and list some of the major explanations for the rapid growth patterns of sunbelt cities.

4.   Analyze the various perspectives on why urban poverty exists in the United States. State which one you think is most accurate and explain why.

5.   Explain why this chapter concluded that "a growing number of Third World cities are powder kegs just waiting to explode."

ANSWERS FOR CHAPTER 11

DEFINITION OF KEY TERMS:

agricultural surplus theory: According to this perspective, cities came into being as a result of a surplus of basic foodstuffs that allowed some people to develop occupations outside of agriculture.

central place theory: From this perspective, cities emerged because farmers needed a central market to exchange and distribute their produce.

trading theory: This theory of city growth states that specialists were responsible for producing the surplus food vital for the growth of cities. Traders introduced new seeds and livestock that resulted in improved crops and a successful agricultural revolution.   This revolution in turn permitted people to develop occupations other than farming.

urbanization: growth in the proportion of people living in urban areas.

human ecology: the area of sociology concerned with the study of the spatial distribution and aspects of human life.

concentric zone model: This model views the city as a series of zones emanating from the center, with each zone characterized by a different group of people (or institution) and activity.

sector model: According to this model of the city, urban zones are wedge-shaped sectors radiating out from the center, or Central Business District.

Central Business District: the major shopping and commercial area of a city.

multiple nuclei model: This model sees the city as comprised of multiple centers or nuclei.   In some cases these nuclei have existed since the origin of the city, while in other instances the nuclei increased as the city grew and diversified.

gentrification: the return of middle and upper-class people to deteriorating central city neighborhoods.

exurbanization: the movement of people to towns beyond the ring of big city suburbs. This process has been referred to as the "suburbanization of the suburbs."

period explanation: According to this perspective, the slowdown and reversal of urban growth that began in the 1970s is a unique and, therefore, temporary distortion of ongoing metropolitan expansion resulting from the convergence of economic and demographic factors.

regional restructuring: the position that views the deindustrialization of the 1970s that hit the winter cities so hard as a component of a new geography of urban growth. Cities will expand in different geographic regions of the country for reasons unrelated to past growth.

deconcentration explanation: According to this perspective, the slow down and reversal of population growth in many of the country's largest cities is a fundamental break with past trends.   More people are deciding to live in smaller cities and semi-rural areas.

domestic colonialism: According to this primarily Marxist view, the inner cities were systematically exploited by the bourgeoisie in the same way that African and Asian countries were exploited by the colonial powers beginning in the 19th century.

primate cities: cities which have one giant metropolitan area at least twice as big as the nation's second largest city, that serves as the country's economic, political, and cultural center.   These cities typically are found in Third World nations such as Mexico, Bangladesh, and Egypt.

KEY PEOPLE:

Robert Park and E. W. Burgess first introduced the term "human ecology" to U.S. sociology.   They also were instrumental in developing the concentric zone model of urban growth.

Homer Hoyt rejected the notion that cities were arranged in concentric zones and developed the sector model to explain the growth patterns of cities.

Fred Williams, a contemporary sociologist, offered three explanations for the relocation of tens of thousands from urban areas to rural and semi-rural towns: the period explanation, the regional restructuring position, and the deconcentration explanation.

Georg Simmel (1858-1918) examined the influence urban structures had on individuals and concluded that life in the city forced people to selectively respond to the almost overwhelming amount of stimuli with which they were bombarded.   As a result of this "overstimulation," people interact with one another on a more superficial level.

Louis Wirth (1857-1952) was interested in everyday, observable patterns of interaction in cities.   Wirth believed that the greater size, heterogeneity and density of city life led to numerous, impersonal, "secondary" type relations, as opposed to the warm, intimate, personal contacts or "primary" relations characteristic of rural life.

Herbert Gans constructed a typology of inner city residents that included cosmopolites (intellectuals, professionals, students, writers and artists who want to be near cultural facilities), the unmarried or childless, ethnic villages, the deprived, and the trapped and downwardly mobile.

William H. Whyte, an urbanologist, conducted research on street people, including shopping bag ladies, beggars, and three-card monte dealers.

Edward Banfield wrote the 1974 book The Unheavenly City Revisited in which he argues that the poor have no one to blame for their situation but themselves.   According to Banfield, the poor are lazy, dirty, and have numerous other negative attributes.   As a result of their values, attitudes and behavior, the poor live in a self-perpetuating "culture of poverty."

C. Wright Mills believed that social problems should be viewed using the sociological imagination -- the ability to recognize that maladies such as poverty afflicting a significant number of people cannot be explained at the individual level of analysis (the unemployed are sick, lame, lazy, etc.), but rather these problems are rooted in the social structure of society.

Paul Harrison wrote Inside the Third World and noted that "hell is a city." In this book he dramatically described the problems of Third World cities such as Calcutta.

ANSWERS TO MULTIPLE CHOICE QUESTIONS:

1. c   The agricultural surplus theory states that cities came into being as a result of a surplus of basic foodstuffs that allowed some people to develop occupations outside of agriculture. Response "a" is the "central place theory." Response "b" is the "trading theory." Response "d" is not directly related to the agricultural surplus theory. (365)

2. d   As cities developed, the division of labor became more complex, increased the types and forms of human interaction, and no longer revolved around hunting and gathering. Thus, response "d" -- all of the above -- is the best answer. (365)

3. e   The first cities were located on trade routes and on important waterways (responses "a" and "b"), so response "e" -- only "a" and "b" -- is correct. Response "c" -- near major highways -- is incorrect because no major highways existed at that time. (365-366)

4. c   Cities prospered as a result of the Industrial Revolution. The fall of the Roman Empire, the Dark Ages, and the Great Depression all were times when cities did not prosper. (366)

5. b   The area of sociology concerned with the form and development of the community in human population is human ecology. (368)

6. a   The concentric zone model views the city as a series of zones emanating from the center, with each zone characterized by a different group of people and activity. (368)

7. d   Cities such as Los Angeles and Chicago with numerous centers of manufacturing, retailing, and education have patterns of urban development best described by the multiple nuclei model. (370)

8. d   Suburbanization in the United States was the result of prosperity and technological advancements, increased ownership of automobiles, and affordable tract housing and federally-insured loans. Response "d" -- all of the above -- is the best answer. (371-372)

9. b   Sociologists refer to the return of middle and upper-class people to deteriorating central city neighborhoods as gentrification. (372-373)

10. c   The movement of people to towns beyond the ring of big city suburbs is called exurbanization. (373)

11. a   Sunbelt cities have grown the most rapidly since the mid-1970s. (374-375)

12. a   Low wage rates, lack of unionization, and tax incentives for corporations all have contributed to the growth of sunbelt cities. (375-376)

13. b   The period explanation sees the slowdown and reversal of urban growth that began in the 1970s as a unique, temporary distortion of ongoing metropolitan expansion resulting from the convergence of economic and demographic factors. (379)

14. c   Georg Simmel argued that life in the city forced people to selectively respond to the almost overwhelming amount of stimuli with which they are bombarded in a rapidly changing, culturally-diverse environment. (381)

15. e   The homeless are not one of the categories in Gan's typology of inner city residents. All other responses are among his five categories. (382)

247

16. c   From a conflict standpoint, street people are victims of a capitalist society that cannot provide employment for all who want to work. (382)

17. d   The theory of "domestic colonialism" argues that the inner cities are systematically exploited by the wealthy; that suburbanites who work in the central city but live in the suburbs do not pay their fair share of the costs of maintaining the city; and that the wealthy take advantage of the inner city's minority work force by paying them low wages. Response "d" -- all of the above -- is correct. (384)

18. e   Primate cities exist in Third World nations such as Mexico and Bangladesh (response "b") and are one giant metropolitan area at least twice as big as the nation's second largest city (response "c"). Response "e" -- only "b" and "c" is correct. (387)

19. a   According to the text, the most serious and debilitating problem facing Third World cities is the lack of housing. (391)

20. b   In Africa and Asia, a disproportionate number of migrants are young, single males. (392)

ANSWERS TO TRUE-FALSE QUESTIONS:

1. True (365)
2. True (365)
3. False -- Rome was the first known city to have approximately one million people. (366)
4. False -- Cities which developed during the Industrial Revolution had major problems with overcrowding, poverty, and disease very quickly. Many migrants simply traded rural for urban poverty. (366-367)
5. True (368)
6. True (368)
7. True (370)
8. True (371)
9. False -- Suburban growth rates in the U.S. slowed down with the onset of the Great Depression. (371)
10. False -- Exurbanization is the movement of people to towns beyond the right of big city suburbs. Gentrification is the return of middle and upper-class people to deteriorated central city neighborhoods. (372-373)
11. False -- According to some theorists, the Sunbelt cities, not the Winter cities, have benefited more from federal expenditure patterns. (377)
12. False -- Over the last two decades, tens of thousands of people have moved from major urban areas to rural and semi-rural towns, not from rural to urban areas. (379)
13. True (380)
14. False -- Racial, ethnic, and religious minorities are concentrated in cities. (380)
15. True (381)
16. True (382)
17. True (383)
18. True (384)
19. False -- Rapid urban growth in Third World nations is the result of natural increase (births over deaths) and rural-to-urban migration. Some researchers estimate that up to 75 percent of urban growth in poor countries is produced by migration. (384)
20. False -- The text indicated that Third World cities are powder kegs just waiting to explode. As cities continue to grow and living conditions deteriorate, the number of people looking for some way out of their misery can only increase. (391-392)

ANSWERS TO MATCHING:

1.   D
2.   A
3.   E
4.   G
5.   I
6.   H
7.   C
8.   J
9.   B
10.   F

CHAPTER TWELVE

MODERNIZATION

Chapter 12 analyzes the process of modernization -- the transformation from a traditional, usually agrarian society, to a contemporary, industrially-based state. The chapter looks at ways in which people in modern societies are different from those in more traditional nations and discusses the relationship between modernization and religion. Evolutionary and world system theories of modernization are presented and critiqued. The chapter assesses the likelihood of a new global economy occurring in which the "fast" economies of the developed world increasingly dominate the "slow" economies of the developing world in a phase of "electronic imperialism." Next, the problems of women in the Third World are explored, and the effects of modernization on their lives are discussed. Finally, the chapter presents a number of the internal and external obstacles faced by Third World nations in their drive toward modernization. The chapter concludes that "sustainable development" will be the greatest challenge as we approach the 21st century.

LEARNING OBJECTIVES:

As you read Chapter 12, use these learning objectives to organize your notes. After completing your reading, briefly state an answer to each of the objectives, and review the text pages in parentheses.

1.   Identify the personal qualities and characteristics of "modern man." (403-404)

2.   Explain how the biological sciences influenced 19th century theories of social change. (405-406)

3.   Compare and contrast evolutionary and modernization theories. (405-406)

4.   Define Tonnies' "Gemeinschaft" and "Gesellschaft," and Durkheim's "mechanical solidarity" and "organic solidarity." (406)

5.   Discuss the major criticisms of modernization theories (409)

6.   State the assumptions about the modern world made by world system theorists. (410-411)

7.   Define "neocolonialism" and explain how it affects economic development in Third World nations. (414-416)

8.   Differentiate between "fast" and "slow" economies, and note their role in "electronic imperialism." (417-420)

9.   Discuss "devolution" and explain how it is related to violence in Third World nations. (424-426)

10.   Describe some of the major problems confronting developing nations today. (426-435)

OUTLINE

I. INTRODUCTION

    A.   <u>Modernization</u> is the term used to describe the transformation from a traditional, usually agrarian society, to a contemporary, industrially-based state.

        1.   Modernization research has focused more on economic growth than on the development of other institutions and patterns of behavior in society.

        2.   The economic development of today's now rich countries (NRC's) and of less-developed countries (LDC's) is related to four primary aspects of industrialization:

            a.   Economic growth through transformations in energy (from human and animal power to machines);

            b.   A shift from primary production (agricultural and mining) to secondary production (manufacturing);

            c.   Growth in per capital income; and

            d.   An increase in the division of labor (diversification of occupations).

    B.   Industrialization is a powerful mechanism of social change affecting the intellectual, political, social, and psychological aspects of society, which in turn is affected by these same dimensions.

        1.   Modernization is a very uneven process of development, with some institutions changing faster and farther than other institutions, social values and modes of interaction to which they are related.

        2.   Social scientists became interested in modernization in the aftermath of World War II.

II. MODERN MAN

    A.   Although discussions of modernization usually are focused at the institutional level (such as the transformation of society's political, cultural, and economic organizations), the fundamental unit of change in any group or social system is the individual.

    B.   Alex Inkles identified these characteristics of "modern man":

        1.   Openness to new experience both with people and ways of doing things;

        2.   Increasing independence from traditional authority figures such as parents and priests;

        3.   A belief in the power and effectiveness of science and medicine, with a corresponding disregard of a fatalistic view of life;

        4.   Ambition for oneself and one's children to be upwardly mobile and successful; and

        5.   A strong interest in community affairs as well as local, national, and international affairs.

    C.   Inkles and his associates concluded that formal education was the most powerful variable in determining how an individual scored on the modernization scale. After the school, the factory was the second most important organization in changing a person's personality or character to ways which are more adaptive of life in a modern society.

    D.   Religion is another important area of individual (and societal) change in the transformation from a traditional to a modern world view. As societies modernize, they become increasingly secular.

251

1. <u>Secularization</u> is the process whereby worldly institutions and values become more important than religious institutions and values.
    a. In a secular society, people believe that they can understand, change and control their world through biological, physical, and social sciences.
    b. Individuals are less likely to resign themselves to fatalistic attitudes often associated with religious views.
2. There is a lack of agreement about the relationship between modernization and secularization: some believe that modernization inevitably produces secularization while others do not believe this to be true.

III. MODERNIZATION THEORIES

A. Evolutionary Models
    1. The founding fathers of sociology reasoned that if biological laws could explain the evolution of animals and human beings, social laws could be identified that explained development and progress in human societies.
    2. <u>Auguste</u> <u>Comte</u> (1798-1857) and <u>Herbert</u> <u>Spencer</u> (1820-1903) believed that societies evolved or passed through recognizable stages.
        a. Comte thought that societies evolved as they passed through three <u>inevitable</u> and <u>irreversible</u> stages.
        b. Spencer thought that societies pass through a series of stages as they become increasingly complex and interdependent. He believed that <u>societies</u> <u>developed</u> <u>in</u> <u>response</u> <u>to</u> <u>their</u> <u>social</u> <u>and</u> <u>natural</u> <u>environments</u>.
    3. <u>Ferdinand</u> <u>Tonnies</u> (1855-1936) stated that there were two societal types, <u>Gemeinschaft</u> and <u>Gesellschaft</u>, each with a unique set of characteristics and patterns of social organization.
        a. <u>Gemeinschaft</u> societies are traditional societies based on primary relations.
            (1). Family and kinship relations are paramount.
            (2). Social control is a function of shared values, norms, and religious beliefs.
        b. <u>Gesellschaft</u> societies are contractual, impersonal, and characterized by secondary relations.
        c. Tonnies predicted the rapid demise of <u>Gemeinschaft</u> societies and the rise of <u>Gesellschaft</u> types of organizations.
    4. <u>Emile</u> <u>Durkheim</u> (1858-1917) characterized societies as being either in a stage of "mechanical solidarity" or "organic solidarity."
        a. Societies based on <u>mechanical</u> <u>solidarity</u> have a minimum division of labor and little role specialization, and the people share a common world view.
        b. Societies characterized by <u>organic</u> <u>solidarity</u> have a complex division of labor, and people have different experiences and are less likely to view and interpret events in the same manner.

B. Impact of Classical Theorists
    1. Most evolutionary theories are <u>unilinear</u> -- societies would undergo a similar (if not identical) set of transformations, resulting in the emergence of the modern industrial state.
    2. Contemporary sociologist Neil Smelser developed a modern "dual stage" model of development:
        a. Development is the transition from traditional societies to modern societies on the following dimensions:

(1). Technological change moves from the simple and traditional toward the use of scientific knowledge.
(2). Agricultural transformation occurs from subsistence farming to specialization in cash crops and the use of wage-labor for agricultural work.
(3). Industrial transition is from human and animal power to machines for mass production and making a profit.
(4). Demographically, people move from farms and villages to urban centers.

b. As a result of these transformations, human groups become increasingly differentiated, and higher levels of education and specialized training become essential.
(1). Social cohesion is now more a function of mutual need than of shared values.
(2). Social disturbances -- such as outbursts of violence, and religious and political movements -- reflect the unevenness of large-scale social change.

C. Rostow's "Take-Off" Model
1. Economist W. W. Rostow delineates five stages of economic development which culminate in a successful "take off":
   a. Traditional setting: using traditional technology the economy has a limited potential for production; there are large subsistence sectors and few developed markets.
   b. The existence of preconditions for growth: widespread desire for growth, a degree of mass literacy, and a central government. Development of an infrastructure to support economic expansion is important.
   c. The "take off:" industrial technology develops rapidly in a few economic sectors and between 5 and 10 percent of the gross national product (GNP) is reinvested in economic growth.
   d. The drive to maturity: application of high technology across many sectors of the economy
   e. The mature industrial economy: a diverse mass consumption economy develops.
2. The "take off" period for developing nations -- such as Iran and India -- in the post- World War II era is relatively short when compared with the same period in Great Britain and other now-rich countries.

D. Criticisms of Evolutionary Models:
1. They only tell how the process of modernization occurs and not why it occurs in the first place.
   a. These theories do not explain why social transformation occurs in some societies.
   b. They do not explain why the process occurs at various rates, and if and when the process can be reversed.
2. They present change as smooth and gradual when, in actuality, development in most Third World nations is filled with strife and conflict.
3. They ignore the possibility that patterns of development in the 20th century were different from those experienced by the NRC's as they began industrializing over 150 years ago.
4. They ignore the role of the states, classes and other social actors in the process of modernization and tend to imply that "inexorable forces" cause this process to occur by focusing almost exclusively on the internal mechanisms of social change.

5.	Evolutionary/modernization theory is ahistorical because it ignores the unique history of each country which must be taken into account in explaining and predicting its developmental path.

## IV.	WORLD SYSTEM THEORY

A.	Immanuel Wallerstein
1.	As the foremost world system theorist, Wallerstein makes three assumptions about the modern world:
a.	Since approximately 1500, the modernizing countries of Europe had contact with most of the nations of the world, with contact after 1800 taking the form of colonial empires and colonized nations.
b.	After 1900, these empires gradually dissolved, although control was maintained by European powers as a result of their domination of world trade.
c.	In the contemporary world, global economics are dominated by an interdependent, capitalist world economic system of trade and investment.
2.	Based on the Marxist notion of classes and class conflict, world system theory views the world as one large, interrelated, interdependent society with an upper, a middle, and a lower class made up of countries:
a.	The international upper class is called the "core;"
b.	The international lower class is called the "periphery; and
c.	The international middle class is known as the "semi-periphery."
3.	The result of this stratification system is an international division of labor where lower class countries (periphery) work at the least desirable jobs for low wages and enrich the upper class (core) societies.
4.	This international system of stratification came about as a result of colonization, which occurred in two waves:
a.	The first wave was centered in North and South America and lasted from the 16th century to the early 19th century and occurred when the European powers -- France, England, Spain, and Portugal -- destroyed or forcibly moved indigenous Indian populations to make way for settlers and institutions from the core, and the transplanting of slaves from Africa.
b.	The second wave was centered in the Americas, as well as India and Asia, and lasted from the late 19th century to the mid-20th century. This wave was based on domination and control through political occupation.
c.	A third wave of lesser magnitude than the first two began in the early 1970s. It does not involve formal colonial rule, but rather economic and arms dependence of peripheral countries.
5.	The second wave, or period, of formal colonization (1870-1945) is the most important for our understanding of development currently taking place in Third World nations.
a.	During the second wave, a mad scramble for territory occurred as a result of the mistaken belief that the world was running short of raw materials and agricultural products. Also, capitalism is driven by a profit motive requiring continual growth and expansion.
b.	Colonial expansion ended in 1910 when the world was "filled up." World War I occurred as a result of the demand for raw materials and new markets, coupled with an arms build up.

254

      c.   After a post-war economic recovery, the world capitalist system was on the verge of collapse in the 1930s because of an economic depression in the U.S. and other core nations.

      d.   World War II was not an ideological struggle, but an attempt to control and alter the world system, and the U.S. emerged as the undisputed leader of the capitalist world system.

6.   Third World nations (especially former colonies) did not benefit from contact with the west as modernization theory assumes, but took a significant economic step backwards.

      a.   According to some theorists, underdevelopment occurred in less-developed countries at the same time and in the same way as development did in the richer industrial countries.

      b.   From this perspective, <u>underdevelopment</u> <u>and</u> <u>development</u> <u>are</u> <u>not</u> <u>two</u> <u>separate</u> <u>stages</u> <u>or</u> <u>phases,</u> <u>but</u> <u>flip</u> <u>sides</u> <u>of</u> <u>the</u> <u>same</u> <u>coin.</u>

      c.   The core nations did not cause the <u>initial</u> poverty in under-developed nations; however, the exploitative relationship between the core and periphery nations did create "lopsided economies and a low pace in economic diversification" in the periphery.

B.   Colonialism and Modernization

1.   According to one variation of world system theory, the world modernized in the latter half of the 19th century and the first half of the 20th century, and at the end of this period, there were economic winners and losers:

      a.   The core countries won, while the losing peripheral nations will never successfully transform their economies to the level of core states no matter how long and hard they work.

      b.   The peripheral nations are unable to fully modernize because the exploitation did not end with the demise of colonialism in the post World War II era, but rather, economic domination of the periphery by the core continued via <u>multinational</u> <u>corporations</u> (neocolonialism).

2.   This neocolonialism occurs as follows:

      a.   More investment capital flows out of Third World nations to core nations than flows into these peripheral countries from core countries.

      b.   Countries subject to external control from multinational corporations cannot control their own surplus capital for investment.

      c.   Quality of life has gone down in many poor nations, as economic penetration of these countries by multinational corporations increases.

      d.   Core countries operate to further their own growth and profits, and have little interest in the economic or social development of their host nations.

C.   Overspecialization

1.   Many former colonies are economically overspecialized as a result of having been developed in a lopsided manner that would benefit the needs of the core.

      a.   Economies are centered around the production of a few cash crops or raw materials they trade and sell in the international marketplace.

      b.   When the price of these crops or products begins to fall, the countries that are economically dependent on these products can experience a rapid and severe decline in revenue.

2. Developed countries help keep underdeveloped nations in the role of raw material exporters by controlling their access to technology and capital from the outside world.
3. Agricultural overspecialization also is problematic because many primary food producing countries cannot hope to see their markets expand significantly, no matter how healthy the economy of the developed world.

D. Internal System of Stratification
1. High rates of poverty and misery in Third World nations have been attributed to their internal system of stratification:
   a. Typically, there is a class structure dominated by a small economic elite whose political and financial interests are tied to the core.
   b. This class structure creates a very unequal income distribution when compared with core countries, in which the opposite process of class formation occurred.
2. One researcher states that the more dependent a Third World nation is on the core economically, the greater the degree of internal income inequality.

E. Criticism of World System Theory (WST)
1. Problems with WST:
   a. Carlos Rangel argues that all countries have progressed in many ways -- including economic growth, health, education, consumption, etc. -- as a result of the impact of international capitalism.
   b. Thomas Sowell and others believe that the plight of many Third World nations is more a factor of internal problems -- including inefficient, corrupt governments -- rather than of external exploitation.
   c. While WST is correct in its criticism of modernization theory for neglecting a country's ties to the outside world, WST did not take into account numerous internal mechanisms of change.
   d. WST has been criticized from a scientific perspective because the theory cannot be easily tested and thus becomes a "catch-all" explanation for all of the problems of the Third World.
2. WST has made a valuable contribution with its explanation of the relationship between developing and developed nations and correctly points out the long-term consequences of this type of relationship.

V. THE NEW GLOBAL ECONOMY?

A. Alvin Toffler believes that "fast" economies of the developed world will increase the economic gap between these nations and "slow" economies of the developing world.
1. In fast economies, advanced technology speeds the entire business cycle.
2. In the slow economies of less developed countries, lack of advanced technology and investment capital, combined with traditional attitudes, make these nations noncompetitive with the fast economies.
3. If Toffler is correct, fast economies will severely undercut the less developed countries major asset in the world marketplace -- cheap labor.

256

B. Electronic Imperialism
1. Fast societies are predicted to increasingly dominate the slow societies as NRC's become information societies in the post-industrial era (as we enter a stage of electronic imperialism).
2. Some theorists believe that Third World nations will fall even farther behind as a result of high technology and computers because information technology can be applied only to <u>existing</u> manufacturing plants, offices, and services.
3. Electronic imperialism also will have significant cultural affects:
   a. Prolonged exposure to television programs and commercials with a "Western consumer-oriented culture" will alter people's values to some extent.
   b. Such cultural imperialism could significantly devalue local tradition, especially among the young.
   c. The resulting feelings of relative deprivation could lead to political instability.

VI. WOMEN IN THE THIRD WORLD

A. While women in developed nations also may be exploited and physically abused by males, the rate and intensity of such exploitation and abuse is significantly greater in the Third World.
1. For example, dowry deaths or bride burnings occur in India when the bride's family does not pay an agreed-upon dowry of money and/or goods to the groom.
   a. Often the bride is killed by being burned alive in an unavoidable "kitchen accident."
   b. The groom is now free to try for another marriage -- and another dowry.
   c. In 1987, at least 1,786 dowry deaths were known to Indian police.
2. Females are even discriminated against before they are born. Until it was forced to stop, an Indian sex-detection clinic advertised that aborting a female fetus now was better than spending money on the young woman's dowry later, for instance.

B. Education
1. In rural areas of developing nations, a young girl's labor is viewed as more important than her education.
   a. As a result, many women over age 25 have no schooling whatsoever in these countries.
   b. When Third World women are allowed to pursue an education, they overwhelmingly are channeled into traditional female majors in the humanities, education, and the fine arts.
2. There is a direct relationship between women's levels of education and their reproductive activities.
   a. Education is the most effective way to reduce child mortality, and as child mortality goes down, the birth rate drops.
   b. Educated women want smaller families than women with little or no schooling.
   c. Educated women are most likely to have jobs, and thus smaller families.
   d. Education can help break deeply-rooted cultural expectations of pregnancy at an early age (under 16), as well as the pattern of repeated childbearing at short birth intervals.

257

C. Reproductive Capacity and Control
  1. The reproductive capacity of women is socially-defined and controlled.
     a. In developed countries the number of children a woman has is typically a joint decision made with her husband.
     b. In traditional societies women are under tremendous economic and cultural pressure to have large families.
        (1). In Asian countries, a woman gains security and respect by bearing sons to take care of her when she is old.
        (2). In Muslim societies the failure to bear sons is cause for a man to consider finding a new wife.
  2. Pregnancy in developing countries is more likely to be a physically draining, possibly life threatening ordeal.
     a. Numerous short interval pregnancies, coupled with inadequate diet, pose serious health problems for women in these nations.
     b. In many developing societies women eat only after men and boys have eaten, resulting in high rates of malnutrition and anemia in pregnant women, who then face even greater likelihood of maternal mortality.

D. Political Sphere
  1. Females have been the last major population group to be given the right to vote.
  2. Women have been excluded from political office, especially at the highest levels of government.
  3. In many developing nations women still are discriminated against on a daily basis as a result of religious and customary law.
     a. In Saudi Arabia, segregation based on gender is part of that country's legal system.
     b. Although Zimbabwe outlawed other types of discrimination, gender discrimination is not included.
     c. In many developing nations, women are legally denied access to land ownership and any other income- producing property.

E. Effects of Modernization
  1. Modernization has been a positive force for millions of Third World women in terms of education and health care; however, modernization also has produced a new set of problems for these women.
     a. For example, in Bangladesh rural males who migrate to cities in search of employment often abandon women and children who must fend for themselves in economically depressed areas.
     b. The abandoned women are forced to survive alone in poor villages and often are victimized again by the forces of modernization.
        (1). Traditional markets for domestic handicrafts have been undercut severely by mass produced factory items.
        (2). In the factories where women work alongside men, they often do so for significantly less money.
        (3). When the women return home, they face another full day's work taking care of their families.
  2. Modernization has not kept women from being both beasts of burden and sex objects.
     a. There is now more emphasis on physical beauty in some Third World nations.
     b. In Bangladesh, for example, women are increasingly deserted by husbands in search of younger, more attractive mates.
  3. The modernization of agriculture has left women increasingly dependent on males.

258

        a.   Mechanization and training have been aimed almost exclusively at men, and women have been by-passed by the new labor saving technology.

        b.   Agricultural innovations and policies may not be the only cause of female poverty in developing nations, but they have helped make women the largest group of landless laborers in the world.

    4.   The development process may not only increase the existing disparity of wealth, status, and power between men and women but also can function to legitimate these inequalities as well.

VII. DEVOLUTION AND THE RISE OF NATIONALISM

Devolution is the surrender of powers to local authorities by the central government. In the developing world today, many nations are attempting to withdraw from existing political states.

1.   A nation is a group of people with a common history and culture.

2.   A state is a political entity occupying a designated territory with a government that has the authority and ability to use physical violence against citizens who resist its law.

B.   According to Bernard Nietschmann, World War III has been fought on a continuing basis since 1948 and has already claimed the lives of millions of people.

    1.   Violent clashes between those groups seeking more autonomy or independence, and governments blocking any such move have claimed the lives of millions of people over the past 40 years.

        a.   For example, over one million people were killed in a three year period in the bitter nation/state confrontations between Nigeria and the indigenous Biafran nation.

        b.   Likewise, in Zaire, the province of Katanga has been fighting to become a separate state for over 30 years.

    2.   Although World War III is well underway in developing countries, industrial states are not immune to these same conflicts.

        a.   Canada has been faced with demands for an independent Quebec.

        b.   Northern Ireland has long sought sovereignty from the British Empire.

        c.   Most Soviet republics are or have been pushing for increased autonomy or independence.

C.   Nationalistic movements cause developing nations to spend badly needed funds to defeat separatist movements instead of improving the quality of life for millions of desperately poor people.

VIII. PROBLEMS AND SOLUTIONS

A.   Corruption

    1.   Although all countries have some degree of corruption, Third World nations can least afford the monetary and psychological costs of rampant bureaucratic corruption by dishonest officials.

    2.   Corruption demoralizes people and causes them to have little faith in their institutions, and it also hampers modernization.

        a.   Examples of widespread and entrenched governmental corruption are evident in Mexico and India, as well as many other countries.

        b.   Widespread poverty does not inevitably lead to corruption, but it appears to be related to it from the standpoint that people may feel that they should "get what they can when they can get it."

B.   Economic Strategies
    1.   When the United States was modernizing, industry was <u>labor</u> <u>intensive</u> (in need of unskilled and semi-skilled workers); however, today industry has become <u>capital</u>-<u>intensive</u> (requiring enormous amounts of money) and fewer, but more highly skilled and trained workers.
    2.   Most Third World nations cannot afford to build modern, high-tech factories, and these nations have large populations of young, undereducated people streaming into the cities looking for work.
    3.   A large amount of <u>investment</u> <u>capital</u> is needed to compete successfully in a global economy.
        a.   The modernization process moves very slowly if a country's industrial output is limited to low priced goods.
        b.   The success of Japan, Hong Kong, Singapore, Taiwan, and South Korea was the result of their ability to penetrate the world market for big ticket items such as steel, automobiles, and sophisticated electronic equipment.
    4.   Developing nations have to complete against the economic superpowers of North America, Europe and Asia, as well as each other.

C.   Distribution of Wealth
    1.   Some theorists believe that economic development initially leads to a more <u>inequitable</u> distribution of income before this trend is subsequently reversed; however, this does not appear always to be true.
        a.   In Brazil and Mexico economic growth led to more inequitable distribution of income;
        b.   But in Taiwan and the Ivory Coast, the income distribution improved as a result of economic growth.
    2.   Other theorists argue that it is not rapid growth per se that leads to more inequality, but rather the <u>form</u> that growth takes.
        a.   In the absence of any mechanisms to redistribute economic growth -- such as land reform, income transfers, and taxation -- the existing system of inequality is perpetuated in some countries.
        b.   Four major factors may affect a country's distribution of wealth:
            (1).   Population growth, which results in agricultural land being subdivided generation after generation, makes it increasingly difficult for farmers to maintain an adequate standard of living.
            (2).   Education and literacy have a favorable impact on a country's distribution of income because schooling presumably leads to increased productivity.
            (3).   Agricultural mechanization may lead to higher yields of food, but it also displaces workers and contributes to the nation's unemployment.
            (4).   Land ownership also is a factor in the distribution of wealth in developing nations.

D.   The Political Sphere
    1.   While a democratic form of government as opposed to a totalitarian system certainly makes a difference in terms of individual freedoms and liberty in a given society, neither political orientation is a guarantee of developmental success or failure.
        a.   For example, Marxist China has made significant strides, while Marxist Cuba has been an economic failure requiring large amounts of financial support from the Soviet Union.

b.   Many other variables -- such as population growth -- have to be taken into account in any explanation of the relative developmental success or failure of countries.

2.   Although a nation's political system per se is not the crucial factor in the modernization process, one theorist argues that four political factors are absolutely essential if modernization is to occur:

a.   Political stability is essential because a climate of civil wars, revolutions, and palace coups undermines the modernization process by draining the country's treasury and resources and by preoccupying people with their own safety and well-being.

b.   Modernization must be the government's top priority.

c.   A strong central government must be committed to intervene in virtually every aspect of the modernization process.

d.   The government must insure that economic development is directed in favor of the many and not just the few.

E.   The International Context

1.   All countries are part of an international economic system characterized by periods of prosperity and periods of slow growth and stagnation; however, Third World nations are more strongly impacted by changes in the international marketplace than are economically-diverse and industrially- powerful developed nations.

a.   During the 1960s, the world economy was flourishing and many Third World nations made significant economic strides.

b.   By the late 1970s and early 1980s, this period of expansion was over, economic growth sharply declined, and development in most Third World nations was adversely affected.

2.   While internal factors such as political stability and a disciplined work force may be <u>necessary</u> conditions for sustained economic growth, they are not in and of themselves <u>sufficient</u> conditions for prosperity.

a.   Successful modernization requires that there be an international market that is buying what a specific country is producing.

b.   The selling price must be high enough to meet expenses, to make a profit, and to expand.

F.   Price of Oil

1.   The price of oil on the world market is an important factor in the modernization process.

2.   Although the cost of oil is important in developed countries, a poor country that produces only a small fraction of its own fuel must spend hard earned cash to import the oil it needs to survive and compete in the global marketplace.

G.   Economic Assistance

1.   Some developing nations will not be able to modernize without the sustained economic assistance from developed nations.

2.   When the world economy was expanding rapidly, many developing nations borrowed large sums of money but were able to make their loan payments and to make economic progress.

a.   Now many developing nations are unable to make their payments, and collectively they owe the world banks over one trillion dollars.

b.   Third World nations now have to compete with newly democratic Eastern European countries and the economic crisis in the Soviet Union for financial assistance.

3. Developing nations also have been victims of a 45 year old superpowers' arms race.

H. "Sustainable Development"
   1. During this century, there has been incredible economic and population growth, resulting in a dramatic drain on oil, natural gas, and other natural resources.
   2. At the same time, there has been a tremendous increase in overall environmental pollution and degradation spawned by this growth.
      a. Most developing nations and large sectors of primarily industrial states have "resource-based economies" -- economies whose productivity is dependent on the use of the soil, forests, fisheries, water, parks, and the use and export of raw materials.
      b. The question arises as to whether all 165 nations can modernize without seriously -- if not totally -- depleting these resources.
      c. The problem of resource-based economies is especially serious for Third World nations because these countries are vulnerable to the international market and because their resources are being consumed much faster than they can be replaced.
   3. The modernization of Third World countries -- as well as continued development in NRC's -- raises questions not only of what can be done, but also of what should be done.
   4. Since the economy and the environment are interdependent components of the developmental process, "sustainable" modernization must be the central focus of our attention as we approach the 21st century.

GLOSSARY OF DIFFICULT-TO-UNDERSTAND WORDS

Page	Line	Col.	Term from Text	Explanation
401	1		poignant	moving, touching
401	2		spiral	curve, winding
401	5		jute	a fiber used to make sacks, burlap, or twine
401	7		minuscule	very small
401	14		looms	taking shape on the horizon
402	1		gut wrenching	violent twisting in the stomach
402	4		agrarian	agricultural
402	4		inasmuch	since
402	25		prompted	moved to action, urged
403	17		fatalistic	all events are fixed for all time and therefore humans have no power to bring about change
403	17		upwardly mobile	to move up the social stratification system, the term usually refers to movement between social classes
404	20		vice versa	changing the order
405	4		secular	relating to the world, not bound by cannon (church) laws
405	7		paramount	dominant
405	13		inexorable	not flexible
405	22		shrines	a place or object defined as sacred and where people direct their devotion
405	25		eradicated	done away with
405	36		descent	the evolutionary processes which have resulted in the human species

Page	Line	Col.	Term from Text	Explanation
406	7		quest	search
406	11		depicted	described
406	16		denotes	stands for
406	23		demise	death
406	24		ascendancy	domination
407	21		renders	gives up
407	24		cohesion	sticking together
407	26		outbursts	breaking out
407	29		vested interest	people who have a special interest in a social arrangement
407	33		multistage	many stages (steps) in a development, conducted by stages
407	36		delineated	described
409	3		ascendancy	domination
409	7		anew	in a new form
409	22		strife	struggle
409	29		inexorable	not flexible
409	38		vacuum	state of isolation from outside influences
410	2		enmasse	as a whole
410	10		inquiry	seeking information
410	29		antiquated	dated, old, archaic
410	30		leftist	radical political position
410	41		plight	difficulties
410	42		deteriorated	become worse
412	9		bourgeoisie	those who own the means of production (factories), wealthy class
412	9		proletariat	the workers who sell their labor--work in the factories owned by the bourgeoisie
413	5		forcibly	used force to
413	13		peripheral	located away from the center--developing nations
413	31		signaled	indicated
413	41		ravaged	destructive
413	47		undisputed	not debate, not questioned
414	14		initial	beginning
414	24		demise	death, stopping
415	30		lopsided	not balanced
416	4		hemp	an Asian plant whose fiber is used to make rope
416	32		neocolonial	where a great power indirectly maintains influence in economic and political policies over other areas or people
417	4		periphery	external countries--poor nations
417	8		aberrations	variations
417	9		antagonistic	opposing
418	12	B	lentils	beans or peas or their seeds
418	15	B	betel nut	a mildly narcotic nut grown in Asia
418	23	B	husked	to take off the outer layer or shell of a seed
419	15		antiquated	old, advanced in age
419	37		dwindling	decreasing, less
420	1		indigenous	native

GLOSSARY OF DIFFICULT-TO-UNDERSTAND WORDS (CONTINUED)

Page	Line	Col.	Term from Text	Explanation
420	3		horrendous	horrible, dreadful
420	9		lagged	moves slower
420	10		ushered	brought in
420	17		rudimentary	elementary
421	7		nutritional anemia	lack of vitality resulting from poor food (nourishment)
421	7		afflicts	injures
421	15		mutilated	harmed, permanently injured to cause lasting damage
421	18		grotesque	not natural, not normal, gruesome
421	20		nuptial	marriage
421	24		bereaved	suffering the death of a loved one
421	40		deprivation	withholding access
421	45		fatalism	events are fixed in advance and humans have no control in bringing about change
422	40		maternal mortality	death of women from childbirth
423	27		myriad	very large number
423	36		skewed	slanted
424	13		arbitrarily	without reason
424	42		shambles	wreckage, state of great disorder or confusion
425	6		protracted	drawn out, prolonged, extended
425	10		secede	withdraw
425	13		dissidents	differing with an opinion or group
426	10		sporadic	occasional, infrequent
426	13		agitated	worked restlessly, attempt to shake people up
426	37		rampant	widespread
427	5		nepotism	hiring of relatives
427	5		peddling	selling
427	27		condone	pardon or overlook, to treat as of no importance
427	47		labyrinth	maze
428	25		alleviated	eased, relieved
428	37		intermittent	coming and going at intervals, occurring again and again
428	42		debilitating	weakening
428	43		equitable	dealing fairly and equally with all concerned
429	9		inegalitarian	not an equal, marked by difference in social and economic standing
429	23		adverse	not favorable, not fortunate
430	15		intrigue	plotting, scheming
430	19		intervene	interrupt, get involved
430	26		merit	value, quality
430	28		petrochemicals	a chemical derived from petroleum or natural gas
430	35		destitute	needy, down-and-out, poverty stricken
430	45		stagnation	no activity
431	4		strides	advances
431	22		turbines	a rotary engine started by a current of fluid (water or steam)
432	12		sluggish	very slow
432	28		thawing	becoming less hostile

GLOSSARY OF DIFFICULT-TO-UNDERSTAND WORDS (CONTINUED)

Page	Line	Col.	Term from Text	Explanation
432	31		alleviating	relieving, easing
432	42		inasmuch as	in view of the fact that
433	4		vagaries	not predictable
435	2		depleted	used up
435	5		jeopardize	risk
435	14		wagering	risking, taking a chance on
435	15		staggering	overwhelming
435	16		sustainable	support for
435	25	A	stagnation	no activity
435	36	A	dire	extreme
436	9	A	shambles	confusion
436	17	A	lucrative	producing wealth
436	35	A	abyss	bottomless pit
436	39	A	extricate	free, untangle
437	35	A	threshold	beginning, point of departure
437	39	A	strenuous	hard, straining, tough
437	14	B	sewage	waste matter carried off by underground pipes
437	22	B	solvents	a liquid substance capable of dissolving other substances
437	23	B	pesticides	a poisonous agent used to destroy pests
437	32	B	cesspool	an underground catch basin for collecting sewage
438	5	A	maquila	off-shore assembly plants
438	29	A	dubious	questionable
439	26	A	acquiesce	to accept or comply, assent
439	34	B	lucrative	profitable
440	6	A	devastated	laid waste to
440	10	A	shambles	confusion
440	42	A	deficit	shortage
440	11	B	fledgling	inexperienced
440	43	B	spectacular	sensational, impressive, dramatic
440	45	B	salient	noticeable
441	45	A	vigorous	strong, dynamic
441	3	B	meddler	interfering, getting in the way
441	22	B	sorely	painfully
441	25	B	compel	force
442	2	A	consensus	general agreement
442	4	A	docile	obedient, able to manage, submissive
442	26	A	reprisal	revenge, retaliation
442	12	B	sprawled	spread, lying spread out

KEY TERMS TO DEFINE:

After studying the chapter, define the following terms. Then check your work by referring to the answers at the end of Chapter 12 in the Study Guide.

modernization

secularization

unilinear theories of change

world system theory

core societies

peripheral societies

semiperipheral societies

devolution

state

nation

KEY PEOPLE:

Alex Inkles

Auguste Comte and Herbert Spencer

Ferdinand Tonnies

Emile Durkheim

Neil Smelser

W. W. Rostow

Immanuel Wallerstein

Alvin Toffler

SELF-TEST

After completing this self-test, check your answers against the "Answer Key" at the end of Chapter 12 in this Study Guide and in the text on the page(s) indicated in parentheses.

MULTIPLE- CHOICE QUESTIONS

Select the response which best answers the question or completes the statement:

1. The transformation from a traditional, usually agrarian society, to a contemporary, industrially-based state is referred to as: (402)
    a.   development.
    b.   modernization.
    c.   secularization.
    d.   devolution.

2.	Which of the following is <u>not</u> one of the primary aspects of industrialization? (402)
	a.	decrease in the division of labor
	b.	economic growth through transformations from human and animal power to machines
	c.	a shift from agricultural and mining to manufacturing
	d.	growth in per capita income

3.	According to Alex Inkles and his associates, "modern man" is: (403)
	a.	open to new experiences.
	b.	increasingly independent of traditional authority figures.
	c.	less fatalistic and more inclined to accept science and modern medicine.
	d.	ambitious, seeking to improve his standing in society and interested in community, national, and international affairs.
	e.	all of the above.

4.	Secularization is: (405)
	a.	the process by which a society is transformed from a traditional, usually agrarian society, to a contemporary, industrially-based state.
	b.	the process by which powers are surrendered to local authorities by the central government.
	c.	the process by which religious institutions and values become more important than worldly institutions and values.
	d.	the process by which worldly institutions and values become more important than religious institutions and values.

5.	Which theory of modernization was based on the idea that if biological laws could explain the development of animals and human beings, social laws could be identified that explained the development and progress of human societies? (405)
	a.	the "take-off" model
	b.	the theory of colonialism/neocolonialism
	c.	evolutionary theory
	d.	world system theory

6.	Which of these theorists believed that as societies evolved they passed through three inevitable and irreversible stages? (406)
	a.	Auguste Comte
	b.	Emile Durkheim
	c.	W.W. Rostow
	d.	Immanuel Wallerstein

7.	According to Ferdinand Tonnies, _____ societies were traditional societies based on primary relations. (406)
	a.	core
	b.	Gemeinschaft
	c.	Gesellschaft
	d.	colonial

8.	Durkheim's concept of "organic solidarity" referred to: (406)
	a.	societies which relied on agricultural production for economic livelihood.
	b.	societies characterized by a minimal division of labor, little role specialization, and a common world view.
	c.	societies characterized by a significant division of labor, much role specialization, and few shared values.
	d.	none of the above.

9. Which of these theorists compared economic development to an airplane moving down the runway, building up speed and momentum as it prepares to take off? (407)
    a. Neil Smelser
    b. Alex Inkles
    c. Immanuel Wallerstein
    d. W. W. Rostow

10. All of the following are criticisms of evolutionary/modernization theory, except: (409)
    a. these theories tell us how the process of modernization takes place but not why it occurs in the first place.
    b. these theories are overly critical of capitalism and do not acknowledge that even the most backward countries have made progress as a result of international capitalism.
    c. these theories view change as smooth and gradual when, in actuality, it usually is neither.
    d. these theories are ahistorical because they do not take into account the history of specific nations in explaining and predicting their developmental paths.

11. According to the text, the foremost world system theorist is: (411)
    a. Neil Smelser
    b. Alex Inkles
    c. Immanuel Wallerstein
    d. W. W. Rostow

12. In world system theory, the peripheral societies are: (412)
    a. economically overspecialized, relatively poor and weak societies subject to the manipulation and direct control of rich nations.
    b. industrial, economically diversified, rich, powerful nations relatively independent of outside control.
    c. nations attempting to industrialize and diversify their economies
    d. none of the above

13. In world system theory, the core societies are: (412)
    a. economically overspecialized, relatively poor and weak societies subject to the manipulation and direct control of rich nations.
    b. industrial, economically diversified, rich, powerful nations relatively independent of outside control.
    c. nations attempting to industrialize and diversify their economies
    d. none of the above

14. World system theory is based on which of these theoretical perspectives? (412)
    a. functionalism
    b. symbolic interactionism
    c. evolutionary theory
    d. Marxist conflict theory

15. Economic domination of Third World nations by multinational corporations has been referred to by some world system theorists as: (415)
    a. good business practices.
    b. secularization.
    c. deindustrialization.
    d. survival of the fittest.
    e. neocolonialism.

268

16. "Overspecialized" economies in Third World nations are characterized by: (415)
    a. too much division of labor among workers.
    b. too little division of labor among workers.
    c. production of too many different types of crops and products to be able to effectively sell them in the international marketplace.
    d. production of too few types of crops or raw materials to sell in the international marketplace.
    e. none of the above.

17. According to Alvin Toffler, _____ economies have advanced technology which speeds the entire business cycle from the rapid movement of investment capital to the delivery of the final product. (417-419)
    a. Gemeinschaft
    b. Gesellschaft
    c. primary
    d. secondary
    e. fast

18. Some theorists predict that electronic imperialism will occur when: (420)
    a. all societies have enough technological capability to engage in "information processing" wars.
    b. now rich countries become information societies in the post-industrial era.
    c. the gap between rich and poor nations narrows.
    d. there are more television signals than available air space.

19. According to the text, which of the following is the most accurate statement about the oppression of women? (421)
    a. Women no longer are exploited and abused in developed nations, but they still are exploited and abused in Third World nations.
    b. Women are exploited and abused in developed nations, but they are not exploited and abused in Third World nations.
    c. Women are exploited and abused to about the same degree in both developed and Third World nations.
    d. Women are exploited and abused in developed nations, but the rate and intensity of exploitation and abuse is significantly greater in Third World nations.

20. Numerous studies have shown that _____ is the most effective way to reduce child mortality. (421)
    a. education
    b. medicine
    c. technology
    d. birth control

21. The process by which power is surrendered to local authorities by the central government is called: (424)
    a. revolution
    b. evolution
    c. devolution
    d. convolution

22. According to the text, World War III is: (424)
    a. going to occur in the Middle East.
    b. a continuing struggle between nations and states.
    c. not likely because of the possibility of human annihilation.
    d. many years away.

23. When the United States went through the modernization process, industry was: (427)
    a. labor intensive (in need of unskilled and semi-skilled workers).
    b. in need of many highly skilled and trained workers.
    c. capital intensive.
    d. in need of enormous amounts of investment capital in order to complete in the global economy.

24. "Sustainable" modernization seeks a balance between: (432-435)
    a. capitalism and communism.
    b. communism and socialism.
    c. the economy and the environment.
    d. First World and Third World nations.

TRUE-FALSE QUESTIONS:

T   F   1. Modernization research has focused more on economic growth than on the development of other institutions and patterns of behavior in society. (402)

T   F   2. Social scientists became interested in modernization in the aftermath of the Industrial Revolution. (402)

T   F   3. Alex Inkles and his associates concluded that formal education was the most powerful variable in determining how an individual would score on the modernization scale. (404)

T   F   4. Gesellschaft societies are characterized by relations that are contractual, impersonal, voluntary and limited. (406)

T   F   5. Most evolutionary theories were unilinear. (406-407)

T   F   6. Sociologist Neal Smelser predicted that if modernization were carefully planned, the process could occur with relatively little disruption to a society. (407)

T   F   7. To W. W. Rostow, a successful "take-off" culminates when a diverse mass consumption economy develops. (407-408)

T   F   8. World system theory focuses on the political and economic interdependence of the world's nations. (410-411)

T   F   9. W. W. Rostow is the foremost world system theorist. (411)

T   F   10. According to world system theory, an international division of labor exists. (412)

T   F   11. World system theorists believe that underdevelopment and development are two separate stages or phases of modernization. (414)

T   F   12. Some world system theorists argue that peripheral nations will never successfully transform their economies to the level of core states no matter how long and hard they work. (414-415)

T   F   13. Most Third World nations have very little internal stratification. (416)

T   F   14. World system theory has been widely tested and verified by numerous researchers. (416)

T   F   15. Dowry deaths largely have ceased in India as a result of recent legislation. (421)

T   F   16. There is a direct relationship between women's levels of education and their reproductive activities. (421-422)

T   F   17. In Saudi Arabia, segregation based on gender is part of that country's legal system. (423)

T   F   18. The text concludes that widespread poverty inevitably leads to corruption in Third World nations. (427)

T F 19. In most countries, economic development leads to a more equitable distribution of income. (428)
T F 20. Third World nations are more strongly impacted by changes in the international marketplace than are First World countries. (430-431)

FILL-IN QUESTIONS

Fill in the blank with the word or phrase that best completes the statement.

1. For Ferdinand Tonnies, _____ societies were traditional societies based on primary relations. _____ societies were contractual, impersonal and characterized by secondary relations. (406)

2. For Emile Durkheim, societies based on _____ solidarity had a minimal division of labor. _____ solidary held together modern societies which were characterized by a complex division of labor. (406)

3. _____ theory focuses on the political and especially the economic interdependence of the world's nations. (410)

4. According to world system theory, _____ societies are industrial, economically diversified, rich, powerful nations. (412)

5. _____ societies are economically overspecialized, relatively poor and weak societies subject to the manipulation and direct control of rich nations. (412)

6. Nations midway between the rich, powerful nations and the relatively poor and weak societies are _____ societies. (412)

7. Alvin Toffler believed that the division between capitalism and socialism will be replaced by a split between _____ and _____economies. (419)

8. _____ is the surrender of powers to local authorities by the central government. (424)

9. A(n) _____ is a political entity occupying a designated territory with a government that has the authority and ability to use physical violence against citizens who resist its laws. (424)

10. A group of people with a common history and culture is a _____. (424)

ESSAY QUESTIONS

1. Discuss Alex Inkles' research on the impact of modernization on people in developing nations, and explain how he defined the "modern man."

2. State the major assumptions of modernization theory and note several major criticisms of this perspective.

3. Explain world system theory and list several major criticisms of this view of modernization.

4. Analyze the impact of modernization on the lives of women in Third World nations. Specify ways in which some of the women may have been helped by modernization, and ways in which they may have been harmed by this process.

5. Describe some of the major problems faced by developing nations and indicate possible solutions -- if any -- for these problems.

ANSWERS FOR CHAPTER 12

DEFINITIONS OF KEY TERMS:

modernization: The term used to describe the transformation from a traditional, usually agrarian society, to a contemporary, industrially-based state.

secularization: The process whereby worldly institutions and values become more important than religious institutions and values.

unilinear theories of change: Theories predicting that societies would undergo a similar (if not identical) set of transformations, resulting in the same end product: the modern industrial state.

world system theory: The perspective that examines the relationship between the developed and developing nations of the world. According to this theory, the developed nations become rich in large measure by systematically exploiting the poor and militarily weak nations of the world.

core societies: Those industrial, economically diversified, rich, powerful nations relatively independent of outside control.

peripheral societies: Economically overspecialized, relatively poor and weak societies subject to the manipulation and direct control of core nations.

semiperipheral societies: Those nations midway between the core and the periphery. These nations are attempting to industrialize and diversify their economies.

devolution: The surrender of powers to local authorities by the central government.

state: A political entity occupying a designated territory with a government that has the authority and ability to use physical violence against citizens who resist its laws.

nation: A group of people with a common history and culture. A nation may or may not be a political state.

KEY PEOPLE:

Alex Inkles, a contemporary sociologist, and his associates identified a set of personal qualities they believed accurately characterized "modern man." They conducted studies to determine if the process of modernization had an effect on the values and behavior of people in developing nations. Inkles and associates concluded that formal education was the most powerful variable in determining how an individual scored on the modernization scale. According to their research, the school was the most important organization in changing a person's personality or character, and the factory was second in importance.

Auguste Comte (1798-1857) and Herbert Spencer (1820-1903) were evolutionary theorists. Comte believed that societies evolved through three inevitable stages of development. Spencer thought that societies passed through a series of stages as they became increasingly complex and interdependent.

Ferdinand Tonnies (1855-1936) put forth a "dual stage" theory of social change. For Tonnies, there were two societal types, Gemeinschaft (an informal, traditional society based on primary as opposed to secondary relations) and Gesellschaft (a large urban society based on contractual, impersonal, voluntary and limited relations). Tonnies predicted the rapid demise of Gemeinschaft societies and the corresponding ascendancy of Gesellschaft type organization.

Emile Durkheim (1857-1917) was another dual-stage theorist. He divided societies into those characterized by mechanical solidarity -- with a minimal division of labor, little role specialization, and a shared common world view -- and those characterized by organic solidarity -- with significant division of labor as is found in large, complex societies.

Neil Smelser, a contemporary sociologist who utilizes an evolutionary perspective, sees development as the transition from traditional societies to modern societies in terms of technological changes, transformations in agriculture and industry, and the movement of people from farms and villages to urban centers. As a result of these changes, human groups become increasingly differentiated. Social cohesion now is more a function of mutual need than of shared values. His theory predicts social disturbances and unrest among people because of these changes.

W. W. Rostow, a contemporary economist, developed one of the more influential theories of modernization, which he called the multi-stage "take off" model. He compares economic development to an airplane moving down the runway, and the take off occurs when a developing nation reaches a point of self-sustaining growth.

Immanuel Wallerstein, the foremost world system theorist, examined the relationship between the developed and developing nations of the world. According to this theory, the developed nations ("core") became rich in large measure by systematically exploiting the poor and militarily weak nations ("periphery") of the world. Nations midway between the core and the periphery are the "semiperipheral" societies which are attempting to industrialize and diversify their economies.

Alvin Toffler, a sociologist who has specialized in writing about the future, believes that capitalism and socialism are no longer the central dividing line between societies, but rather that fast and slow economies will become the dividing line. Now rich countries have fast economies, and less developed countries have "slow" economies which are hampered by "tradition, ritual, and ignorance." These nations are no match for the speed and efficiency of fast economies. Toffler believes that less developed countries need to strengthen their agricultural sectors so that they will be able to feed their growing populations and to slow the rural-to-urban migration.

ANSWERS TO MULTIPLE CHOICE QUESTIONS

1. b   The transformation from a traditional, usually agrarian society, to a contemporary, industrially-based state is referred to as modernization. (402)

2. a   Response "a" -- decrease in the division of labor -- is not one of the primary aspects of industrialization; there is an increase in the division of labor with industrialization. Responses "b," "c," and "d" all are associated with industrialization. (402)

3. e Alex Inkles and associates defined "modern man" as: Response "a" -- "open to new experiences;" Response "b" -- "increasingly independent of traditional authority figures;" Response "c" -- "less fatalistic and more inclined to accept science and modern medicine;" and Response "d" -- "ambitious, seeking to improve his standing in society and interested in community, national, and international affairs." Thus response "e" -- all of the above -- is the best answer. (403)

4. d Secularization is the process whereby worldly institutions and values become more important than religious institutions and values. Response "a" is the definition of "modernization." Response "b" is the definition of "devolution." Response "c" is a reversal of the correct response. (405)

5. c The evolutionary theory of modernization is based on the idea that if biological laws could explain the development of animals and human beings, social laws could be identified that explained the development and progress of human societies. (405)

6. a Auguste Comte believed that as societies evolved, they passed through three inevitable and irreversible stages. (406)

7. b According to Ferdinand Tonnies, Gemeinschaft societies were traditional societies based on primary relations. (406)

8. c Durkheim's concept of organic solidarity referred to societies characterized by a significant division of labor, much role specialization, and few shared values. (406)

9. d W. W. Rostow compared economic development to an airplane moving down the runway building up speed and momentum as it prepares to take off. (407)

10. b Responses "a," "c," and "d" are criticisms of evolutionary/modernization theory. Response "b" -- these theories are overly critical of capitalism and do not acknowledge that even the most backward countries have made progress as a result of international capitalism -- is a criticism of world system theory. (409)

11. c According to the text, the foremost world system theorist is Immanuel Wallerstein because he pioneered this perspective, which is viewed by many sociologists as the most sophisticated approach to explaining global inequality. (411)

12. a In world system theory, the peripheral societies are economically overspecialized, relatively poor and weak societies subject to the manipulation and direct control of rich (core) nations. (412)

13. b In world system theory, the core societies are industrial, economically diversified, rich, powerful nations relatively independent of outside control. (412)

14. d World system theory is based on Marxist conflict theory. A central component of this theory is the Marxist notion of classes and class conflict; however, the "classes" are not made up of groups of people, but of countries. (412)

15. e Economic domination of Third World nations by multinational corporations has been referred to by some world system theorists as neocolonialism. (415)

16. d Overspecialized economies in Third World nations are characterized by production of too few types of crops or raw materials to sell in the international marketplace. When the prices begin to fall on these crops, the countries can experience a rapid and severe decline in revenue. (415-416)

17. e According to Alvin Toffler, fast economies have advanced technology which speeds the entire business cycle from the rapid movement of investment capital to the delivery of the final product. Developing nations tend to have slow economies which are noncompetitive with fast economies. (417-419)

18. b Some theorists predict that electronic imperialism -- the increasing

domination of slow societies by fast societies -- will occur when now rich countries become information societies in the post-industrial era. As a result, the wealth gap between the rich and poor nations of the world will increase. (420)

19. <u>d</u>   The most accurate statement is "Women are exploited and abused in developed nations, but the rate and intensity of exploitation and abuse is significantly greater in Third World nations." (421)

20. <u>a</u>   Numerous studies have shown that <u>education</u> is the most effective way to reduce child mortality. (421)

21. <u>c</u>   The process by which power is surrendered to local authorities by the central government is called <u>devolution</u>. (424)

22. <u>b</u>   According to the text, World War III is a struggle between nations and states which already is taking place. In the Third World today, there are a significant number of nations attempting to withdraw from existing states and create their own independent political entities. (424)

23. <u>a</u>   When the United States went through the modernization process, industry was labor intensive (in need of unskilled and semi-skilled workers). Today the modernization process is capital-intensive (requiring enormous amounts of money), and it requires fewer, but more highly-skilled and trained workers. (427)

24. <u>c</u>   "Sustainable" modernization seeks a balance between the economy and the environment. (432-435)

ANSWERS TO TRUE-FALSE QUESTIONS:

1.   True (402)
2.   False -- Social scientists became interested in modernization in the aftermath of World War II. The new world order dominated by U.S. economic and military power, coupled with the crumbling of European colonialism, prompted researchers to take a closer took at the Third World. (402)
3.   True (404)
4.   True (406)
5.   True (406-407)
6.   False -- Smelser predicted that transformation from a traditional to a modern society would not occur without paying a price. Social disturbances such as "mass hysteria, outbursts of violence, and religious and political movements" reflect the unevenness of large-scale social change. (407)
7.   True (407-408)
8.   True (410-411)
9.   False -- Immanuel Wallerstein is the foremost world system theorist. Rostow's "take-off" model is evolutionary/modernization theory. (411)
10.   True (412)
11.   False -- World system theorists do not believe that underdevelopment and development are two separate stages of phases of modernization. They believe that underdevelopment and development are flip sides of the same coin because the rich countries could not have become that way without exploiting the poor ones. (414)
12.   True (414-415)
13.   False -- Most Third World nations have an internal system of stratification. These countries typically have a class structure dominated by a small economic elite whose political and financial interests are tied to core countries. (416)
14.   False -- World system theory has not been widely tested and verified because it is not comprised of interrelated propositions, and thus is not easily tested. This theory is a grand historical "vision," a socio-historical model meant to apply to a plurality of situations, but it has become a catch-all explanation for everything that is wrong with the Third World. (416)

15. False -- Dowry deaths have not ceased in India. In 1987, Indian police recorded 1,786 dowry deaths. (421)
16. True (421-422)
17. True (423)
18. False -- The text does not conclude that widespread poverty inevitably leads to corruption in Third World nations. It does acknowledge that people living in unstable and uncertain economic climates are much more likely to do what is necessary to survive, even if that means engaging in rule violating behavior. (427)
19. False -- In most countries economic development may lead to a more _inequitable_ distribution of income. Some theorists believe that economic development _initially_ leads to a more inequitable distribution of income before this trend is subsequently reversed and begins to improve. (428)
20. True (430-431)

ANSWERS TO FILL-IN QUESTIONS:

1. Gemeinschaft; Gesellschaft (406)
2. Mechanical, organic (406)
3. World system (410)
4. Core (412)
5. Peripheral (412)
6. Semiperipheral (412)
7. Fast; slow (419)
8. Devolution (424)
9. State (424)
10. Nation (424)